HOPE FOR ALL SEASONS

Biblical Expressions of Confidence
in the Promises of God

DANIEL J. SIMUNDSON

Easter, 1991

To Suttons
We think of you often
as we remember our wonderful
stay at Tantur. We pray
you may know God's blessings
and comfort in your life.

AUGSBURG Publishing House • Minneapolis

Shalom,

Dan + Sally
Simundson

HOPE FOR ALL SEASONS
Biblical Expressions of Confidence in the Promises of God

Copyright © 1988 Augsburg Publishing House

Scripture quotations unless otherwise noted are from the Revised Standard Version of the Bible, copyright 1946, 1952, and 1971 by the Division of Christian Education of the National Council of Churches.

Library for Congress Cataloging-in-Publication Data

Simundson, Daniel J.
  HOPE FOR ALL SEASONS.

  1. Hope—Biblical teaching.   I. Title.
BS680.H7S55   1988   234'.2   88-22290
ISBN 0-8066-2362-4

Manufactured in the U.S.A.   APH 10-3140

1   2   3   4   5   6   7   8   9   0   1   2   3   4   5   6   7   8   9

To the Point Roberts Pioneers,
especially Runa, Laugi, Jonas, and Elsa.

CONTENTS

PREFACE

The Bible is a book of hope. But it also includes a long chronicle of sin, pain, conflicts among humans and between God and humanity, occurrences of untimely and unwelcome death, and countless other examples of suffering. The Bible does not ignore or suppress the reality of suffering when it speaks of hope. Rather, the themes of suffering and hope must be seen together. Suffering would be unbearable if we had no genuine word of hope, no way to make sense of the pain or (probably even more important) maintain confidence in the goodness and power of God. And hope would not be necessary if there were no suffering, if we did not sense that things are not right, if we did not long for something better.

In earlier books *(Faith Under Fire: Biblical Interpretations of Suffering* and *Where Is God in My Suffering?),* I attempted to sort out what the Bible says about suffering and to make connections between the experience of our biblical ancestors and our own struggles with suffering. The emphasis was on the theme of suffering, though there was also some effort to move beyond suffering to give hints of the hope which gave strength and comfort to the biblical writers. In this book, the emphasis is on the other side of this double theme of suffering/hope. It is, of course, easier to analyze the problem of suffering than it is to instill hope. It is, similarly, easier to talk about hope, to lay out the biblical expectations for the future in some sort of orderly fashion, than it is to move another human being (or even oneself) from despair to hope. Nevertheless, we have been promised that God's Spirit will speak to us as we study the Scriptures. And so, with that assurance, we will examine the biblical words of hope and trust that God will not only enlighten our understanding but will also increase our hope.

Sometimes hope comes easily. In times of trouble, it is more difficult to hope. When all is going well, when it is easier to hope, one is less in need of hope. When past and present experiences make it more difficult to hope, that is the time when hope is most needed. In times of suffering or other unpleasantness, we begin to question whether we will ever see the good things of life again. Will God keep his promises? Will God take care of the hungry and the dispossessed of the world? Will God protect my nation, my loved ones, myself from all the dangers of this world? Will God heal our diseases? Will there ever be peace in the world, whether in one's own family or between warring nations? Will the good people finally be rewarded and the evil people punished? Is forgiveness really possible? Can the world be a better place? Is it naive optimism to hope for much improvement in this world? Or must we wait till the next world for the fulfillment of our hopes? Are all earthly hopes doomed to failure?

Such questions troubled our biblical ancestors just as they continue to disturb us. We should be able to find help in our own efforts to find hope by identifying with them in their struggle with questions like these.

There is an intellectual content to the biblical hope. Hope is a noun. We will put in categories the various things for which they hoped: the necessities of life, protection from danger, justice, community, and life after death. But hope is also a verb. To hope is to live through times of naivete, disillusionment, and sometimes, despair, while trying to be confident that the future will be better. To hope is to trust in the God who will walk with you into that unknown future. In our study of hope then, we must take into account not only the *content* of the biblical message of hope, but also the *process* that a person goes through during a life pilgrimage of success and failure, good and bad, fulfilled and unfulfilled hopes.

My special thanks to the board and administration of Luther Northwestern Theological Seminary for their granting of a sabbatical leave for working on this book. Thanks also to Lutheran Brotherhood for their generous financial support of theological education in general, and particularly, for the award which they granted to me. Thanks to all those friends, family, and colleagues who have encouraged me in this project, especially those in St. Paul, Minnesota; Point Roberts, Washington; and Tantur, Jerusalem, and most important of all, my wife Sally, who has been with me in all those places.

1

THE
NECESSITY
OF
HOPE

Human beings must have hope. Without hope, there is no tomorrow, only a fear-ridden or boring present. Without hope, one lives in dread of what will come next or is stifled with a meaningless life that is not going anywhere except to the grave.

Hope is an elusive word. It is both a noun and a verb. It is the thing hoped for, and it is the process of living in hope. Hope is closely connected to words like trust, confidence, or faith—a belief that the system will work, the good will be rewarded, the story will have a happy ending. For religious persons, hope is centered in one's faith in God, not merely in a vague optimism that "things will turn out all right." If one is convinced that God is good, God is at work in the world, and God is on my side, then hope is easier to maintain even in times of distress, disappointment, and suffering. Unfortunately, such experiences often affect one's trust in God, so that hope becomes more difficult at the very times when it is most needed.

As we move through life, hope changes for us. We are continually reevaluating what we think is possible, letting go of certain hopes and turning our attention in other directions. We know that we cannot abandon hope altogether, and so we work frantically to put back together a life of hope when previous

11

expectations have left us disillusioned. The content of what is hoped for may change. And our trust in the one who fulfills our hopes (whether "the system," parents, government, or God) may also be strongly challenged, driving us either to a restatement of faith or a loss of confidence.

A young man faces the future with optimism. He has prepared himself well for his career. He has been taught that the system rewards people properly. He expects to find a good job, work hard, move up through the corporation, and eventually make a lot of money. By the time he is in his middle years, his naive optimism will have tarnished somewhat, depending on his personal history. Sometimes the brightest and best do not receive the greatest opportunities and rewards. Sometimes one must live with tensions between what is best for the job and what is best for the family. A person's moral values are not necessarily shared by the supervising executives. Even with success and monetary rewards, one may still feel empty. The goals have been achieved, hopes have come true, but something is still missing. As one advances in years, death becomes a more and more certain reality. What does one dare to hope for in the face of that eventuality?

A young man in a developing country has joined the revolutionary forces. He is filled with hope for his country once the tyrannical military dictatorship has been overthrown and the authentic leaders of the people take office. He has tied his whole life to that hope, giving up a promising law career, living on the run and in danger of his life, even separated from his young wife and baby. His father is greatly distressed by his son's behavior. The father has been around long enough to be properly cynical about the fate of all "revolutions of the people." He has lived through at least four of them. All politicians are alike. Revolutionaries quickly become like the ones they replace—or worse. His son is foolish to give up his life for such idealistic hopes. The only sensible goal in life ought to be to survive (and maybe even do fairly well) in spite of which tyrants are currently running the government. He had hoped his son would learn that. Now he has little hope for his son.

12

The South Dakota farmer used to pray for good weather. He had been taught that God would answer prayers like that. But he has now lived through too many years of rain coming at the wrong time (or not at all) and the devastation of hail and wind. Why should he pray for the right kind of weather? It won't make any difference. It is as if God is too busy to bother with things like that, though in Bible times, it seemed that God was much more active in responding to people's needs. Maybe, he thought with a mixture of cynicism and attempted humor, there are now more people in cities praying for good weather for picnics or the beach than there are farmers praying for rain. It is really great weather when you are having a drought.

A middle-aged woman was very ill with cancer. "Have hope," her friend said. "God can do anything if we have enough faith. Didn't Jesus heal illnesses of those who came seeking his help? Don't block out the Spirit with your cautious faith. Hope for the impossible. Doctors don't know everything." And so she hoped for healing from her illness. And she prayed. And she mustered up as much faith as she could. And she kept up a good front for the family. And she got worse and worse. And then, at some point, she's not even sure when, her hopes began to change. She stopped banging her head against the wall. She knew her friends meant well, but she had to move away from the script they had written for her. She stopped hoping for restored health in this life. She stopped praying for that. Now she hoped that the days left to her would be good ones, that her family would have the strength to move on from their grief, that the pain would be bearable, that she would not be alone when she died, that God would forgive whatever wrong she had done, that she would still exist as a real person after her death.

And so hopes change as one moves through life. But one cannot live without hope.

Like all people, our biblical ancestors lived in hope. Through them, we can learn about the God in whom they hoped, the content of their hope (what God promised to do for them), and the process of living a life of hope where actuality often does not live up to expectation. Like them, we may need to move from one kind of hope to another as we work to maintain hope in the face of cruel reality. A study of what the Bible says about hope could be organized according to (1) what we hope *in* (i.e., what we can learn about a God who can be trusted), (2) what we hope *for* (i.e., the specific promises given by God to provide for our needs in the present and the future), or (3) our hope *in spite of* (i.e., the process of living through different stages of hope as our life progresses). Our primary method of organization will be to center on the biblical promises (number two), what we can expect from God on the basis of past performance and assurances about the future. As we look at each of these, we will notice how the experience of Israel and the early Christians affected the way that they hoped (number three). Underlying our whole discussion is the basic question of whether or not God can be trusted (number one). In the light of this, the following are preliminary thoughts about hope. They present the underlying point of view and the method of organization of this study. We will return to them again and again as we explore in more depth several specific biblical hopes.

The Relationship between Faith and Hope

We have already noted a close relationship between faith (or trust) and hope. Dictionary definitions of hope speak of hope both in terms of content (hope *for*) and in terms of confidence or trust (hope *in*). There are nonreligious forms of hope in the future—such as capitalistic or communistic theories of economics, blind trust in authority, various utopian or idealistic ideas about human nature. For a religious person whose faith is centered in the Bible, such hopes are doomed to failure because they are too shallow and idolatrous and too optimistic in the face of human sin and the reality of death. For such a religious person, the primary basis of hope is trust in God, the confidence that God will see that we have a good future. Since the future is unknown (though there is, of course, much speculation about what it will be like—in biblical times and up to our own day), to have hope is to put our future in God's hands and to be assured that God will be on our side and in the long run will see that everything works out for the best. As long as that faith is strong, hope comes rather easily. When our faith wavers, perhaps tested by severe trials and suffering, then it is harder to be hopeful about the future. As we begin to wonder if God is really going to help us, then the future becomes much more frightening.

Hope and trust are so interrelated that translators have sometimes been uncertain which word to use to translate a particular Hebrew word. There are several Hebrew words which are read as "hope" in English. (There is more consistency in words for hope in the Greek New Testament.) The Septuagint, the ancient pre-Christian translation of the Hebrew Scriptures into Greek, translates the Hebrew word *baṭaḥ* into the Greek word for "hope" *(elpizein),* though most modern English translators render it as "trust." That is, the Septuagint has used the word "hope" where the thought is of trust and refuge in God.[1]

And so, hope is really a matter of faith. What kind of a God do we have? Can God be trusted with the future, with the unknown? Can we turn over to God all those matters over which we have no control? What strengthens faith will increase hope. What weakens faith will also diminish hope.

Our Needs and God's Promises

God has promised to fulfill certain needs that we have—both in the present and in the future. If they are being met in the present or have been met in the past, we are more likely to expect God to continue to provide as we move to the future. To be hopeful is to believe that what you need will continue to be provided. Some of these needs are:

The necessities of life. We need air, water, food and land on which to live and raise crops. These are the very basics. Without them, life cannot even exist. There are many places in the Bible which speak of God the Creator who provides his children generously with the gifts of life. The first two chapters of Genesis

15

speak of the wonderful creation in which God takes pride. The humans are to have dominion over all the creatures, using them to fulfill their needs and eating of the plants for their nourishment. Many psalms praise God for these gifts of creation. Fall festivals, such as our Thanksgiving, praise God for the bounty of the land. God even sent manna and water to the Israelites in the wilderness, bread and meat to the prophet Elijah in times of drought, and a miraculous multiplication of bread and fish to the crowd listening to Jesus.

Much of the Old Testament is preoccupied with land—the longing for a place where the wandering Hebrews can settle down, ground which they can call their own, where they can live in freedom without having to answer to foreign oppressors. When the land is lost, prophets emerge to speak words of hope that God will again restore it.

Protection from danger. God has promised to keep his people from all danger. This is true for the people as a whole and for individuals within the society. On a corporate level, the people of Israel and the Christian church claim to be God's special people, whom God will keep and protect through the ages of time. Sometimes God does this by acting directly to save us from enemies that might hurt us, even giving victory over hostile nations. Or God may send us leaders who will judge fairly and protect the weak. When human leaders fail us, the hope is that a future, perfect king, the Messiah, will come to defeat all the powers that can harm us.

On an individual level, we have also come to believe in a God who will protect us from all danger—from accidents, from illness, from an early death, from despair and loneliness. We pray for protection before a long trip or serious surgery. Perhaps the most common prayer of all is for healing from affliction or illness. We ask God to keep safe our loved ones when we are separated from them. Sometimes, people speak of guardian angels who watch out for the ones whom God loves. And, of course, we want protection from that most fearsome danger of all—death and what comes after.

A moral order—a world that makes sense. If we are to face the future with hope, we need to know that the world makes moral sense, that God is a righteous judge, that God is truly in charge, that the good will finally be rewarded and the evil will be curtailed and punished. In short, we need to know that somewhere in the future (we hope earlier rather than later) the "good guys" will win. It would be hard to be hopeful if we could not see any sense to the world, if there were no evidence of God at work, if innocent people suffered continually and wicked people flourished and there were no end to it. Why should a young person looking ahead at life ever choose to do the right thing if there is no reward in it? If it doesn't make any difference to God which way we choose, then why should we bother? Better to live only for self and get whatever you can out of your life in the present.

Community. It is hard to be hopeful without some sense of community, the assurance that we will never be completely alone, totally abandoned, or obliterated as a person. We need community on two levels. We need a sense of communion with God *and* with other humans. As long as one still feels God's presence and concern, there can be hope. But often, in times of deep trial and despair, one begins to feel forsaken by God. And, also on the human level, the presence of loving, caring persons in our life can bring hope. But it is difficult to maintain hope when one feels condemned and alienated from the love of others.

One of the greatest fears about death is the fear of the loss of community—being cut off from those we love, facing the unknown completely on our own. One who has a strong sense of communion with God and with other humans, both living and already dead, finds death easier to face. And in our expression of hope for what comes after death, we Christians believe that somehow communion with both God and others will not cease.

God has promised these things. We want to trust that God will continue to provide them, and as long as we still believe that (faith and trust in God), we are able to maintain hope for the future.

Various Stages in Life with Regard to Hope

With regard to our confidence that these needs will be met, many human beings go through three stages in their lives. They are of different length for different people and the movement is not necessarily a smooth transition from one stage to another without some doubling back and forth.

First stage—naiveté. At the beginning of their life journey, many people believe that everything will go well for them throughout life. They expect that God will provide the basic necessities. God will keep our nation safe from danger. God will keep me well, and in case of illness, God will answer my prayers for healing. The world makes sense, and if we live like we should, we will be rewarded with a good, long, happy life. We can count on other people to support us and surely God would never turn away from us.

We start life with these hopes, with the confidence that all will be good. This stage may last a long time for those who have relatively comfortable lives or for those who are so optimistic they cannot even see when things are falling apart. Some will work hard to maintain this view of the world, even if they have to beat down and deny the real facts.

Second stage—disillusionment. This stage may come early for some people, later for others. In our day, many move into this stage rather quickly, becoming cynical about the world, the motives of those in authority, the dangers to our environment, and the threat of nuclear annihilation. "What hope is there if the world blows itself up before I am old enough to vote?"

For others, the disillusionment may come in very personal ways—grief, losses, disappointments. Perhaps the end of naiveté comes with the death of a parent, the betrayal of a relationship, a chronic illness or some other physical characteristic which is unwanted and unchangeable. Maybe it comes in a spiritual crisis, where God who had seemed so near and so kind becomes remote, unreal, or unkind.

Most people move in and out of this stage at least some times during their life. This is the time when it is a real struggle to hope. Those things that one needs in order to have hope in the world are under attack. Trust in God has been questioned. Great efforts are made to find explanations that will allow confidence in God to continue. If God does not provide what he has promised now, how can I have the confidence that God will do so in the future? And if I cannot be sure of that, how can I have hope? Can I continue to hope any more in *this* world? If there is to be hope at all, must it now shift to things *beyond* this world in order for me to continue to trust God?

Which way is one to go in times of great disillusionment? The second stage is not a pleasant place to be. But one cannot return to the simple faith of the past, as if the experiences that had challenged hope had never occurred. A person may become doubtful that God's promises will be achieved this side of the grave or the second coming. The tension pulls one in two directions—between the desire to find hope again in this world and skepticism that that will ever happen. Many persons have found a resolution to this dilemma by returning to trust in God, with or without evidence of God's activity on their behalf. After considerable struggle, they have returned to a new naiveté in which their relationship with God has been restored, even though their situation in this world has not improved and probably will not. It is as if they have returned to stage one with regard to hope as trust *in* God, but they have moved to stage three with respect to the things which they hope *for* (i.e., those hopes will be fulfilled only in some time beyond this life). So they continue to live out their life with a faith that has been tested, hammered out in diversity, able to deal with unpleasant reality, and probably stronger than ever. We shall see biblical examples of this in several places, including the movement from complaint to praise in the lament psalm and in Job's response after his confrontation with God.

Third stage—give up on this world and look to the next. In the third stage a person abandons all hope that the ambiguities of life will be resolved in this world. There will always be droughts, floods, political tyrannies, accidents, illnesses, injustice, betrayal, and loneliness in this sinful world. And so one is wrong to put his or her hope in the things of this world where one is certain to be disappointed. The problem is to prevent loss of our hope *in God* even if what we had *hoped for* in this life may never come to be. In this stage, we look to the next world for all things to be made right.

Ultimately, it is indeed the case that hopes limited to this world are doomed to be dashed. Certainly, as individuals, we all must die. But do we sometimes move to this stage too soon? Surely we do not want to treat this world as if it is insignificant, as if it is only evil and a place where God has no influence, as if it is only something to endure until we die or Jesus returns, as if we did not have some responsibility to try to make it a better place to live. There is hope even for this world and for its betterment, though it is finally the case that complete fulfillment will not be possible within the limitations of the created world as we know it now.

As our biblical ancestors thought about the promises of God, they too went through these various stages. Though it is an oversimplification, the biblical story moves through these stages from times of optimism, through confusion and disillusionment, to new hope and, finally, to a hope that transcends what takes place on this earth. The Old Testament tends to push for hope that will be seen in history, whereas the New Testament sees the completion of hope in an eschatological vision of the future. That is to say, in the tension between stages two and three, the Old Testament is more likely to be in stages one or two, whereas the New Testament has moved closer to three. We will look at how the various biblical promises pass through these three stages as the biblical story unfolds.

How Words of Hope Are Heard

Hope is heard and understood differently depending on which of these three stages we find ourselves. Someone who is still in the naive stage, who has never been truly hurt, who still believes

20

that the good always win and God will always provide and prayers will always be answered, may sound hopelessly out of touch with reality to one who has experienced great loss or disappointment. One who is in a desperate struggle (the second stage) trying to hold on to hope may be turned off by the smiling optimist who promises that "everything will be all right" and "if you just have enough faith, God will give you what you want."

Job's friends (still living in the first stage) insisted that good people are always rewarded and only those who deserve it are punished. They wanted things to work that way, and of course, since they were well and successful, it was easier for them to believe it. By insisting on this, they hurt Job (who was struggling in the second stage). They condemned him by insinuating that he deserved his terrible misfortunes.

The biggest problem for those who have moved past the naive stage is to know what to hope for anymore. They don't want to give up on this world completely. They want to believe that God can provide, protect, judge righteously, and never forsake them. But their personal experience has made all that doubtful, and they are having a hard time trusting God to do anything for them in this world. And all the pleading on the part of their friends that they should just have more faith only makes them feel worse. They cannot again return to a simple trust that they may have had at an earlier time. There have been too many negative experiences, too much water over the dam. To their pious friends, they may look as if they have "lost their faith," and so their zealous comforters try to persuade them to return to a way of thinking which is now impossible for them.

And so some struggling Christians look on their earnest brothers and sisters as being overly naive. And, from the other side, those who struggle are labeled as doubters, skeptics, overcautious—unwilling to trust the power of God's Spirit to work in the world. And so we argue about who are the "true and faithful" Christians because we are standing at different stages of life in our understanding of hope.

For a Christian, hope finally has to move to the third stage and not try to return to the first one. There will be a new age.

Jesus will come again. All the bad things about life will be defeated once and for all. Even death does not have the last word. Though a Christian's ultimate hope reaches beyond what this world can offer, one may find new hope within the pains and struggles of this life. Many of our ancestors in the faith have attested to that. They describe a hope that has been tested in fire and has become even more certain. Hope can flourish even in the midst of events that may seem to the world to be hopeless.

When is the right time to give up on this life and fasten our hopes on something beyond? This is not an easy question to answer. It will come up again and again as we review the promises and hopes of the Bible. We probably err on both sides. We try to manipulate people and events and force the kingdom of God into earthly institutions. We cling to earthly hopes when we should let go and trust God, even as we die. We expect some last-minute miracle or we devise all sorts of technological marvels to postpone the final moment of death as if we can actually avoid it. On the other hand, the church has often been accused, and rightfully so, of being more interested in the next life than in this one. We have preached "pie in the sky," teaching people to be submissive and willing to deny their hopes for this world in the hope that all will be fulfilled in the wonderful life that is to come. People struggling for freedom have often been offended by words that seem to legitimate their present situation and frustrate their hopes for a better life in the present.

2
HOPE
FOR THE
NECESSITIES
OF LIFE

The people of the Bible received certain promises and assurances from God. At times, those things promised by God, either to the people as a whole or to individuals, seemed not to be forthcoming. Then the problem was how to cope with the deprivation, how to come to some understanding of God's participation in their negative experiences that allowed for continued trust (and, thus, hope) that God would continue to provide what had been promised.

In this chapter we shall look at God's assurances that the people would have land and they would have favorable weather and sufficient rain for growing the food necessary for life to exist.

The Land

The theme of land runs through the Old Testament. It is promised, given, lost, promised again and partially regained. Hope for the return to the land is one of the most common Old Testament ways of expressing hope for the future.

God will provide land, a space

The creation. In the beginning there was no land. There was only watery chaos. In order for life to exist, God acted to make a space, to separate the waters by means of a firmament (Gen.

1:6-8). Then those waters under the heavens were gathered together in one place so that there would be dry land where humans and others of God's creatures could live (Gen. 1:9). "And God saw that it was good" (Gen. 1:10b). The creation story speaks of land in general, not the promise of a specific piece of geography. That will come later. But here, at the very beginning, the theologians who have left us this creation story remind us that the land is a gift of God, made possible by God's (and only God's) gracious activity on our behalf.

The creation very quickly became a disappointment to God, and there was a danger that the land would be taken away, covered over again by the waters of the flood, reverting again to a formless chaos where human life would no longer be possible. But God saved Noah and established a covenant with him and his descendants, promising "that never again shall all flesh be cut off by the waters of a flood, and never again shall there be a flood to destroy the earth" (Gen. 9:11). There will always be land, though how it will be divided up among earth's inhabitants remains a crucial issue throughout biblical times and into our own day. Later in the biblical story, God's people will be removed from their land because of idolatry, disobedience, and perversion of justice. But no more will God remove the land itself. Though God has promised never again to destroy the earth with a flood (which should be a hopeful word), one wonders if God might still destroy the world by some other means or if God might allow humans to destroy the earth through their own deviousness.

The promise to Abraham. Abram's family had already wandered from Ur to Haran on their way to Canaan, looking for land (Gen. 11:31). They settled in Haran rather than continuing to Canaan. God came to Abram and told him to leave his own country and his kinfolk and head toward a new land which God would show him. God said, "And I will make of you a great nation, and I will bless you, and make your name great, so that you will be a blessing" (Gen. 12:2). In the priestly version of the covenant with Abraham, God says, "And I will establish my covenant between me and you and your descendants after you throughout their generations for an everlasting covenant, to be God to you and to your descendants after you. And I will give to you, and to your descendants after you, the land of your so-journings, all the land of Canaan, for an everlasting possession; and I will be their God" (Gen. 17:7-8).

A sinful and divided humanity (as shown by the fall, the murder of Abel, the flood, the Tower of Babel) was in desperate need of a new start. And God moved to choose Abraham, the first step in God's activity to redeem the fallen human race. Abraham and his descendants would be the ones through whom God's will and God's character would be made known. Abraham would, thus, become a blessing for all the families of earth (Gen. 12:3). But for Abraham to live and have descendants and become a large enough nation to have any influence at all, he must have a land. God promised to provide that land if Abraham would have the courage to pack up and move west into the unknown. The basic covenant, the promise that God would be with Abraham and make him a blessing, was very closely tied to the promise of land. The land became a visible symbol of the promise that God had made. Though Abraham remained a sojourner in a foreign land, with little actual property other than a burial site (see Gen. 23 and Gen. 49:29-32), his descendants continued to hold God accountable for this promise and they lived in the hope that someday it would be fulfilled.

The gift of land after the exodus. The biblical story takes a large detour into Egypt when Jacob and his sons follow Joseph there. Though prospering for a time, the Hebrews were later made slaves by a king who did not know Joseph (Ex. 1:8). Now they were worse than aliens or sojourners, who might have been treated with some respect even though living in someone else's land. They became slaves who were forced to build someone else's cities. What had happened to the promise to Abraham to become a great nation in his own land? Though it might appear to be so, God had not forgotten. When God promises something, you can rest assured that it will come about—even though it may take several generations. God saw and heard the affliction of the Hebrew slaves and called Moses to be his accomplice "to deliver

25

them out of the hand of the Egyptians, and to bring them up out of that land to a good and broad land, a land flowing with milk and honey, to the place of the Canaanites, the Hittites, the Amorites, the Perizzites, the Hivites, and the Jebusites" (Exod. 3:8). (We should make note here of a persistent problem whenever human beings claim divine sanctions for their rights to the land—someone else already lives there.)

As Moses led the wandering people through the wilderness, it was hope for the "promised land" that kept them going. When they were discouraged, they were reminded that God would not renege. When they were rebellious or faint-hearted, their crisis of faith was presented as a reason for the delay in reaching the land. Nearly all would die before they reached their destination (Num. 14:20-24).

In Joshua and Judges, we read (in accounts difficult to harmonize) of the takeover of the long-promised territory. The Joshua account, with its warfare and violence, is difficult material for many of us. To be sure, God's promises about land were fulfilled but at a high price for our image of a loving God who is concerned for all humanity and is not the God of one nation over against all others. Since the promise was very particular and earthly, talking about real nations and real pieces of geography, the inevitability of conflict, and even violence, was there. We shall need to return again to some issues raised by our contemporary application of these promises about land.

Deuteronomy and the deuteronomic history make some very important points about the land. The land which the people were going to possess was promised to Abraham, Isaac, and Jacob (Deut. 1:8). That is, God had kept his promises (though the wait was too long for many generations who had died in the meantime). The land was a gift. The people should have had no illusions about their worthiness to earn such a prize. Rather, the wickedness of the nations who preceded them was so great that God drove them out (Deut. 9:4-5). (This is at least a partial explanation for why others were dispossessed in order to make room for the Israelites.) And the deuteronomic traditions make clear the conditionality of the acquisition of the land. The promise

26

had been fulfilled. But the people had something to say about whether or not they would continue to live on the land (e.g., Deut. 4:40). God gave them the land, though they didn't deserve it, and God could remove them from it again if they should merit that.

How to understand and cope with the loss of land

God's people found hope in the promise that they would have a place to call their own, that they would not forever be wanderers on the face of the earth, vulnerable to the whim of the local authorities who may or may not tolerate their presence. That hope kept them going through the days of the ancient patriarchs and through the time in the wilderness. Under David and Solomon, their position on the land was made secure. God had accomplished what was promised. But it did not stay that way. The kingdoms divided after the death of Solomon. The fortunes of Israel and Judah had their ups and downs, but finally Israel, and then Judah, were destroyed as nations and many were sent into exile, again becoming homeless people with no land. How did this turn of events fit with God's promises? The theologians were confronted with the task of explaining how God could still be trusted, how the people could still hope in a good and powerful God in spite of the fact that God's promises had either been delayed interminably (as in the case of Abraham and to a lesser degree in the 40 years of wandering in the wilderness) or had apparently been withdrawn (as in the case of the exile). How were they to explain the disparity between what God wants for the people and the reality of life in this world?

In a world of sin, things are seldom as they should be. Genesis 1 speaks of dry land where crops grow and animals live and humans have dominion over it all. Genesis 2 paints an idyllic picture of a beautiful, well-watered garden where the human being can live a good life by tilling it and keeping it (Gen. 2:15). But in the real world, it is not always so. Life is hard. Many do not have land at all. Even for those who do, the crops do not always come easily. What went wrong is symbolized by the story of the fall.

The responsibility for the gap between what God intended and what actually came to be lies with the humans. They did not trust God. They ate the forbidden fruit in the hope that they might overcome their human limitations and discover what only God knows. And because of their action, all humans pay the consequence. "Therefore, the Lord God sent him forth from the garden of Eden, to till the ground from which he was taken. He drove out the man; and at the east of the garden of Eden he placed the cherubim, and a flaming sword which turned every way, to guard the way to the tree of life" (Gen. 3:23-24).

The loss of land is the result of specific sins. God can still be trusted. God has kept his end of the bargain. The promises are still intact. The problem is with us. We have sinned. We have turned away from the true God to follow false gods. We have not dealt justly with the poor and weak and needy in our own society. This was the primary interpretation of the exile—offered by prophets and historians. It left the people with a basis of hope. God had not acted arbitrarily. God had even sent warnings through prophets and other messengers, but the people had not heeded. The deuteronomic historian is particularly forthright in drawing connections between the sins of the people and the loss of their land (see especially 2 Kings 17 and 2 Kings 24:1-4). As long as the people were willing to accept this interpretation, they could find some comfort. God was still reliable. Though they had strayed away from God before, perhaps they could avoid future disasters by being more relentless in their pursuit of God's law. If they would repent and not repeat the mistakes of the past, there was still hope.

Lamenting can be a proper reaction to loss of land. In a lament, one may or may not accept responsibility for the calamities that have arrived. If one accepts the deuteronomic view that the dashing of hopes is understandable as a working out of God's justice, then perhaps repentance is the best response. But often the loss, the suffering, seems way out of proportion to the crime or even seems to fall heaviest on those who are least culpable. And so part of a lament may be a protestation that God has been uncaring, unjust, or simply inattentive to what has transpired. The book of Lamentations contains a series of carefully constructed prayers that mourn the fate of Jerusalem and the land of Judah. Though there are admissions of guilt (as in Lam. 1:18), there are also times when God's justice is challenged. In Lam. 2:11-12, there is at least the insinuation that babies should not have to suffer so cruelly. Habakkuk (in 1:12-13) wondered why a just God could look on and remain silent while the wicked (probably meaning Babylon) swallowed up the one who was more righteous (i.e., Judah). One could add up many such examples, particularly from the lament psalms.

One of the most important tasks when one's initial hopes have been destroyed, when disillusionment has set in, when naiveté has ended, is to reevaluate one's faith in God. What had you expected from God? How did you understand those promises? Have you been deceived? Has God been unfair? What can you still expect from this God who has not granted what you thought he had promised? The lament is a very important biblical resource for doing this kind of work as one struggles with his or her relationship with God and tries to return to an attitude of trust. Strangely, though the words of the lament often seem excessively skeptical or even hostile toward God, they may be of much value to us as we struggle to recover hope when all has gone wrong.

Look to the past as a ground for hope. In times of trouble, biblical religion looks to the past for assurance. When the land has been lost, the old promises are again brought to our remembrance. God is faithful and does not take back what has been given. A time of exile is a time for digging in, hanging on tightly to those ancient promises, reciting over and over the stories of Abraham and Isaac and Jacob, and remembering how God heard the anguish of the Hebrew slaves in Egypt and delivered them. Remember that they, too, sometimes lost their nerve as they wandered in the wilderness. The history shows that when they rebelled, trouble came. But God has always been faithful, and we must trust that the future will be as the past. The high point of the book of Lamentations comes in the middle of the book. "Remember my affliction and my bitterness, the wormwood and

29

the gall! My soul continually thinks of it and is bowed down within me. But this I call to mind, and therefore I have hope: The steadfast love of the Lord never ceases, his mercies never come to an end; they are new every morning; great is thy faithfulness. 'The Lord is my portion,' says my soul, 'therefore I will hope in him' " (Lam. 3:19-24).

For one who is still in the first stage, not yet hurt in a profound way, such a statement of trust and hope might come easy. To one who is still struggling, these words may seem naive, representing a stage of trust to which they think they can never return. But, when hammered out in the midst of adversity, surrounded as they are in the book of Lamentations by horrible and vivid descriptions of the reality of suffering, they become a profound witness to the staying power of faith and hope in God. This is a return to the past, to a God who has been faithful, but not to a simple naiveté that hides its head from calamity and refuses to challenge ancient theological positions—and even God himself.

A return to the land as a way of expressing hope

The exile was not the end of the story. God had not forever abandoned the people. Prophets arose to revive the hope of the people and to tell them that the ancient promises of land for God's people were still intact.

God will return the people to the land. Prophets who spoke to the exiles promised them that they would return. The ancient land of promise which had temporarily been taken from them would be restored. It would be a glorious return, accompanied by singing and great joy (Isa. 35:10). The travel would be easy, with no dangerous beasts along the way (Isa. 35:9). As if prepared by a builder of modern freeways, the valleys and hills would be levelled out and the highway would be straight and smooth (Isa. 40:3-4). Jeremiah spoke several times of the return of the people from distant lands so that the nations of Judah would again exist in their own place (Jer. 3:18; 16:14-15; 23:3; 30:10). Jeremiah even defied every law of real estate investment by redeeming the field of a kinsman just as the Babylonians were about to take control of the whole country. This symbolic act portrayed God's promise that people would again buy and sell land in Judah (Jer. 32:15). God would gather the people from all the countries to which God drove them in anger (Jer. 32:37). Ezekiel, too, promised a revival of the people, though they were as dead and disconnected as bones strewn throughout a valley, and a return to their land (Ezek. 37:11-14).

These were very specific hopes expressed by the prophets. They were not talking about land in general, any piece of real estate where the Jews could start out again. They were talking about a particular place on the east end of the Mediterranean, where Abraham had migrated from Haran, where the Hebrew slaves chased out the Canaanites, and where David and his sons ruled for several centuries. This was very much a "this worldly" hope. Were the prophets promising too much? Could a defeated and dispersed nation actually come back to life? In a sense, it has happened twice, though perhaps less gloriously than some prophets might have hoped. Under the Persians, exiles were allowed to return to resettle the land and to rebuild the temple and the city wall. The glories of the days of David and Solomon were never reached again. In fact, no son of David ever sat on the throne again. For most of the centuries following the Jews' return, their land remained as occupied territory for one mighty empire after another—the Persians, the Greeks, and the Romans. But it was a fulfillment nonetheless. The community continued in its own land and, of profound significance for Christians, eventually was the setting for the birth of Jesus, son of Mary.

After centuries in which the Jewish people were scattered throughout the world and there was no Jewish state, the state of Israel was founded after World War II. Many have associated this recent development with the ancient prophetic promises and have seen it, too, as a fulfillment of God's promises to give his people a land. Those with a more pronounced apocalyptic bent have identified this return to the land as one of the signs of the end times and have included it in their calculations of the nearness of Christ's return and the coming of the new age.

31

Christians have used these promises to speak of the coming age. The New Testament (and the Christian church) have usually spiritualized these promises of return to the land. We Christians have not been so concerned about the Holy Land as a sign of God's promises being fulfilled in the world. For Christians, the supreme manifestation of God's presence in the world is in the incarnation, the appearance of God in the form of a real human being, not in the people of Israel or the holy city or the temple. And so these promises about God providing a land, a place of rest and security, space to call our own, are usually interpreted as a final hope after we die. Our true home toward which we travel in our pilgrimage through life (as ancient Israel traveled through the wilderness of Sinai) is a heavenly home which far surpasses anything that earth can offer. (See chapters 3 and 4 of Hebrews; also Heb. 11:8-16; Phil. 3:20.) And so what was a very real hope for this world among the people of the Old Testament (and for many present-day Jews) has been reinterpreted by Christians. Now the imagery of land is read allegorically or symbolically or spiritually as a future time of rest and safety—a time and place that transcends our human experience. Hymns and other poetry that express our hope for life after death have found rich imagery in these ancient promises of a "land" for God's people.

> Jerusalem, whose towers touch the skies,
> I yearn to come to you!
> Your shining streets have drawn my longing eyes
> My lifelong journey through.
> And though I roam the woodland,
> The city, and the plain,
> My heart still seeks the good land,
> My Father's house to gain.
>
> *(Lutheran Book of Worship* 348,
> text copyright © 1978)

> Jerusalem, my happy home,
> When shall I come to thee?
> When shall my sorrows have an end?
> Thy joys when shall I see?
>
> *(Lutheran Book of Worship* 331)

32

When I tread the verge of Jordan,
Bid my anxious fears subside;
Death of death and hell's destruction,
Land me safe on Canaan's side.
Songs and praises, songs and praises,
I will raise forevermore, I will raise forevermore.
(*Lutheran Book of Worship* 343)

Jesus, still lead on, Till our rest be won;
And, although the way be cheerless,
We will follow, calm and fearless;
Guide us by your hand
To our Father's land.

If the way be drear, If the foe be near,
Let no faithless fears o'ertake us,
Let not faith and hope forsake us;
Safely past the foe
To our home we go.
(*Lutheran Book of Worship* 341)

Contemporary use of promises of hope for the land

This world or the next? In times of trouble, people want whatever they have lost to be restored. And so it was with our biblical ancestors. So far in this chapter, we have been talking about land, whether in general or the specific part of the world where David reigned and Jesus was born. Their first hope was that their fortunes would be reversed and they would recover what they had lost *in this life*. Perhaps after a period of struggle, some of them became resigned to the likelihood that what was lost was forever lost in this world and they would live the rest of their life in Babylon or Egypt or elsewhere in exile. If there was going to be a restoration, it would have to come after their death, either for their descendants or for themselves in some future life. That transition from focusing on "this world" to the next seemed to take place between the Old Testament and the New. As was already pointed out, the very particularistic hopes for the land of Israel are not read literally anymore by most Christians. If Christians use these ancient texts at all, they may draw analogies to their own time and place (e.g., God brought the Europeans to North America and gave them this "promised land") or, as already mentioned, they spiritualize the "land" of these promises to be our ultimate rest, our home with God when we have completed our earthly pilgrimage. Used in this way, these passages can still have enormous power and are hope-producing (as the hymns mentioned above) even though understood in ways far different from their original intention.

This question will come up again and again as we recite the various biblical words of hope. Are we still to take these hopes literally when they are so specific in their promises to ancient people that they no longer apply to modern people in different lands? Can we still hold out for some hope for this poor old earth and human history, or must we always be postponing our hopes for real improvement to some future beyond death and human history?

The modern state of Israel. Though most Christians find little significant meaning for themselves in the promises to give Abraham and Sarah and their descendants the land of Israel and to return exiles there from ancient Persia, there are at least two religious groups who find profound meaning, in our day, in these ancient promises. They have become wonderful assurances to them that God is still at work in the world, God always keeps promises, and therefore, we can count on God to go on to complete other promises that we can find in the Bible or our religious tradition. The return of Jews to Israel and the revival of a Jewish state have been such events to many in the Jewish community and to a considerable number of conservative Christians. After nearly 2000 years of living as "sojourners" in other nations, the Jews now have a land of their own again. To be sure, most Jews are quite happy to be citizens of other countries, but the terrible experience of the holocaust under Hitler and continuing eruptions of anti-Semitism in various parts of the world have led many to appreciate the existence of a land (*the* land—the place of the ancient promises) where any Jew can go and be home. And many conservative Christians have also rejoiced in the founding of modern Israel. God will bring about what God has promised. Now they can return to biblical prophets and apocalyptic literature with the assurance that just as this specific event was foretold and came to pass, so other prophecies will surely happen. Further, when coupled with other "signs" of the end time, some have been rather bold in expecting the end of the world in a short time.

This common interest in modern Israel has made strange bedfellows out of Jews and Christians. It is, of course, difficult, as it is in all ages, to say with any certainty what part God has played in the movements of nations on the world scene. We may want to claim God's participation in the founding of Israel, but we would hardly want to accuse God of directing the events that led to Hitler. Whether or not it is God's will that Israel be again a national state cannot be proved but only believed. And for those who choose to believe, these Old Testament promises about a land for the descendants of Abraham have given them support for their position.

Analogies to our continuing needs. There would seem to be another way to read these promises that is still worldly without the necessity of reading them as if they are only about the land of Israel. God knows our needs. Just as those ancient nomads needed a place of their own, a land to raise their crops, someplace that was home, so it is still true in our time and place. And so God wants to provide us with a home. God still feels compassion for the homeless, the stranger, the lonely, the refugee, the modern-day exile.

One has only to look in the newspapers or watch the evening news on television to be reminded of how many homeless people there are in this world—"boat people," Palestinian camps in Lebanon or the Gaza strip, street people in the slums of huge cities, Central American refugees hiding in towns along the Texas or California border. The list could go on and on. By analogy, their situation is like that of the ancient Hebrews. And so the promise of God to give a home to Abraham or the Hebrew slaves or the exiles in Babylon is a reassurance that God still cares for people like that and will work on their behalf to provide them a land. Perhaps we need to remind ourselves of God's promises to such

35

people so that we, like Moses, may join with God to bring about what God has promised.

Some have lost their land and may never be able to return. The old Latvian may finally be resigned to the reality that his country will never be free during his lifetime. But even though he may not see it, he still has hope. He has hope for himself and his future with God even beyond death. But he also has hope for this world—that someday his beloved land will be free of oppression. Maybe it will happen in the next generation or the next century. But it will happen. And that hope gives him strength, even though he won't be there to see it.

Others have lost their land in very individual ways. The century-old family farm has gone bankrupt. Four generations have lived a good life on this piece of God's earth. No one else has ever farmed it. And now it is owned by the huge bank that has sold it to a holding company that makes everything from cigarettes to soft drinks to women's dresses. The farmer's hope for the future is shattered. He feels he is a failure. He has let down both past and future generations. He cannot imagine anyone else living on his place. There is no chance he can ever get his farm back. What can he do? Is there any hope? It is as if he is living through his own time of exile, searching for words of hope, wondering if God will help provide a place for him to begin again.

Dangers of nationalism.   Can any people claim a divine right to a certain parcel of land? Though God intends land, a place, space, a home, for all, how is the limited amount of world real estate to be divided? There are, of course, many world conflicts where different groups claim title to the same land. The situation becomes much more difficult when these groups each claim that their right of ownership goes back to an edict given by God himself. Who is to arbitrate such disputes? What if one God was the God of Islam and the other the God of the Hebrews? What if one God was the Roman Catholic God and the other the Anglican God? Do those who got there first have priority? But what if my family has been there 2000 years and yours 2500 years? There are probably some people living in Israel today whose ancestors were there even before Abraham. Certainly American Indians lived here in North America long before any Europeans showed up. Does that mean the whole continent should revert to them?

Obviously these are questions not easily answered. Quoting from ancient prophecies to support one's case probably is not going to convince the opposition, who may also think God is on their side. It is difficult to walk a narrow line with regard to God's promises about land. We want to believe that God is concerned for our earthly home as well as our heavenly home. But to claim special divine favor on our own people or land, to believe that God has put my people here to stay forever, is to pin my hopes on earthly matters. To do so is dangerous because earthly hopes will fail us. To do so is idolatrous because it seduces us into trusting something other than God himself.

Good Weather and Sufficient Food

There is no more basic need for human beings (and other creatures for that matter) than food. Without food, obviously, we would have no future. And so our hope for the future must include the nourishment that our bodies need. And, as part of this hope, we need the right kind of weather—neither too much nor too little rain, no destructive storms, no early frosts—to produce that food.

The Creator God promises to provide our basic needs

Creation stories—Genesis 1–2. Again we return to the creation stories. The Creator God is responsible for all that there is. The creation was a good thing, intended for the use and enjoyment of God's creatures, particularly the humans who have special status as God's stewards, assuming dominion over all the other creatures (Gen. 1:28; Psalm 8:5-8). God made all sorts of vegetation, each producing its own kind in orderly fashion (Gen. 1:11-12). God made the sun and moon to give light, order the seasons, and (in the case of the sun) make plant growth possible.

And then God brought forth all the living creatures. God said, "Behold, I have given you every plant yielding seed which is upon the face of all the earth, and every tree with seed in its fruit; you shall have them for food" (Gen. 1:29). God also provided food for all the beasts and birds and creeping things. Everything that has the breath of life will be fed by God (Gen. 1:30).

In Genesis 2 God began the creating process by causing a mist to water the ground in order for the previously barren earth to produce (Gen. 2:4b-6). Man was then created so that he could till the garden that God planted (Gen. 2:7-8). "And out of the ground the Lord God made to grow every tree that is pleasant to the sight and good for food" (Gen. 2:9a). Then God formed all the beasts and birds and brought them to the man to help him and to be named by him. Again, it is clear that the human is on a different level than the animals. The human has dominion over the animals (Genesis 1), but he needs a relationship with one that is his own equal. And so God created woman and man.

This is the way it is supposed to be. God the Creator has made a good world. It is constructed in such a way that all God's creatures will be provided with what they need. The plants are there for humans and other creatures. It is a little less clear whether some animals are meant to serve as food for other animals. Both Genesis 1 and 2 clearly put animals in a lower category than humans and subject them to human domination. Those of us who read these creation stories should have confidence (and, thus, hope) that our future needs will be provided. God has made the world that way.

Psalms of praise and thanksgiving. This confidence in a God who continues to provide daily sustenance is seen clearly in the worship of ancient Israel, most notably in the psalms of thanksgiving and praise. "The eyes of all look to thee, and thou givest them their food in due season. Thou openest thy hand, thou satisfiest the desire of every living thing" (Psalm 145:15-16). Psalms of thanksgiving acknowledge that it is God who has made the world and has made it fertile. "Thou visitest the earth and waterest it, thou greatly enrichest it; the river of God is full of water; thou providest their grain, for so thou hast prepared it" (Psalm 65:9). "The earth has yielded its increase; God, our God, has blessed us. God has blessed us; let all the ends of the earth fear him!" (Psalm 67:6-7). "Rain in abundance, O God, thou didst shed abroad" (Psalm 68:9a). Such praise and thanks to God comes easy when the weather is right and the crop is good. Each new year, the farmer again plants the seed, trusting (and hoping) that God will again perform the miracle of mixing seed and soil and sun and rain to produce the food that we need. One can only wonder and be grateful to a God who has created a world like this to meet our needs. Ancient Israel had thanksgiving harvest festivals, and though it has lost prominence in the Christian church year, it has returned through the back door in national holidays of Thanksgiving.

If God is to be honored when the crops are good, then how does one think about God's promises to deliver food in those bad years of drought, famine, flood, or mass hunger? If God gets credit for the good, must God also be blamed for the bad? And how are we to hope for the future if God provides in some years but not others, or to some people and not others? We will return to this question.

Stories of God's people being fed. There are a number of important occasions in the history of the people when God supplied them food, and those stories were remembered and eventually included in our Scripture. Joseph was sent into slavery because of the hostility of his brothers, but God, working through Joseph, used Joseph's wisdom and strategic placement in Egypt to save many from famine (Gen. 50:20). The slaves who followed Moses out of Egypt and into the wilderness soon began to wonder if they were not better off as slaves. At least they had food to eat (Exod. 16:1-3). God heard their murmuring and sent them manna from heaven. But they were to be absolutely clear that it was God who provided, who both delivered them from Egypt and gave them food in the wilderness. In order to test their obedience, they were to take only one day's portion at a time. If they took more, it would rot (Exod. 16:4, 13-21). Each person had enough for the day and only for that day. One could not, therefore, plan ahead for oneself but had to depend wholly on God to provide for each new day. As Jesus would say, much later, in the prayer that he taught his disciples, "Give us this day our daily bread."

The Elijah and Elisha stories include a number of examples of God providing food. (It is also the Lord who can hold back the rain—1 Kings 17:1, 14. We shall return to that point later.) Elijah was fed by ravens in the wilderness (1 Kings 17:3-6) and then by a poor widow from Zarephath (1 Kings 17:8-16) whose meager portions of meal and oil never failed. Elisha also was involved in some miracles regarding food—a widow of one of the sons of the prophets collected enough oil from one jar to pay off all her debts (2 Kings 4:1-7), he made edible some stew that had a poisonous plant in it (2 Kings 4:38-41), and he fed 100 men from a small amount of bread with some food left over (2 Kings 4:42-44). Since God has promised to provide food, these events are seen as signs that Elijah and Elisha truly were "men of God," and God was at work in their activities.

Jesus, too, was one in whom God showed himself in a particularly novel way—even more so (for Christians) than in Moses and Elijah and Elisha and all the other great holy men of the past. One of the ways in which Jesus showed that God was at work in him was through his miracles of supplying food to the hungry. The only miracle of Jesus that is recorded by all four Gospels is the feeding of the 5000 (Matt. 14:13-21; Mark 6:32-44; Luke 9:10-17; John 6:1-15). As with Elijah and Elisha, this became a sign that Jesus was indeed "the prophet who is to come into the world" (John 6:14). There is continuity here with the Creator God who provides the hungry with food, who made the world that way at the beginning and has continued to show his power and care in this way throughout the history of the people.

But Jesus pushed the matter further. It was not only our material needs that Jesus had come to provide. In John 6:25-35, Jesus did some follow-up teaching after the miracle of the feeding of the 5000. "Do not labor for the food which perishes, but for the food which endures to eternal life, which the Son of man will give to you" (John 6:27). Jesus identified himself as the true

40

bread that came down from heaven that gives life to the world (John 6:32-35). Earlier, Jesus had quoted Deut. 8:3 when confronted with the devil's temptations—"Man shall not live by bread alone, but by every word that proceeds from the mouth of God" (Matt. 4:4).

There is more to life than nourishment for our physical bodies. Most Old Testament texts speak of God providing real food for real humans in order for life to exist. Jesus would not deny that necessity. But he pushed beyond the needs of this life to speak of hope for eternal life—food that will nourish our soul even when the decay of this life has taken over and we have no more to hope for in this life. Once again, the New Testament takes a primarily earthly, literal hope and uses it to speak of hope beyond this life (but the thought was already there, in part, in Deut. 8:3).

The response when the promise seems to have failed

God has promised to provide. But what about those times when our cup does not overflow? If hope is a matter of trust, then the religious community facing famine, starvation, etc., must find some way of reconciling their trust in a God who provides their needs with the reality of their situation.

Remember the past. Times are difficult now, that is true. But they have been difficult before. Our spiritual ancestors had their own times of famine and hardship, but God provided. So bring out the old stories. Tell about Joseph and the manna in the wilderness and Elijah and Jesus feeding the hungry. Tell them again and again so that you never forget what kind of God you know. Perhaps you will need some sort of visible symbol to help you remember. Moses told Aaron, "Take a jar, and put an omer of manna in it, and place it before the Lord, to be kept throughout your generations" (Exod. 16:33; see also Heb. 9:4). According to Paul, Jesus on the night he was betrayed took bread, "and when he had given thanks, he broke it, and said 'This is my body which is for you. Do this in remembrance of me' " (1 Cor. 11:24).

Many find comfort in the present and hope for the future in remembering what God has done for them in the past—both in the past of our religious community that helps us remember through stories and rituals and sacraments, but also in our personal histories where God has been with us in times of doubt and struggle. But hope may still evade others, though they meditate on God's great deeds in the past. They cannot resist the question, "But what has God done for me lately?"

Lack of food may be the result of sin. There are many efforts in the Bible to make some sense out of God's failure to provide our basic needs. If we can come to some reasonable explanation that protects God's justice and mercy, then it will be easier to continue to hope in this God. If the fault lies with us humans and not God, then the promises are still intact and hope continues.

The stories of creation are followed by the story of the fall. The world is not the way it was intended. The punishment on the man and woman included a cursing of the ground which will grow thorns and thistles and yield its fruit only after great effort (Gen. 3:17-19). We cannot jump immediately from the wonderful promises of Genesis 1–2 to our present day. Something has intervened. In this world, human sin has corrupted the system so that all are not fed as God would want.

Sometimes people are hungry because of the sins of others who have not kept the commandments of God to take care of the defenseless, the poor, the widow, and orphan (as in Deut. 14:28-29 and numerous other places in Deuteronomy and the prophets). These persons remain hungry through no fault of their own. And God is not responsible for their hunger. On the contrary, God has left us with commandments that speak to their needs. The problem is with those of us who have not acted to share with them what God has given us.

It may be that the people have brought their famine on themselves by their sinful ways. There are passages that speak of God's bounty as a conditional gift. This does not mean that we are good enough to earn it, but we can be bad enough for God to take it away. God provides food for *those who fear him* (says Psalm 111:5a). Ahab accused Elijah of being the one who troubled Israel, but Elijah turned that accusation back on Ahab (1 Kings

18:17-18). The drought and famine was a result of Ahab's sin in allowing Baal religion to flourish in the nation. The terrible suffering and starvation of women and children during the siege of Jerusalem was interpreted by Jeremiah (and others) as the consequence of the sin of the nation. Not all people in the nation were equally guilty—some may have been quite innocent—but in a corporate society in which all are interconnected, the sin of one or a few can have devastating effects on the whole people. Deuteronomy had reminded the people not to become overconfident in their time of prosperity and forget that it is God who had given the food and the flocks. Since these things were God's to give, then God can also take them away if they go after other gods (Deut. 8:11-20).

Some texts indicate that God uses hunger and famine to teach the people so that they may turn back to God before it is too late and complete destruction comes. God let the people hunger in the wilderness so that they would know that "man does not live by bread alone, but that man lives by everything that proceeds out of the mouth of the Lord" (Deut. 8:3b). Amos promised doom for the people because they had not responded to earlier efforts by God to get their attention. " 'I gave you cleanness of teeth in all your cities, and lack of bread in all your places, yet you did not return to me,' says the Lord" (Amos 4:6).

No explanation but hang in there. One of the Hebrew words often translated as "hope" really means to wait *(yahal).* There may be no good explanation why things have gone wrong. One remembers the past and hopes that God will act again. One may or may not be able to pin the problem to human sin, whether others' or one's own. Often, hope is simply waiting—even with a kind of grim determination that "I will hang in there come hell or high water until things get better." Such a sentiment is shown in Hab. 3:17-18: "Though the fig tree do not blossom, nor fruit be on the vines, the produce of the olive fail and the fields yield no food, the flock be cut off from the fold and there be no herd in the stalls, yet I will rejoice in the Lord, I will joy in the God of my salvation." Similarly, with a stiff upper lip and dogged resolve, Job responded to his first series of calamities with, "Naked I came from my mother's womb, and naked shall I return; the Lord gave, and the Lord has taken away; blessed be the name of the Lord" (Job 1:21).

Such examples of piety fill us with admiration (perhaps) or skepticism (if one is still struggling with disillusionment and smashed hopes). How can one be so confident in God's providence when all the evidence seems to be running to the contrary? A person might envy such a faith—or wonder if it is "for real."

Lamenting may be a proper response. As stated earlier with regard to loss of the land, the lament is a common biblical way of responding to loss, whatever form that loss may take. It provides a process for keeping in touch with God, letting one's feeling and thoughts be known, and working through the relationship with God that has entered a time of trial. Though the content of the lament may be an expression of hopelessness, it may (as it usually does in the liturgical form of lament in the Psalter) lead one eventually back to renewed hope.

Biblical expressions of hope often speak of food and prosperity

In times of desperation, as hope begins to emerge again, those who are called to articulate that hope often resurrect the promises of the past. So it was with God's promises with regard to the land, and so it is with the renewed confidence that the Creator God will move to provide all our needs for nourishment. When they spoke of hope for the return of prosperity and abundant food for all, the prophets of the Old Testament seemed most often to be hoping for such things yet in this world. But, in some of them, there was a longing that seems almost beyond anything this world could offer—more like an eschatological vision of an ideal life of abundance and security.

The end of the book of Amos (9:11-15) promised crops so abundant that "the plowman shall overtake the reaper and the treader of grapes him who sows the seed" (9:13). Jeremiah promised that after the time of starvation and destruction, "again you shall plant vineyards upon the mountains of Samaria; the planters shall plant, and shall enjoy the fruit" (Jer. 31:5). The time of abundance and prosperity and security would return (Jer. 33:6-9). The wonderful oracle in Micah 4:1-4 ends with the promise of a time of peace when everyone will sit under his own fig tree (Isa. 2:1-4 duplicates most of this same oracle but not the part about the fig tree).

As we move toward the apocalyptic (or near-apocalyptic) material in the Old Testament, the hope for a feast prepared by God becomes a bit more dramatic, perhaps coming only after a terrible battle in which evil forces that impede God's promises are removed once and for all. Ezekiel 39:17-20 speaks of a rather bizarre sacrificial feast that God was preparing upon the mountains of Israel, where flesh would be eaten and blood would be drunk. In the so-called "Isaiah apocalypse," we read, "On this mountain the Lord of hosts will make for all peoples a feast of fat things, a feast of wine on the lees, of fat things full of marrow, of wine on the lees well refined. And he will destroy on this mountain the covering that is cast over all peoples, the veil that is spread over all nations. He will swallow up death forever, and the Lord God will wipe away tears from all faces . . ." (Isa. 25:6-8a). Ezekiel's vision of the new Jerusalem imagines a river flowing from the temple that would purify the stagnant waters so the fish would thrive and trees that grow along its banks would never fail to provide fruit (Ezek. 47:1-12).

And so the end time becomes like a glorious feast in which all our wants will be provided. Jesus told parables about the kingdom of heaven being like a feast or a wedding—sometimes with warnings not to refuse the invitation and not to arrive too late to get in. In the night in which he was betrayed, Jesus, who was also concerned for real food for real people, gave the ultimate food to his followers. Of course we need food for our physical bodies, but we need even more because those bodies will one day fail us. In the words of the precommunion liturgy used by my church, "Let the vineyards be fruitful, Lord, and fill to the brim our cup of blessing. Gather a harvest from the seeds that were sown, that we may be fed with the bread of life. Gather the hopes and dreams of all; unite them with the prayers we offer. Grace our table with your presence, and give us a foretaste of the feast to come" (*Lutheran Book of Worship*, p. 107).

Theological and pastoral observations

Hope for this world or the next? Again we are left with the question of how much can we hope for in this world. Do the hungry of this world have a right and a realistic hope that their plight will improve? Is it possible to remove starvation and famine? Is it possible to distribute the world's resources so that no one is in desperate want? Probably not—in this world of sin. And so there is logic in moving to understand God's promises of life-giving bread as a future eschatological hope. But can we not have both? We should not abandon our hopes for this world too soon, especially if by doing so, we are excusing our inability to share what we have in abundance with others.

Skipping over stage two. We have spoken of the tension between hopes for this world and the next, the difficulty in knowing when to move between the second and third stages of hope. There are some who try to avoid this tension by moving directly from stage one to stage three—from a naive hope that God will provide everything that we need in this life to the belief that God will provide all we need in the next life. That is, they try to avoid the struggle of trying to understand and deal with a world in which there is not always enough land and enough food. When all goes well, they speak of a God who provides everything. When confronted with examples to the contrary, they immediately jump to the next life as the only truly significant concern. And so, if God blesses you, you are free to enjoy that. If God does not bless you, it doesn't matter anyway because God will give you your reward in heaven.

This perspective sometimes surfaces in certain attitudes toward conservation of natural resources. God has given us the earth to use for our own pleasure. Conservation is for pessimists, prophets of doom, those with no hope. If someone protests that we are using up our soil, water, air, oil, trees, etc., in a reckless manner, the reply is either a naive trust that God will continue to provide no matter what we do *or* the world will end anyway before everything will be used up. Thinking similar to this was even expressed by a recent Secretary of the Interior of the United States.

Famine and starvation as a consequence of sin. As we have mentioned, there are a number of biblical texts which, in the struggle to understand why God is withholding the gifts of creation, interpret crop failure, terrible weather, starvation, and famine as God's acts of judgment against a faithless people (or, in some cases, even against individual families or persons). The disaster, then, is intended to be a catalyst to bring people to repentance and to give them the incentive not to go against God's law the next time.

Such texts can be a problem. A hailstorm or tornado or flood or drought is seen as God's judgment. People wring their hands and feel guilty and try to discover what they have done wrong to put them in such a situation. The final nail in the coffin for some of those farmers who have lost their land was a series of disastrous growing seasons. Are they to believe that God is punishing them for something—or maybe is trying to teach them something? Or, to turn it around, is the successful farmer to believe that he deserves his good fortune? Does the wealthy nation understand that it has God's favor in a way that poor countries do not? One must be careful not to be too simplistic in applying such theories to explain away misfortune and to protect God's image for the sake of future hope.

Hanging on to hope against the evidence. We looked at Habakkuk and Job as examples of those who were determined to trust God and have hope even though the world was falling in around them. Are they examples of piety to be admired? Or might we be suspicious that they were merely "whistling 'Dixie' while Atlanta burns," hiding their heads in the sand, pretending that all was still okay, when deep down inside it was not?

Timing seems to be a very important matter in understanding submission to God and trust in God even when everything is going wrong. Often, in times of disaster, people will still talk the old way, say the old words of hope, trying to convince themselves even as they fear they are slipping into doubt and fear about the future. For some, hope may seem to vanish for a time (maybe even a long time) and they can no more say those words of trust. If they talk of God or to God at all, it can only be in words of complaint and lament. But, strangely, these persons often return to hope. And, as they return, they say the same words which they had said before. The first time, there was a shallowness, a naiveté to their expression of hope. It had not yet taken seriously enough the depth of the loss. Perhaps it was still holding out for some earthly manifestation of God's activity that would somehow prove that God could be trusted after all. But then, as the depths were reached, God was even there. Now nothing that can happen can remove hope because it truly does transcend events and blessings of this life. In chapters 1 and 2, Job perhaps spoke too quickly of his immovable trust in God. His stoic submission was premature. It took many chapters of debate with his friends and himself, much complaining and lamenting, and finally, some rather pointed words directly from God, before Job was able to return to submission to God. The words he says at the end of the book (42:1-5) are, on the surface, not that different from what he said at the beginning (1:21). He still had no explanations for his suffering. His trust was still dependent on his relationship with God, not on tangible evidence. But now that relationship had been hammered out through his experience. Now he lived in hope that could deal with his misfortune. In the epilog (42:7-17) at the end of Job, his fortunes were restored. But the change in Job had already taken place prior to that time. My guess is that Job would have lived the rest of his life in hope, even without the happy ending.

3
HOPE
FOR
PROTECTION
FROM DANGER

The world is certainly filled with many things than can hurt us. We could spend our whole lifetime living in terror about what is coming next. There are the threats to our whole nation from outside enemies or from our own unscrupulous leaders who misuse their power and authority. There are countless dangers that can come to hurt us individually—illnesses that medical science cannot seem to defeat (even new diseases that arise out of nowhere), automobile accidents, loss of employment, violent criminals and terrorists, destructive storms, floods, or earthquakes. One has only to peruse the morning newspaper to imagine a whole litany of peril that one may have to face that very day. A child dies in her sleep. An innocent bystander is run over by a drunk driver. A plane crashes, killing more than 100 persons. Often there seems to be no point to it. The stupid, freak accidents are particularly hard to understand, and they drive home the terrifying insight that we are all, at all times, exposed and vulnerable to all sorts of calamities. If one has a supernatural world view, then one can add a myriad of unseen enemies (demons and evil spirits and other hostile cosmic forces) to the ones that are visible. No wonder that the future can seem to be a very fearsome place—both to those who have already felt the sting and know what it is to be profoundly hurt, but also to others who live in dread because they suspect that their present run of good fortune is too good to last. And, of course, the last great threat that we will all have to face is death. How will we experience that and what comes after? Even though we survive the dangers of this life relatively unscathed, there is no way to avoid the ultimate threat to our person (unless, of course, the world should end before we have to die).

And so we look to God to protect us from danger as we move to the future. As we look at the biblical record, we see that God's people lived with promises from God that God would protect them from what could hurt them. They found comfort and hope in those promises, though not without struggle and with some adjustments in how they understood these words of hope. Again, we shall see the transition through stages of naive optimism about this world to disillusionment to new hope which must look beyond this world. For those in the first stage, the hope is that God will keep them away from danger. For those who have already been hurt (defeat by an enemy, illness, etc.), the hope is that God will deliver them from the danger and restore them. At this point, they may wonder for a time why God allowed the hurtful thing to happen, and then the focus will turn toward some future act of God which will defeat the enemy that has temporarily won the battle.

At times, it was hoped that God would act directly to protect us from danger. At other times, it was recognized that God acted through intermediaries (angels, humans—such as judges and prophets and kings and healers) to protect or deliver us from what can hurt us. Similarly, it was thought that sometimes God would act directly to raise up leaders to meet specific times of crisis (as in the days of the judges), but in other times there was confidence that God worked on our behalf by setting up specific institutions (such as the Davidic kingship, the priesthood and its rituals, the Christian church) to be mediators of God's activity in the world. In a time of distrust of all human institutions, hope again returns to God who will have to act directly in order to bring about the final victory over all that can harm us (as in the apocalyptic thought world).

We will divide biblical texts which express the hope that God will protect us from danger into two categories: (*a*) hope for the people as a whole, the nation, the community and (*b*) the hope of the individual for God's protection.

God's Response to Threats against the Whole People

God called out a people, saved them from slavery, formed them into a community, and promised to be with them to protect them from enemies. Those of us who are acquainted with the biblical tradition have borrowed from their understanding of how God protects his chosen people when we speak of God's involvement in our own national life and our assurance that God will save our nation.

Oppression in Egypt

God saw the affliction of his people in Egypt and came down to save them from their oppressors. This is the primary story of God's deliverance from those who would enslave us, force us to do their will, use us in order to benefit themselves. Though such tyranny may continue for a time, as it did in Egypt, God will eventually intervene to save his own from their oppressors. God was their king and the only one whom they were to serve. Even the mighty pharaoh could not withstand the power of God on behalf of the lowly, despised, enslaved. The king of Egypt would be forced to let God's people go.

God enlisted Moses to be the intermediary in the release of the captives. But God was the real actor. Moses claimed no special talent, had already fled from Egypt in fear, claimed that he could not even speak in a way that would persuade anyone to do anything (Exod. 4:10-17), and, in short, was very reluctant to take on this assignment. Never mind. God would take care of it. There would be mighty signs, not least of all the crossing of the sea with Egyptian troops in hot pursuit, making it clear to the community of believers that this escape was definitely God's work.

The signs of God's intervention are much more obvious here than in many other biblical stories. It becomes the story to recount again and again to remind ourselves what kind of God this

51

is. God has the power and the will to free us from danger. We take that story with us as we face the future, secure in the faith that God who created a people by freeing them from their task-masters will continue to act in like manner as we face new dangers to our existence as a people.

This is very much an "earthly" hope. God works within this life to bring deliverance. The Egyptians were real people. The Hebrew slaves did not have to remain in that servile situation until released finally by death. God was moved by their plight in this life and was unwilling to let this continue any longer. The time for salvation was now—not in some future century or future world.

The example of the exodus, the hope in a God who acts on the side of the poor and oppressed, has inspired many revolu-tionary movements who have thought that they, too, deserved freedom in this life—and dared to believe that God would sup-port them in their hopes. In our day, liberation theologians and activists on behalf of many social causes have looked at these texts in such a way.

The charismatic individual

Though God may work through the miraculous, as in the case of the plagues on Egypt or the crossing of the sea, God also acts to bring deliverance by selecting certain persons to do the job that must be done. These are people with charisma, the touch of the spirit which has singled them out for special gifts to be used on behalf of the people. Moses was such a person. He was not appointed or elected to an already existing office. He did not inherit a title. He came into a position of authority only because God appointed him. When God saw the situation of the slaves in Egypt, God chose one who would do what had to be done to set them free. God will provide the right person for the right time—the charismatic personality who will suddenly appear on the scene to save the people just when all seems to be hopeless.

As the people of Israel settled into the promised land, they continued to hope for God to provide the leadership that they needed. God was still thought of as the king who was active in the events of their lives. The ideal was to have as little human government as possible so that God's Spirit could act freely, unencumbered by human methods of providing leadership, to raise up God's own choice. To try to manipulate the selection or to borrow human institutions such as monarchy in order to assure an orderly transition of leadership was a sign of lack of faith in God's participation in the process.

And so we read in the book of Judges about a succession of leaders whom God selected to deliver the people in times of danger—Othniel, Ehud, Deborah, Gideon, Jephthah, Samson. The same cycle was repeated several times as the deuteronomic historian tried to make some sense out of the ebb and flow of the fortunes of the people. They turned away from the Lord to follow other gods. The Lord was angry and sent some enemy to harrass them (again we see that God's promises are contingent on obedience; if God does not provide what had been promised, the fault is most likely to be found in the sins of the people). But when the people cried to God for help (as did their ancestors in Egypt), God was moved by compassion to send them a deliverer. God had allowed them to become temporarily subjected to enemies but would not allow them to stay in the predicament. The promise still held. The deliverer fought on their behalf. The enemy was subdued. There was peace until the leader died. Then the people backslid again, turned toward false gods, angered God; an enemy was allowed to prevail; they asked for help; and the whole cycle was repeated.

In order to emphasize trust in God as the king, there was to be as little human government as possible. There was no room to play politics here. When the crisis that led to the judge's appointment had passed, he or she was supposed to withdraw quietly to his or her previous status and not assume to have any permanent authority, especially not any claim that could be passed on to the judge's children. Their thinking went like this: "Let God choose our leaders. We can count on God to send the right person for the job."

This view of the function of government is not strange to many people in our own day. Many still believe that the less government the better. Too much human manipulation only tends to mess things up. Better to let natural selection processes (whether understood as God's activity or capitalistic theories or a kind of "survival of the fittest" or an idealized view of democracy where the voice of the people is "the voice of God") run their course. Don't give the politicians too much power. For such persons, hope for the future of their nation lies in limiting human interference with forces that work best when left alone. Some, like the ancient Israelites, will claim that God works best when humans don't interfere.

Compromise with reality

Finally, the ideal had to deal with reality. To be sure, God is the king and God will send us a deliverer. But the enemy is getting closer. Defeat seems inevitable if someone does not do something. Here we are, waiting for God to act, while the enemy takes advantage of our lack of preparedness, our disorganization, our deficiency of army and weapons. This was the situation of ancient Israel at the end of the period of the judges. The Philistines were threatening to push the people off the land which God had long ago promised to Abraham and his descendants. Samuel, the last of the great charismatic judges, was old and his sons were unworthy to assume leadership (1 Sam. 8:1-5). Something had to be done. And so the elders of Israel met with Samuel and insisted that he appoint a king "to govern us like all the nations" (1 Sam. 8:5). The idea displeased Samuel, but after talking it over with God and giving them a warning of what it would be like to have a king, he finally agreed, with God's consent, to make them a king (1 Sam. 8:6-22). (In the next chapter, 1 Samuel 9, Samuel seems less opposed to the idea of kingship, revealing perhaps that there was a considerable difference of opinion in Israel about the wisdom of proceeding to turn the nation into a monarchic state.)

God had promised to protect the people. So far, God had provided Moses and Joshua and the judges, including Samuel. But the situation was desperate. The people feared to sit on their hands, waiting for God to act, submitting weakly to their enemies without fighting back. And so Israel took a momentous step in appointing a king. In order to protect themselves from outside enemies, they had to make this move. But how could they do this without losing the important truth that God was still the true king, and the human king was only acting at God's bidding? If you give a king enough authority to raise taxes, draft young men for his army, and enforce law and order, you run the risk that the king will assume too much power. He may begin to think he can do whatever he wants without having to answer to God and to the people. He may forget that he is there to serve and protect the people, and he may begin to use the people for his own gain. And then, ironically, the people who had wanted a king to protect them from their enemies will now need protection from their own king.

And so, in this beginning of monarchy, it seems that there was a compromise worked out. The people could have their king. But he had to be appointed by God, through a prophet. And he was not to assume that the job would belong to him and his heirs forever. If he did not live up to God's expectations for a king, then God (still playing an active role in all this) would send a prophet to speak critical words to the king, and if he would not heed them, God's prophet would choose someone else to be the king. And so Samuel chose Saul, then rejected Saul and anointed David. This prophet–king relationship continued between Nathan and David. David was severely criticized by Nathan for his sin against Bathsheba and Uriah (2 Sam. 12:1-14), but the kingdom was not taken away from David. Nathan himself spoke an oracle about David's dynasty lasting forever (2 Sam. 7:11-16), though there is considerable doubt that Nathan would have been that supportive of an eternal dynasty. After the death of Solomon, there are very few recorded confrontations between prophet and king in Judah. The idea of a divinely sanctioned dynasty took over. In the northern kingdom of Israel, however, the prophetic tradition of critiquing the king and even seeking his overthrow in revolution was carried on by prophets like Ahijah (1 Kings 11:29-31; 14:1-20), Jehu (1 Kings 16:1-4), Elijah and Elisha.

There is a clear realism here. Human leadership is needed but cannot be fully trusted. For the sake of order and protection from enemies, we will have a king, but his power must be limited or he will develop pretensions of grandeur. He must be reminded that only God is king. He needs a prophet, an advisor who is close to God and will assure that the king does not become a tyrant, endangering the very people he is supposed to protect.

Most kings would not like this kind of arrangement. They would resent limitations on their power. A pious king like David might listen when the prophet shakes his bony finger at him and condemns his behavior. But other kings might just as likely have the prophet removed, thrown in jail, or even killed to get him out of the way and prevent him from stirring up thoughts of rebellion among the people. And so would be the response of later kings to prophets—e.g., Ahab to Elijah or Jehoiakim to Jeremiah.

Divinely appointed dynasty

Somewhere along the way the idea of an eternal covenant between God and David emerged. The king, as worked out in the compromise, was to be chosen by God through the prophet. But, in the case of Saul, the kingship was contingent on Saul's obedience to God's commands as passed on by the prophet. When Saul failed to follow Samuel's direction, he was removed and the way was prepared for David to be his successor. This was not to be a typical oriental dynasty in which the king's son automatically took the throne on the death of his father. There were too many hazards to that system. A great king may have had a terribly incompetent or cruel son. The sons of some of the priests and judges (including Samuel) in Israel's past had demonstrated that sons often did not live up to the reputation of their fathers.

When David died, his son did succeed him, though it was quite a troubled and bloody story before one of them survived to assume the throne. Though Nathan challenged David, he did not act to remove David from the throne. Probably he could not, even if he wanted to. As noted earlier, Nathan actually was quoted as speaking an oracle that promised an eternal covenant between God and David (2 Sam. 7:11-16). This is a very important passage for the development of the idea of the Davidic dynasty and

God's promises to keep it going forever. In later times, when there was no longer a king on the throne, people would return to this promise and look for a future king, a messiah, whom God would send to save the people.

The king would want to have his subjects believe that he and his family were singled out by God to rule a nation forever. If the people could be convinced that it was part of God's plan for the world that David's family should rule, then they were not very likely to engage in subversive activities to overthrow the king and set up a different government. Who would dare to go against what God had ordained? This was a wonderful way to maintain law and order, to keep people in line, to provide an orderly transition at the time of the death of the king.

The Davidic dynasty lasted for a long time—over 400 years. In the history of the world, that is a very long time for any family to occupy a throne without being removed by some rival family. As the years went by, the people became more and more confident in the eternal quality of this promise from God. Had it not been demonstrated by many years of history? The inviolable character of the promise to the king also became connected with promises about the city of Jerusalem and the temple. God would see that no enemy would overthrow them. They would go on forever. After a close call in escaping total destruction at the hands of the Assyrians in the time of Isaiah, this confidence in God's protection grew even stronger. "Nothing can defeat us. God is on the side of our king and our temple and will protect us forever." When Jeremiah tried to convince the people that the temple and city and kingship were doomed, he was treated as both a traitor and a faithless man who did not believe in God's promises. (See chapters 7 and 26 of Jeremiah.)

Our Bible contains many texts that glorify the king and the Davidic dynasty. Some of them were composed for special occasions like coronations (Psalms 2 and 110; perhaps Isa. 9:2-7) or weddings (Psalm 45; perhaps part of the Song of Songs) or asking for victory in battle (Psalm 20) or giving thanks for victory already achieved (as Psalms 18 and 21; perhaps Psalm 118) or commemorating God's choice of Jerusalem and David (Psalm

132). During the exile and following, these texts (and others that speak of God's promises to David) took on a future orientation. They became part of the promise that God would send a new Messiah, a new son of David who would deliver the people from what oppressed them. In our day hardly anyone would still hold for a literal earthly reinstatement of the Davidic dynasty. Even the Jews who have founded the modern state of Israel have not attempted to set up a monarchy with a descendant of David on the throne. Christians have understood the promise to David in a special way relating to Jesus Christ (more of that later), and Jews have their own ways of talking about the Messiah.

But there is a way in which our hopes for our nation often parallel the hope for an eternal promise between God and David. We, too, tend to absolutize our own way of government, our own nation. We think we have God's special favor as over against other nations. It is hard for patriots of any nationality to imagine that there will come a day when their country (the United States of America, the U.S.S.R., the United Kingdom, France or any other country) will no longer exist in its present form. Like Jeremiah's contemporaries, we resist mightily any prophets of doom who dare suggest that our great and wonderful nation could ever meet a fate like that which happened to ancient Judah. And yet, if any nation ever had God's promises of protection, they did. Are we to claim even more for ourselves than was possible for them?

Continuing prophetic suspicion of authority

The history of the monarchy in Judah and Israel is, in some sense, a continuation of the rival points of view that led to the compromise under Samuel. On the one hand was the need for stability, law and order, that led eventually to the belief in a divine sanction for the house of David. Who would challenge a leader whom God himself had put on the throne? But on the other side was the suspicion of authority, the refusal to grant to mere humans the authority that belongs only to God. As long as there were kings, there would be prophets, reminding the king that God would not tolerate disobedience in the king anymore than in any other human being. A system of government that is too rigid, that picks a leader merely because that person is born in the right family, that does not allow for the removal of bad leadership and the expression of the people's will is dangerous. God protects people from their own leaders by sending prophets.

Perhaps we would be best served if we could keep both these traditions in tension with each other. On the one hand, we have the danger of tyranny on the part of the ruler. On the other hand, we have the danger of chaos, a government constantly being attacked by prophets who are always much better at criticizing than they are at governing. Our U.S. constitution seems to have taken seriously the suspicion of authority that we see in the prophetic tradition. The founders of our system of government were no doubt influenced both by their biblical understanding and their experiences with the nations of Europe. And so our constitution contains an elaborate system of checks and balances. In our history, we tend to swing back and forth between times of submission to whatever our leaders say is right to times of distrust when we scarcely can believe anyone in authority. There are considerable difficulties in being stuck at either end of that spectrum.

Messianic hope

The exile was a severe test of people's faith. Many of the beliefs that had held the community together and given it hope were shattered. The naive stage had ended with a vengeance. Those who had hoped in a God who would demonstrate his power by keeping their nation safe from all foreign enemies now had to go back to the drawing board. Those who had believed that God would always give them a king from the house of David as a symbol of the everlasting promise to watch over the people now had to think of some other source for their hope. Could they still trust in God? Was this not an indication that God's promises meant nothing? The facts were simple. God had promised an eternal kingship. Now there was no king. The promise had failed. Was God too weak to provide what had been promised? Or was God uncaring? Surely God had not lied. What went wrong?

Prophets like Jeremiah and Ezekiel (and earlier ones like Amos,

Hosea, Micah, Isaiah) helped provide some rationale for dealing with this. Had not Jeremiah warned them? God was not weak or arbitrary or unjust. There was always some contingency to the promise. God could not allow sins of the kings and the people to go unnoticed. The end of the nation and the kingship was the result of the sin of the people. They had brought it on themselves. That line of reasoning helped people move through the trauma of the loss of their dreams. It enabled them to continue to trust in God.

But now what? Would God remain angry forever? Was it all over between God and the people? Again, the prophets helped the people turn toward the future. Some of the same prophets (such as Jeremiah and Ezekiel) who had uttered words of doom now began to speak words of hope. God had not broken his promises. God would continue to protect and keep his people. They would not perish. They would return to their land (we have already looked at examples of that promise). And they would have new leadership—better than they had ever had before. The ancient promise to David was still intact. Though temporarily sidetracked by the people's sin, it had not been retracted. God does not break promises. Someday God would send a new king, a Messiah (the anointed one) who would reign with justice and make his people prosper in peace. Some texts very specifically connect this new ruler with the line of David (as Isa. 11:1-5; Jer. 23:5-6; 33:14-26; 30:9; Micah 5:2-4). Other prophets, such as Ezekiel and Isaiah 40–66, do not tie their hopes so closely to the emergence of a new king from David's line. Earlier texts that had been sung to celebrate events in the life of the king, especially those having to do with his coronation (as Psalms 2 and 110 and Isa. 9:2-7), now became future-oriented, words of promise about a wonderful new king who would restore the fortunes of the people, protect them from outside enemies, and maintain justice within.

Most of the prophets were probably thinking of a real king who would sit in Jerusalem and rule the country as David had done, but even better. That is to say, this was still an earthly hope for most of them. However, their experience with past rulers had been so bad—only David and perhaps a couple of others that were worthy of any praise at all—that maybe it would take more than an earthly king to bring about God's kingdom on earth. Ezekiel suggested that God himself would have to assume the role of the shepherd of the people. No human being had been up to the job (Ezek. 34:7-16). There was a movement back toward God's direct participation in the governing of the people. The human intermediaries had failed. The institution of kingship had sunk in the flood of human sin.

On various levels, we still look for a "messiah," one who will come riding in on a white horse and save our nation from peril. We want to believe there is such a person out there, perhaps born in a humble out-of-the-way place (like Bethlehem). Maybe such a one will be like one of the great leaders of the past—a new Washington or Jefferson or Lincoln. We are ready to believe and follow such a person if one will appear and promise us relief from our troubles. Others of us are more cynical. In this world, at least, there are no "messiahs," no quick fixes, no guarantees that a strong and safe nation will continue forever. The one who hopes for an earthly messiah will, sooner or later, be disappointed and will be forced to move from one stage of hope to another if hope is to be maintained at all.

Apocalyptic hope

Older biblical views sought to find ways in which God could still act through the human institutions of government. If God would not send leaders when they were needed, then the people would let prophets choose the king and watch over them. Or, if God would designate a specific family to rule, then they would know that they could safely submit themselves to that authority. But now the Davidic dynasty had been broken. In spite of some renewed optimism on the part of some prophets, things were not going very well for those who had returned from exile to Jerusalem. The glorious days of David and Solomon were not going to be repeated. Most of the time what was left of Judah was dominated by some foreign superpower (Persian or Greek or

Roman), and their own leaders were really pitiful. How could God possibly be at work in such rotten human institutions?

The thinking went like this: "The whole world is corrupt. All rulers are evil. There is a complete split between the kingdom of God and the kingdoms of this world. God does not work in the institutions of the world as presently constituted. In fact, they all work against God. The only hope is for God to intervene in order to destroy the evils now in control and to assume more direct control for himself." The sustaining hope with such a world view is that God will take such action soon. Christ and the heavenly armies will defeat all that is evil (as in Rev. 19:11-21).

There seem to be a number of people in our own day who hold such dismal hopes for our world and its human governments. With this hope for the future, there would be at least two ways one could go: (1) One could choose quietism and submission to authority. The powers that presently rule the world are only temporary, and they are too strong for mere mortals to resist anyway. So, one should make the best of a bad situation, live as well as possible, try to survive without losing all integrity. (2) A person may decide to work to destroy the present system of government in order to speed the arrival of the new day. God is the main actor in the overthrow of the present world, but God may enlist his followers to pick up their arms and follow. People who are deeply immersed in this apocalyptic frame of mind are more likely to be found in vicious, tyrannical, totalitarian societies. But they can be found anywhere, at least partly because even the best of governments is not perfect, and there are people in every society with real or imagined reasons to hate and distrust the authorities.

King Jesus and his kingdom

We Christians call Jesus the Messiah, the anointed ruler whom God has sent into the world to save us from what can hurt us— sin, evil, the devil, death. But in the minds of many, the "Messiah" was to be a political leader, one who would drive out the Roman oppressors, bring back Judah's independence, and rule the people in peace and justice. It is no wonder that many did not accept

Jesus as the Messiah. He did not fit their expectations for what a messiah is supposed to do. He ran away when they tried to make him king (John 6:15). Perhaps their hopes for him were raised again when he rode into Jerusalem on the back of an ass, like the king mentioned by Zechariah (9:9). But a few days later he was dead. What good is a messiah who is dead? How will the enemies be defeated and the people protected if their king willingly allows himself to be put to death by the very authorities that he should be defying? It was too much to grasp. It didn't make sense. Those whose hope for a messiah was still firmly attached to a specific political agenda for this world saw little reason to call Jesus the "Messiah." Hadn't Jesus himself declared that his kingdom was not of this world? (John 18:36).

The king whom God sends does not rule by force but by love and forgiveness. This king does not destroy his enemies but loves them. He does not inflict suffering on others but assumes their suffering on himself. This is a strange king indeed. It is something different for this world. It has an unreal, idealistic, future quality to it. Kings don't survive in the real world by living like this. Perhaps Jesus shows us more of what God is like than what earthly kings are capable of doing. But, if the human ruler is to be God's representative on this earth put here to watch out for God's people and see them safely through times of danger, maybe there is much to learn from the meek and loving and forgiving Jesus. Such rulers would be welcomed by some of us now, in this world, before the final age arrives.

Jesus' kingdom is not of this world. It is not tied to the fortunes of any specific nation-state—whether ancient or modern Israel or the United States or any other political entity. Promises of an eternal covenant, hope in a God who will never abandon the people whom he has called for his own, are still valid. They transcend the kingdoms of this world. They even transcend the survival of the worldly institution of the church. They are trustworthy for all time and beyond. Individual kingdoms will come and go, but the kingdom of God is forever.

God Will Protect the Individual Believer

Individuals within the society also face a myriad of dangers as they walk through life. There are many things out there that can hurt us. The believer finds comfort in God's promises to go with us into our future, to protect us from danger, to deliver us from illness or other destructive situations, and finally, to see us safely through the most hazardous trip of all—death.

As we look at examples of biblical texts on this subject, several questions reappear, as they do whenever we examine the biblical words of hope. What does God actually promise? Will God protect me from dangers in this life? If so, how come bad things still happen to me and my loved ones? Does God heal diseases? Are there some that God can heal and others not? When do I give up on seeking deliverance from God in this life and begin to focus on the next? How tightly does God control everything that happens in the world—a car skidding on the ice, the hands of a drunk on the steering wheel, the flick of the knife by a surgeon, the invasion of a virus into the cells of my body? Am I unrealistic to expect God to protect me and heal me from all harmful things? Or, am I showing lack of faith to doubt God's healing power in even the most pessimistic diagnosis?

These anecdotes illustrate our dilemma with similar questions:

It was a terrible morning at the seminary. A member of the community had died the night before in an automobile accident. The word was passed around during the first two hours of class, but many had not yet heard of the tragedy until the announcement was made at the beginning of chapel service. The congregation was stunned. How do we respond? The worship service must go on. Surely, Christians worship in bad times as well as good. But what had been planned by the participants a week earlier was not necessarily any longer appropriate. The sermon was abbreviated and modified to speak at least partially to this occasion. Then we proceeded with the morning prayers as written in the liturgy. The words of the concluding collect jumped out at me: "O Lord, almighty and everlasting God, you have brought us in safety to this new day; preserve us with your mighty power. . ." (*Lutheran Book of Worship*, p. 136). I couldn't hear the rest of it. How could we pray this prayer? We had just begun to mourn the death of one who was not brought safely to this new day. So, where was God in all of that? And, if this person was not protected, then how do we go on with the rest of the prayer asking God, with his mighty power, to protect us in this new day and all the new days? Can we expect more from God than this accident victim received?

The businessman had not found peace in the two years since the plane accident. He never was very fond of flying, even though his job required him to do so several times a month. He usually said a little prayer just as the plane took off and again as it landed. He did it automatically. Somehow it made him feel a little better. He would never forget that day two years ago. He was delayed at the office and then was stuck in traffic. When his plane was taking off, he was still two miles from the airport. He was furious. The only thing worse than flying was time spent waiting in airports. Then he saw a big column of smoke off to the left. Only after he entered the terminal did he realize what had happened. His plane had crashed. If he had been on time, he would be dead. For the first few weeks after the event he felt grateful, though somewhat guilty because he was alive and all those others were dead. He was a religious person, and it was hard for him to understand what part God had to play in all this. He thanked God for saving him. But then, why hadn't God saved all those others? He knew there were people on that plane who were probably better human beings than he, maybe with more important work to do, perhaps with families that were even more in need of them than in his own case. Why should he be alive? Does God have some purpose in this? Does God have something that he should do? If so, he doesn't know what it is, and he feels tremendous pressure because nothing that significant seems to be happening in his life and work. Maybe it was just a freak accident and just blind luck on his part. Maybe God had nothing to do with it. He almost wishes he could believe that to take some of the pressure off his back.

Every Sunday morning she watched all the religious programs on television. She was in bed most of the time. She had not been out of the house for a year or so, and the last time she was in church was two years before the present pastor arrived. He came to see her once in a while, but she depended on television for her worship life. She loved the music and the messages were uplifting. But she always felt a little uncomfortable when they started reading the letters or giving testimonies from people who had been healed from their diseases. Some of them even claimed to have recovered from the same ailment that had kept her an invalid all these years. At first, she found some hope in the accounts of their miraculous cures. But lately, they only depressed her. She had prayed to be healed. Her pastor prayed for it. Many of her friends remembered her faithfully in their prayer groups. How come all those other people get results but she didn't? Do they know some better way to pray? Have they been more deserving? Do they have more faith? Does God really keep promises? She did not know what to hope for anymore. She really doubted that she would ever be able to live a normal life again. But couldn't it get better than this? Her disease probably wouldn't kill her—at least for a long time. What did she have to look forward to? Is there any relief this side of death? She did believe strongly in a life after death and expected to find release there. That faith kept her going. But what about the meantime?

The character of God is to deliver us from trouble

There are many biblical texts which portray a God who is determined to protect us from trouble and to rescue us if we have already gotten into trouble. This is true with regard to the whole society, as we have seen, but also is true for the dangers which confront the individual. There should be no doubt about God's intention. Though there are times when trouble comes anyway, we should remind ourselves that our suffering and hurt is not what God wants for us. However we resolve the intellectual dilemma of a good and powerful God who rules a world where dangers abound, we should hold fast to the belief that God wants only the best for us and eventually will achieve that.

Even fallen sinners are objects of God's care and protection. Throughout the Bible, much of the trouble that comes to the world is ascribed to human sin—the sins of others (both past and present) and our own. The story of the fall at the beginning of the biblical account already makes this point. Though punishment came for those sins of Adam and Eve and their children, God was quick to move to ameliorate the problem, to bring some protection from the hostile world in which the humans now found themselves. Immediately following the curses on the serpent, woman and man, the Lord God Almighty "made for Adam and for his wife garments of skins, and clothed them" (Gen. 3:21). The man and woman had gotten themselves into a horrible mess. God would not pull them out of it. There would be many perils in the life that they now were forced to live, away from the security and bounty of the garden. But God had not abandoned them. God was still with them, even willing to take on the humble task of making garments for them. This is a lovely message of God reaching out to offer assistance to us as we struggle through our earthly life.

Similarly Cain, the first murderer, was punished for his grievous sin against his brother. He would be a fugitive and wanderer on the earth (no land), tilling ground that was reluctant to yield its fruit (Gen. 4:12). Cain protested that his punishment was more than he could bear (Gen. 4:13), and as a fugitive and wanderer, he would likely be slain by anyone who found him (Gen. 4:14). And God listened to him and acted to protect him. If anyone hurt Cain, they would be subject to God's vengeance (even sevenfold—Gen. 4:15a). Further, God put a mark on Cain "lest any who came upon him should kill him" (Gen. 4:15b).

Even in a fallen world, where human beings hurt one another and bring suffering down on themselves, God will act to protect us from at least some of the dangers that could befall us. In this life, at least, God will not remove all the threats. The curses on Adam and Eve are still in effect. Cain is still a wanderer without land and often without food. But God is not absent. God has not turned away from them. God still wants to ease their burden as much as possible in their life situation. Some protection can come from God even in this life.

Psalms of lament and thanksgiving expect God to work for our well-being. Psalms of lament ask for help from God in times of trouble. They expect God to hear them and to do something about their problem. Sometimes they wonder why God doesn't act quicker or they feel that injustice has been done in allowing trouble to come at all. But they turn to God because there is no place else to turn. God is the ultimate authority. If God cannot help, then no one can. The typical lament form merges with the psalm of thanksgiving and/or praise, confident that God has heard and already anticipating that God will take action to remedy the situation. The psalm of thanksgiving recognizes, after the deliverance from some danger, that it is God who has been the deliverer.

The following examples are typical of many lament psalms, especially those in the first part of the Psalter:

O Lord, how many are my foes!
Many are rising against me;
many are saying of me,
    there is no help for him in God.

But thou, O Lord, art a shield about me,
    my glory, and the lifter of my head.
I cry aloud to the Lord,
    and he answers me from his holy hill.
                Psalm 3:1-4

In peace I will both lie down and sleep;
for thou alone, O Lord, makest me dwell in safety.
                Psalm 4:8

In Psalm 27:1-6 we see a lovely expression of this kind of trust:

The Lord is my light and my salvation;
    whom shall I fear?
The Lord is the stronghold of my life;
    of whom shall I be afraid?
                Psalm 27:1

For he will hide me in his shelter in the day of trouble;
he will conceal me under the cover of his tent,
  he will set me high upon a rock.
      Psalm 27:5

Some psalms specifically ask for healing:

Be gracious to me, O Lord, for I am languishing;
  O Lord, heal me, for my bones are troubled.
My soul also is sorely troubled.
  But thou, O Lord—how long?
      Psalm 6:2-3

The Lord sustains him [the one who considers the poor]
on his sickbed;
  in his illness thou healest all his infirmities.
As for me, I said, "O Lord, be gracious to me;
  heal me, for I have sinned against thee!"
      Psalm 41:3-4

Psalm 30 is a prayer of thanksgiving for healing:

O Lord, my God, I cried to thee for help,
  and thou hast healed me.
O Lord, thou hast brought up my soul from Sheol,
  restored me to life from among those gone down to the Pit.
      Psalm 30:2-3

Many biblical narratives tell of God's protection from peril. There are many examples in the Bible of God taking action to protect the faithful from some danger. Most people could prepare their own list of favorite Bible stories of deliverance from an enemy or other hazard to life and limb. Two of the more colorful stories are from the book of Daniel, where God sent an angel to bring about deliverance. The three young Hebrew men emerged unscathed from a furnace so hot that it even killed the mighty men who threw them into the inferno (Dan. 3:19-23). When the king peered into the furnace, he saw a fourth figure (3:25), who turned out to be an angel sent by God to deliver his servants (3:28). In the familiar story of Daniel in the den of lions, God sent an angel to shut the lions' mouths so they did not hurt him (Dan. 6:16-22). In a nice ironic twist, however, those who had accused Daniel were cast into the den and were torn apart by the lions even before their bodies reached the bottom of the den (6:24). No guardian angel for them.

The New Testament contains many stories of Jesus acting to save people from what can harm them. He cast out demons that bring physical illness or mental torment. He stilled the storm and walked on the sea, showing that even the tremendous forces of nature have no ultimate power to hurt us. He healed all manner of diseases. He made the lame walk and the blind see and the deaf hear. He even raised people from the dead and demonstrated through his own resurrection that even this most dangerous enemy is not able to conquer us. Through words and action, Jesus demonstrated a God who is able and willing to save us from every possible hurt.

Such stories remind us again of what kind of God we have. They provide a basis for hope. As God has done in the past, so God can do again, in our own day, and in the future.

God as healer

One of the ways in which God protects and delivers us from danger is by healing us of our diseases. We have already made some mention of texts, both in Old and New Testaments, in which God acted to bring healing. A few more words should be said about our hope for healing.

Health and wholeness are the normal state. Sickness and death are abnormal. God intended a good world, free of suffering and pain and illness. This means that we should never accept loss of health as normal, something to be accepted passively without a fight, a condition easily passed off as "God's will." We should expect health because God wants it for us. Even in times of severe illness, we should look ahead with confidence to a time of health and wholeness again. If that is what God wants, then sooner or later, that will be what God will achieve. The difficult question for us is whether or not it will be achieved in this life.

70

We are invited to come to God to make our requests. God bids us to make our needs and desires known in prayer, even though they be outrageous, flying in the face of all that medical science and past human experience has reckoned to be possible. Our prayers in times of illness are to be honest communication of our deepest fears and hopes. If we want to ask for a return to health even as we lie on death's door, then that is what we should do. We ought not to be so timid that we censor our prayers before we utter them, checking whether or not we think God can accomplish our request.

Sometimes the cure will not come. The answer may be a clear "no," or it may appear that there is no answer at all—only silence and seeming indifference. To be sure, we are invited to ask for anything, to tell God what we really want. But it does not necessarily follow that all our requests will be granted just exactly as we have made them. To believe that we can so manipulate God is dangerous and leaves us terribly vulnerable to dashed hopes. God is no genie in the lamp who is compelled to follow our bidding. There is not that kind of magic in prayer. Even the great heroes of the faith in biblical times occasionally had to deal with a "no" from God. Moses never reached the promised land (Deut. 3:23-28), Jeremiah never had his burden taken away (Jer. 15:18), David's baby died in spite of his impassioned prayers (2 Sam. 12:15-23), Jesus did not have his cup removed but had to endure execution on a cross (Matt. 26:36-46), Paul never had his thorn in the flesh removed (2 Cor. 12:7-10). But each received other things from God—patience, the strength to endure, certainty of God's presence, hope for better things after the ordeal was over, humility, and renewed trust in God. Such lessons do not come easy. One may still be unhappy that the thing most desired is not forthcoming. But the prayer has been heard and God has acted.

A failure to have health restored should not lead to a search for someone to blame. Since health is the normal state, what God really wants for the world, then we assume someone must be at fault if God's intention is not in evidence. "It is human sin that has caused the trouble." That may be profoundly true in a general way, but we must hesitate to blame ourselves when requests for healing are denied. Too often that is exactly what happens. Zealous proponents for faith healing leave one with few alternatives if the result is not good. "Is my faith not strong enough?" "Have I been such a wicked person that God will not grant my prayer?" If we refuse to blame ourselves, as Job, then the most likely other choice is to blame God, who seems not willing to fulfill promises to heal us if we bring our petitions to him. This, of course, is not a happy conclusion either as it drives a wedge between a person and God. As we have been saying all along, hope is primarily trust in God. When one begins to lose confidence in God, then hope is very difficult to maintain.

Healing is more than a return to physical health. It may be that certain physical conditions simply cannot be changed, not in this life anyway. Some afflictions are chronic or terminal. Some conditions are irreversible—a broken spinal cord, blindness, an amputation, a genetic defect, infirmities of old age. And yet there can be healing. One's spirit can be touched, the mind can be enlivened, despair can be replaced with peace and hope, distrust can turn to belief. We can even dare to say that death, which of course must come to everyone some day (no matter how many times one has recovered from prior illnesses), is a kind of healing. For an old man of 90 with failing sight and hearing and barely in touch with reality or a woman in the latter stages of terminal cancer, death is the only kind of healing possible.

When Jesus cured some people of their illnesses, they were real healings. Some suffering was lessened. Jesus demonstrated God's desire and eventual intention to heal the whole creation. But they were more than just isolated miracle cures. They were signs of the coming of God's kingdom, a breaking in of our eschatological hope for a time when all the things that can harm us will be defeated once and for all. For the time being, we still live in a world where sickness and death persist and the answer to our request for healing is sometimes "no." But we have seen Jesus and we know what he did and what he can do, and we await the time when the final age will emerge in all its glory.

72

Theological and Pastoral Observations

Hopes for society and the individual are closely intertwined

We look to God for protection from danger, deliverance from evil and all that can hurt us, and a safe and secure future. But such things are not possible for an isolated individual. A solitary human being needs protection from other human beings, and so we have laws and governments to execute those laws. Our own community or nation also protects us from other peoples or countries who may be hostile toward us. And so, when we have talked about God's promises to protect us, we have had to look at promises and hopes for the whole people and not only at the promises for individual protection and healing. In our highly individualistic society, we sometimes think of hope as a totally personal thing. Will I make it through life safely? Will I be well and healthy and successful? Will God guide and protect me? Will I have a good death and go to heaven? It is natural to be concerned about ourselves, but we are part of a larger community and it is important to remember that our future is bound up with the future of others. If there is no hope for God's people as a whole, then how can there be hope for me as an individual? As God said to Baruch, through Jeremiah, "How can you seek great things for yourself when the whole nation is being destroyed?" (from Jer. 45:5). We shall return to speak more about how our personal hopes are intermingled with our hopes for community.

Our identification with biblical models of government

Religious people have developed different ways of understanding how God works within human government to protect the nation. Most of them resemble some stage in the biblical understanding of how God achieved his purposes in the national life of Israel. Some would like a very unstructured, *laissez-faire,* perhaps almost anarchic system (or lack of system), in which God is free to work out what is best—either by acting directly or more subtly through laws that are built into the created order (such as survival of the fittest, supply and demand). Others still look for a charismatic figure or messiah who can make sense out of our national problems, give us all confidence and hope in his leadership, make us all prosperous and happy, take care of the poor and needy, and it won't cost us anything.

Others have a more authoritarian approach. They believe that their king, or their constitution, or their system of government has been given by God and is the right and true way for every nation to be governed. Therefore, citizens should be obedient and faithful to their own leaders who know best and were chosen by the best of all possible methods. It is interesting that such absolutist claims are made also by believers from other religions besides Judaism or Christianity (such as certain Muslim states) or by those that make a principle of no religion at all (such as communist Russia). Often, those who are concerned that their own way is the only right one are then dedicated to exporting their system of government to other nations.

Still others have given up on the powers of this world completely. There is no hope in seeking a better world through political means. All rulers are equally bad. Power corrupts; the more you have the worse it becomes. Revolutionists are usually worse than the tyrannies they replaced. The best advice is to keep quiet and stay out of trouble and wait out this world, in the hope that things will go better next time. With a little luck, the end of the world might even come soon enough that we can be in on it and avoid having to go through the unpleasantness of dying.

So where do we hang our hopes for our own country? Is God at work in our choice of leaders? Is God's will somehow being done in the way we conduct our national business? What is the best way to try to accomplish that? Perhaps by continuing to keep in tension the ongoing biblical conflict between (a) those who say that government is a gift from God and for the sake of order we should be obedient to the officials and (b) those who mistrust any human leaders because they are sinners and subject to vices such as greed and the itch for power. So far, our American system has been a pretty good way of maintaining that tension. But, of course, God is the real ruler of the world, and we cannot absolutize our way of doing things and build up the false hope that it, unlike any other human institution, will go on forever.

God's control over what happens in the world

The issue of God's power or control of events in the lives of humans, both corporately and individually, is a very complex and difficult one that is close to the center of our biggest theological questions. Though God has promised to protect his people, and many pious folks can recount examples where this has happened, we do not have to look hard to find places where the protection has broken down. God may have saved the three Hebrew children from the fiery furnace, but what about those millions of Jews who were fed to the furnace of Nazi insanity? Where was God then? There seem to be many things happening in the world that God would not want to happen. That was also true in biblical times, of course, as God's people were constantly rebellious and acted contrary to God's will. If people (not to mention demonic forces) are allowed to defy God, then how can we speak of God protecting us from such harmful forces? Why does God let it go on? When will it stop? If God lets evil run its course now, in this day, what are we to hope for the future?

Some may still be in the first stage of hope, trusting that God is ever present, snatching us from danger, fighting off germs, protecting us from the other driver, keeping the airplane's mechanical system in good order. They can speak of God's control as if it were immediate and apparent. Others have had their own experiences of hurt, or they have simply observed too much pain, even among the good and faithful. And so they don't know what to hope for anymore as they work their way through the second stage of disillusionment. They will attempt rationalizations to account for God's failure to prevent evil from winning as they try not to lose their trust in God. Some of them work better than others, and at some times, none of them work. They may still want to believe in a God who, either directly or by means of a guardian angel, watches our every step so that we do not stumble. They want to believe that God will cure the illness even though

75

the doctor says it is hopeless. Even though they know their ultimate hope can only lie beyond this life, they are not ready to give up on this world altogether.

It is easier to live in the first stage and, perhaps, to be a little critical of the one who seems to be too questioning, too doubting, too pessimistic. Or, in a way, it is easier to live only in the third stage, confident that God's power will finally be shown in the end time. The lack of protection for God's children in the present can be dismissed because of the certainty of what is to come. The hardest position to be in, the place where hope is both most needed and hardest to grasp, is in the middle—still in this world, but not in this world; needing some manifestation of God's work in this world but knowing that those who hope only in this world are "of all men most to be pitied" (1 Cor. 15:19).

The possibility of reform of a society

If a government is bad, tyrannical, oppressing rather than protecting its own citizens, is it proper to work to change it? Those in authority may say that any change would bring chaos and loss of order. Business would be discouraged and everyone would be worse off than they were before. If they can get away with it, they may even claim some divine support for their authority. They will preach submission to their rule as the best course for their subjects. And if they don't agree, a little force or other intimidation may be applied.

So, maybe change is impossible without a fight. Those in power won't let go unless forced (as Pharaoh or the Babylonians). Is it proper then to take up arms, maybe even kill many innocent people to make a better society? Since no human government is perfect, how much bloodshed is it worth to replace one imperfect government with another one? Is it perhaps better to remain docile and put up with the existing evil as preferable to the bloodshed that would follow? From a safe distance we may make that kind of decision for someone else. But those people who are convinced that a better life is possible in this world are willing to sacrifice everything, even their own lives, in order to see that it happens.

76

There is a lot of talk about liberation theology these days. There are those who find it to be a helpful way of speaking about God's desire to support the weak and poor against the powerful. They have read the story of the exodus and the words of the prophets and of Jesus. Why should the dispossessed have to wait for the next world to achieve some of God's blessings? They are quite critical of those Christians who have preached submission to authority and patience till the next age when all will be sufficiently rewarded for what they have had to endure in this life. On the other hand, there are those who criticize liberation theology as naive, supposing that humans are actually capable of constructing an ideal society on this earth. They point to the lack of self-criticism and refusal to take sin seriously. So what is the poor peasant who seeks a better life to do?

Again, the delicate balance between hopes for this life and our ultimate hope is difficult to maintain. But we are called to work at it. We are commanded not to ignore the poor and needy in our midst or put them off with promises of "pie in the sky." Neither are we to be so audacious as to believe that our revolution or plan for the betterment of society will actually bring God's kingdom on this earth. But, it may make life better than it has been, and therefore, it is worth doing.

4
HOPE
FOR
JUSTICE

One of the dominant biblical hopes is that this world is a moral place, that right thinking and ethical behavior will be rewarded, that those who do what is wrong will eventually be held to account, and that injustices which occur in this life will eventually be made right. We want the world to be fair, and if we should become resigned to the impossibility of achieving complete fairness this side of the grave, we at least hope for "everything to come out all right" in the next world. Like our biblical predecessors, our hope for the future is closely tied to our trust in God. So it is important for us to believe that God is a righteous God. God will not forever tolerate injustice done to God's faithful servants nor the transient prosperity of the wicked. There will be a time of judgment when God will see that the good and right and true will win out over the bad and wicked and false. Our hope is shaped by our confidence whether or not God will finally do that and whether it can happen in this world or only in the next. This means that this area of hope, like others we are examining, changes for people as their personal experiences move them from naive to other stages of hope.

Why It Is Important to Believe that Justice Will Someday Be Done

As we face the future, our hope for the inevitability of justice becomes a very important ingredient in the way we think and feel about that future. This is true for a number of reasons.

Planning is possible

If the world makes some moral sense, it is possible to make plans. If there are certain cause and effect relationships between what one does and what happens next, then we can analyze our choices, think about the consequences, and make the decision which will lead to the desired result. We can take some control of our lives. We do not live in a world where everything comes completely by chance, where good or bad comes in a totally arbitrary way. If we work hard, there is a better chance that we will be successful than if we are lazy. If we build good relationships with family and friends, there is a good likelihood that we will receive love and support from them. If we love God and try to live a life of service to others, those decisions will bring rewards, though not always material prosperity. If we take care of our bodies, eat the right food, remember to exercise, and learn how to handle stress, we raise the odds of having a long and healthy life. If we are a good citizen, we expect to be treated fairly and with respect by those in authority.

And so it is possible to take some control, to have something to say about the kind of future we will have. The future is not so foreboding if we can do some things to help shape it the way we want it.

Ethical motivation is necessary

If there were no hope for justice, if good was not rewarded and evil was not punished, good people might be less likely to choose the good, and wicked people might be more likely to choose the evil. We teach our children that there are rewards for being good, and there are penalties for doing wrong. That is the way the system is supposed to work. And, as long as it does work that way, people are encouraged to do what is right and discouraged from hurting others within the society. We feel outraged when the moral system seems not to work very well—when crime is committed at high levels of government or business and no one seems to know how to stop it or bring the wrongdoers to justice, when the saintly God-fearing woman suffers one illness after another while the meanest man in town lives to a healthy old age, when the couple who worked hard all their lives for a wonderful retirement are killed in a car accident on their first winter trip to the south. "It is so unfair. They don't deserve it," we say.

If the evildoer discovers that he can get away with it, we fear there will be no end to the mischief that he will cause. And so we insist that there must be justice in the world. And, for those who seem to escape their rightful punishment in this life, we imagine a place after death where they will finally "get what is coming to them." If there is no reason to choose what is right, no fear of the consequences of one's own actions, will anyone ever do what is right? Some tell us that love of God should be enough motivation in itself. Knowing that one is doing what God desires should be enough for the faithful believer, regardless of what rewards or dangers might result. But most of us need a belief in (hope for) justice to move us to act responsibly. Though the world may find our behavior unpopular and may hold back its rewards, we at least want to know that God will one day right the balance—if not in this world, then in the one which follows.

The present state of injustice will be remedied

Our first two points are particularly important to those who are still in the first stage of hope, the innocent and confident stage in which one can still believe that good is always rewarded and the wicked will be punished and if we can have stronger laws and tougher judges the wicked will finally decide to stop doing bad things. For those who have already seen and felt the injustice of the world, either in their own lives or in the lives of others, it is important to hang on to the hope that there will be justice someday. The present situation of the world cannot be the last word—where innocent children are beaten and sexually molested, where a majority of a nation's citizens are subjected by the minority because of their race, where accidents and illnesses often strike the most innocent, where the wrong people sometimes win the wars. If there is a God at all, if God is good, if God cares even a little about the world that is his own creation, if God has some power over the way the future will unfold, then one must hope that the world as it exists is not the way it will always be. There will be justice one day.

God's goodness and power come together in our hope for justice

And so we hope for a time in the future when God will finally act to demonstrate both that God is good and that God is powerful enough to bring justice into actuality. In the present world it is not always apparent that God is both good and powerful. Perhaps, as some conclude in their struggle with disillusionment, God is neither. Or others assert that God is both, but we can't quite understand the key for how this works. Or maybe God's power is temporarily limited in this sinful world. Or God is both good and powerful, but there is some other explanation—like human sin or our need for discipline—to account for God's seeming indifference to the injustice of the world. Or we must simply admit that we are in over our heads in trying to understand God and are making it difficult for ourselves by projecting human ideas about what is just and what isn't onto God.

Regardless of our ability to come up with a satisfactory explanation for the lack of justice in this world at the present time, it is very important for us to believe in a God who will one day act with both power and love to remedy all the wrongs that have been allowed to continue. If God cannot, or will not, do that, then it is very difficult to feel secure in our hope. Though God's goodness and power may be prevented from its full expression in this world, we hope for a time when there will be no more limitations, no more explanations, no more injustice. To hope is to trust that God will one day do just that.

Let us now look at some examples of biblical texts which speak to this hope for justice to those in each of the three stages of hope—naiveté, disillusionment, and hope beyond this world.

Hope for Justice before the Calamity Strikes

Many biblical texts express the confidence that this world makes moral sense, God is in charge, good will be rewarded and evil punished, and we can control our future by making proper moral decisions. These are texts which may or may not be helpful to one who is trying to be hopeful in the face of adversity. To the naive and untested, they speak profound truth. To those who have suffered, they may sound like hollow promises, as likely to be perceived as condemnation than as comfort.

Genesis 2:17

Theoretically, the first man and woman had a choice. God told them the options. They could eat of every tree in the garden except for one: the tree of knowledge of good and evil. God told them the consequences of their disobedience—they would die. God made a good world. It makes moral sense. If the humans deliberately do what God had just told them not to do, then one could hardly accuse God of injustice.

Could those first humans have chosen otherwise? What if they had trusted God enough to obey? What if they had believed what God told them? What if they had believed that God had their best interests in mind and was not arbitrarily drawing boundaries to prove that God is God and humans are only human? If all that had been possible, then God, who is a God of justice, would not have punished them and the world would have been a much different place than the one we all know.

But, of course, it was not like that. We can no longer think of the world as if it were in some pristine state where each individual can choose right or wrong and expect that consequences will come as orderly as night follows day. There has been too much water over the dam, too many generations of sinful behavior affecting our ancestors and us. We are too connected to one another, both those living and those dead. In a sinful world like this, some who appear undeserving have more than their share of troubles. And it seems unjust. Unscrupulous characters live long and even happy lives, and we wonder where justice has gone. That's the way it is in a world like this.

It is naive to assume that we, at this point in time, face the future with the same options that faced our first parents at the beginning of time. They were not yet sinners (though we might argue whether their transition into that state was inevitable). We are all sinners in a long line of sinners. After the sin of Adam and Eve, the option of naiveté is gone. We cannot start new and fresh and clean. We cannot make choices as if nothing has yet happened. We continually choose the wrong. Or life becomes so ambiguous that there is no clear right or wrong. Or perhaps we choose the right, but we are hurt by others. Regardless of our personal choices, justice will not necessarily follow.

Psalm 1

This wisdom psalm contrasts the fate of the righteous person with that of the wicked person. The one who keeps clear of sinners and their ways while delighting in God's law will prosper like a tree that is supplied with ample water (vv. 1-3). On the other hand, the way of the wicked will perish like chaff in the wind (vv. 4-6). This is an encouraging word to one standing at the threshold of life. God will see that the righteous are rewarded and the wicked are punished. Therefore, it is to your advantage to make the right choice. You can take some control of your destiny. Good will triumph over evil. God is at work in the world. If you want a good life for yourself, make the right decisions. If you join the way of the sinners, you have been forewarned about your fate.

The problem comes, of course, when one suddenly looks around and sees that this has not worked as promised. The person who has faithfully tried to serve God, studied God's Word, been constantly in prayer, and kept clear of sinful behavior, shrivels up like a tree in a drought rather than one planted by streams of water. And, to make matters worse, the wicked are not blown away but are flying around in jet airplanes finding new places to spend their ill-gotten wealth. How then does one understand this psalm (and words like it) which promise that good will win and evil will lose? In some cases, they become a promise for the future. Do not be fainthearted. God's justice will come. Give it time. Though it may seem absent for now, it will come.

Deuteronomy 30:15-20

One could find many examples in the deteronomic history or the book of Deuteronomy which speak of a God of justice who will see that right behavior is rewarded and evil is punished. God, of course, wants us to make the right decisions but will not allow disobedience, immorality, and idolatry to go unnoticed. The decision is up to the people. They have a clear choice before them. They can choose God's way and live, or they can go after other gods and perish. This word is closely connected to God's promise to let them live on the land. The length of their sojourn on the land is directly related to their obedience to God's commands.

The book of Deuteronomy puts this word in a speech by Moses, at the beginning, as the people were about to go over the Jordan to possess the promised land. Like the story of Adam and Eve, Moses' speech laid out the potential that was there at the beginning, if people had just been able to make the right decisions. But, just as the story of the fall was written by humans looking back from a world of sin, so Deuteronomy and the deuteronomic history were put in their final edited form after the people were removed from the land. Again, God, in justice, laid out the options for us, told us what to expect, made it clear what would work and what wouldn't, but we chose the hurtful way anyway.

When seen at the beginning, in the naive stage, these promises of a just retribution for our behavior may be helpful to us as we make plans for how we will live. When all has not gone so well for us, they may provide us a way to face the adversity without losing trust in God. God is still just. God had told us what would happen. The fault is with us. God is still reliable, and we can continue to look to him for justice in the future. Perhaps if we can go back to the drawing board, look at our past mistakes, and try to do better next time, then our future will be a good one. God will reward our renewed endeavors. But this renewed optimism may not last. Finally, one may despair for the fulfillment of justice in this world. Will not people always choose what is hurtful? Will they not always act against God? Though Adam and Eve or the Israelites on the banks of the Jordan were told the consequences of their sin, it did not deter them from their self-destructive behavior. Maybe justice will have to wait till some climactic act of God to sort out the wheat from the chaff, the good from the wicked.

Job 1:1-5; Job 31

The first few verses of the book of Job show Job in his naive stage. He is introduced as a blameless, upright, God-fearing man of great wealth. Among his other blessings, he had seven sons and three daughters. His sons took turns holding feasts at one another's houses on specific days. And when they did this, Job took it upon himself to offer up a sacrifice on their behalf just in case they may have committed some sin, unwittingly, perhaps under the influence of too much wine.

Job had a theology like the writer of the wisdom psalm or the compiler of the deuteronomic history. We can do things to shape our future. We can avoid trouble and ensure a good life by following God's commandments. Job was a perfect and blameless man—God himself said so (Job 1:8; 2:3). Therefore, his good and prosperous life should be no surprise. A good person like Job should be so rewarded. It is only just. And just to make sure that things stay that way, that his children would continue to prosper as he had, Job offered the sacrifice.

Like other "good," "religious" people, Job was outraged when his fortunes took a dramatic turn for the worse. Had he not kept his end of the bargain? In his final soliloquy (in chap. 31), Job went on and on to point out all the evil that he did not do. If he had committed these sins, he could have understood what had happened to him. But since he was an innocent person, he could interpret his disasters only as God's failure to execute justice (as in Job 9:19-24).

At the beginning, before his world fell apart, Job thought that he could have some control over the future. He thought that by choosing to do right and by faithfully adhering to God-given rituals, he could save himself and his family from the perils of this life. He had thus interpreted God's promises to deal justly with humans. He even had texts (as Psalm 1 and the deutero-nomic literature) to support his viewpoint. It would perhaps be too cynical to assume that Job served God only in order to get a reward from God. Satan had tried to make that point with God. We should not doubt the piety of Job, his love for God, his desire to serve, by supposing that it was all done out of selfish moti-vation. Nevertheless, Job did feel a sense of betrayal when all his best efforts to lead a moral life did not protect him from a terrible series of calamities. He did not think he deserved it, and he could point to many persons much more wicked than he who continued to prosper. In this reaction to his suffering, in his move from the stage of naiveté to one of intense struggle to maintain hope and trust in God, Job is very much like many sufferers in our own day.

Job's counselors

Job and his friends started off in the same place. They both believed in God's just retribution in this world. Eliphaz said, "Think now, who that was innocent ever perished? Or where were the upright cut off? As I have seen, those who plow iniquity and sow trouble reap the same" (Job 4:7-8). Eliphaz even re-minded Job that Job had also instructed others along the same lines when they had come to Job for comfort (4:3-4). But now Job was having trouble, and the words that used to seem so true and hope-producing didn't help much anymore (4:5).

Though they had started in the same place, they were no longer in the same place. Job was moving out of his naive stage. Life was not so simple anymore. His own life was evidence to him that justice does not always exist in this world. But his friends still maintained that God was at work, that justice would prevail, that good would win over evil. That could mean that if Job really was as good as he thought he was, then he had nothing to fear because God would see that a righteous person like him would come through this safely (4:6 could be interpreted in such a way). Or it could mean that Job (surface impressions to be contrary) was not such a good person after all. He may have been deserving of his fate and the best course for him would have been to examine himself, find his most serious flaws, repent, and then wait for God to reward his change of heart (as Bildad in 8:5-7 and Zophar in 11:13-20).

The conflict between Job and his friends is a classic example of people who are still in the naive stage of hope trying to counsel someone who has already moved beyond that stage into a desperate struggle to hold onto faith in a good God. By their insistence that all that happens in this world is evidence of God's justice, they caused several problems for Job. The most serious outcome was their condemnation of Job. After all, if God is just, then such terrible things would not have happened to Job without some good reason. He must either have been a sinner of major proportions (sometimes the ones that look the most pious are the worst sinners of all), or God must have been working hard to teach him a lesson. Like Job, many sufferers have felt condemnation from comforters who, speaking naively, have insisted that God's justice is actually occurring in the most horrendous of human experiences.

The book of Proverbs

There is much in the book of Proverbs which contrasts the way of the righteous with the way of the wicked (as, for example, in Proverbs 10). The message is similar to what we have seen in the choice facing Adam and Eve, in Psalm 1, in Deuteronomy 30, and in Job's counselors (and Job himself, before his troubles came). If you do what is right, life will go well for you. If you do what is wrong, you will have trouble. Good is rewarded and evil is punished.

Proverbs is an interesting book. There are many pithy little sayings, some filled with colorful imagery, which appeal to our imagination and speak to our experience. But the book of Proverbs seems particularly attractive to those who are in the first stage of their attitude toward hope. They still hold onto the belief that the world really works, that there is a moral order that somehow survives in this world of sin. If we obey the commandments, life will be good. We can have control. God has promised to work in this world to bring about justice for those who choose correctly.

This biblical book is much less appealing to others who, though they may find delight in occasional quotes from Proverbs, tend to look on the book as too simple, too naive, perhaps even too authoritarian in its insistence on respect for an obedience toward parents and all others in authority. In many ways, the book of Proverbs is like Job's counselors. Therefore, those who have shared some of Job's struggles react to the book of Proverbs as Job responded to the "platitudes" of his friends.

There is a sense in which Proverbs is written for the naive stage. These observations about how life works, what is wise and what is foolish, what leads to a productive life and what is damaging, are laid out for young people to instruct them as they grow up and prepare to take their place as responsible adults. They should know that it does make a difference how they choose to live. Actions do have consequences. You cannot do whatever you want with your life without ever being held accountable for what you have done. There are things you can do to make life better, to raise the odds of having the good life, even though one cannot completely control the future and avoid all unpleasantness. We create a problem when we push these helpful words too far and try to turn them into universal words of truth that are applicable as an explanation for everyone's fortune or misfortune (as Job's counselors did).

Donald Capps has made some interesting observations about the book of Proverbs.[2] He has studied certain specific genres of biblical literature, looked at their original contexts, and tried to match the ancient "situation in life" with contemporary ones. When he did this with the book of Proverbs, he concluded that it could be valuable for premarital counseling. That is a time to make plans, to talk about what one can do to make a marriage work, to make conscious decisions about important matters and not just drift into marriage expecting that all will work out for the best no matter what we do. Proverbs would not be so useful for marital counseling, when the earlier promise has faded, when the relationship has become confused and unhealthy, when further admonitions to dig in and try harder will not work, when a new perspective is desperately needed. The biblical genre that Capps selected for this kind of counseling (for people in the second stage, struggling to renew hope) is the parables of Jesus, not more proverbs.

Reaction to Injustice

What was the reaction of our biblical ancestors when it seemed that there was no justice in the world—when the innocent suffered and the wicked flourished and Israel's enemies prevailed and God allowed it all to happen? Is God a God of justice or not? How long must we wait for the good to triumph?

Looking for an explanation

If hope is closely connected to trust in God, then part of the task of keeping hope alive is to seek an explanation for what has gone wrong which will protect God's reputation as a God of justice. We have already looked at some texts which would help the people to do this. God's intention was to create a good world where justice prevailed. The sin of the human beings introduced all the negative things into the picture. God is not unjust if we were told what to do but refused to take heed. The troubles that have come to the human race are justified, deserved. God is still reliable and true to his promises. Even the fall of the nations of Israel and Judah can be linked to sins of kings and people. God is not unjust. And since that is true, then there is still hope in spite of the defeat that God has allowed at the hands of our enemies.

The problem of injustice becomes more acute when we look closely at individuals. It is easier to speak in broad generalities of the troubles of the whole human race after the fall or the exile of the people because of a sinful society. But what about innocent children? What about pious believers who had always trusted in God but are swept along by the disaster that affects all of society? What about Job? Though we may theologize that we are all sinners and deserving of any trouble we encounter, when we look at individual lives, some people look like worse sinners than others but their affluent and healthy life doesn't necessarily reflect their moral standards. It is at this point that forced application of belief in God's justice, in every individual life, in every trial and tribulation, can be very troublesome. Job's counselors insisted that there was an explanation for Job's troubles. And the most obvious explanation was that Job deserved his fate. Rather than to struggle with Job, to be dismayed at why such a good person should suffer so much, to admit a little confusion about how a good and powerful God could let this happen, they pushed their simple explanations and were forced to make Job look bad. Someone must be at fault, they thought, and it surely can't be God. Job was the culprit, condemned in order to protect his friends' theological synthesis.

Job, of course, did not like the feeling of patronization and condemnation that he received from his friends (see Job 13). He already knew the usual explanations for suffering, but now he found them unsatisfactory to explain his own situation. He accused them of speaking falsely for God (13:7), as if they had taken God's side in Job's complaint about God's justice (13:8). They had painted Job as a sinner to protect their idea of God's justice. According to Job, their "maxims are proverbs of ashes," and their "defenses are defenses of clay" (13:12).

Another way to understand what may at first seem to be a miscarriage of justice is to see it as a learning experience. Our suffering may not, in the strictest sense, be deserved. Nevertheless, as awful as it may seem, it may be of some benefit to us. Both Eliphaz (Job 5:17) and Elihu (Job 33:14-18; 36:8-12, 15) tried this approach on Job. We also see it in other places in the Bible, including Rom. 5:1-5 and Heb. 12:3-11 (quoting from Prov. 3:11-12). Thus God's power and goodness are kept in balance. Though we are hurt, it is for some greater good. God is at work to achieve good things even in our bad experiences. God is just after all and can be trusted.

Such efforts at theodicy (defense of God's justice) are an important task for many as they struggle to make sense of what seems to be a lack of justice in the world. They seek to show that God is just, that God cares and that God has not abandoned direct involvement in the affairs of human beings. But, for one who has gone from stage one to stage two, there are very few explanations that will be completely satisfactory. Like Job, such a person may resist such efforts because they don't explain every example of injustice, and they can sound condemning and offensive. "Don't tell me that I deserve my cancer. Does that make me worse than all those others who don't have this disease?" "So, we are all sinners and deserve whatever might happen to us. Well, then, how come I'm sick and you're not?" "Don't tell me that any good can come out of the death of my loved one. That loss will leave me with a deep sadness till my dying day." "Why do I need to be disciplined so severely by God? Do I have that many rough spots? Even the strictest parents don't punish their children by killing them."

Complaining about the situation

God has promised to deal with us justly. When it seems that that has not happened, our first reaction may be to find some explanation for the incongruity between what God has promised and what has actually occurred. The next step for many is to complain. In some religious circles, there is not much encouragement to do this. The popular conception for how one bears suffering, even if clearly undeserved, is to bear it submissively and trust God to work everything out for the best. Often, one of the explanations which we have just reviewed will accompany the plea to be submissive.

But the Bible, particularly in the lament psalms and books such as Job and Jeremiah and Ecclesiastes, makes it abundantly clear that if we have a complaint with God about God's justice, we have permission to speak to God about it. Many biblical prayers wonder why God continues to let the innocent suffer and the wicked prosper. Habakkuk questioned why God used the Babylonians, who were even worse than Judah, as an instrument of punishment (Hab. 1:12-16). Jeremiah wondered how long the wicked would prosper (Jer. 12:1-4). The writer of Ecclesiastes complained because the same fate comes to all, the wise and the foolish (Eccles. 2:12-23; in contrast to Psalm 1 or Proverbs 10). Job was torn between hoping that God would give him a just hearing and decide in his favor (as in Job 23:1-7) and fearing that God was, in fact, unjust (as in Job 9:14-35). Psalm 10 calls on God to take direct action to save the poor and curtail the work of the wicked person, who has grown arrogant thinking that he is immune from God's judgment. God is looked to as the one who will "rain coals of fire and brimstone" on the wicked (Ps. 11:6) because "The Lord is righteous, he loves righteous deeds" (Ps. 11:7a). Job and his friends carried on seemingly endless conversations about whether or not God would ever punish the wicked. Job said it was not happening now and would not happen (put very eloquently in Job 21). All three of the counselors were absolutely convinced that sooner or later the wicked would have to pay. As Zohar put it, "The exulting of the wicked is short, and the joy of the godless but for a moment" (Job 20:5).

God is expected to execute justice in the world, and if one is not satisfied with the result, then it is only fitting to talk to God about it. Though we are only human, though we cannot claim to understand what God is doing, though we project our limited view of justice on God, still we are right to hold God accountable. God claims to be a righteous God, and if we take God at his word, then we should let God know of our disappointment in the way God has been executing justice lately. We honor God by our complaints because we take God seriously by holding God to his promises. We expect God to hear us, and we are confident that we will be heard and God will do something to remedy the situation. A lament then becomes an act of faith, which still trusts God enough to talk about issues that are deeply troubling, that even dares to confront God. This process helps one continue an honest and open relationship with God—a vital ingredient if hope is to grow.

What will God do now?

What has happened in our past and present is a large determinant in shaping the way we hope. When all has gone well in the first stage, it is easy to believe that good will be rewarded and evil punished in this life. Evidence of God's lack of justice in our past or present makes us struggle. We may, like Job and his friends, search for an explanation that will not tarnish our image of God. Or we may go through a time of complaint, sometimes even to the point of cynicism and bitterness about the way we have been treated by the world in general and God in particular. But then, for many people, sometimes only after a long ordeal, there is a renewal of hope—even for hope in *this* world. God will not leave the poor to be oppressed by unjust tyrants. God will act again to see that justice is done. The innocent will be vindicated. The wicked will be curtailed and punished. Forget the past. Leave that behind.

The typical lament form, having allowed free expression of the complaint, moves on to hope—a certainty of being heard, the promise of vindication. Don't worry anymore about how you got into trouble, whose fault it was, whether or not it was just. Only know with certainty that God will be with you as you move ahead into better times when justice will finally be done. Psalm 77 is a good example of this transition from lament to praise. The psalmist agonized about his present situation and wonders if God would spurn forever, if God's steadfast love had ceased, if God's promises had come to an end, if God had forgotten to be gracious (Ps. 77:7-9). In order to help him put this in perspective, the psalmist recalled God's mighty deeds in the more distant past, both in the work of creation and in the history of Israel (Ps. 77:11-20). Reminding himself of God's acts of justice in the past became a way of moving from gloom about the present to hope for the future.

Often the biblical hope for justice focuses its attention on the fate of the wicked. As mentioned, part of the lament is that the wicked are prospering. As one moves through despair and becomes again hopeful that justice will be done, there is often an articulation of what will happen to the wicked who have temporarily been gloating over their good fortune. Psalm 52 opens with an address to the wicked man who has boasted about "mischief done against the godly" (v. 1). "But God will break you down forever; he will snatch and tear you from your tent; he will uproot you from the land of the living. The righteous shall see, and fear, and shall laugh at him, saying, 'See the man who would not make God his refuge, but trusted in the abundance of his riches, and sought refuge in his wealth' " (Ps. 52:5-7). The psalmist ends with words of confidence about his own deliverance (vv. 8-9). Several psalms with similar hopes for the destruction of one's enemies follow in this section of the Psalter (Psalms 53–60).

As mentioned earlier in the second and third cycles of speeches between Job and his friends, the primary subject under discussion is whether or not the wicked will someday be properly punished. If God is a just God, then it is important not only that the innocent not suffer (the problem with Job himself) but also that the wicked be punished. Job's experience had made him much less confident about God's justice for either the innocent or the guilty. The counselors, still insisting that everything was working as it was supposed to with regard to God's justice, argued that the wicked would one day reap their reward. Perhaps later, when he had finally worked his way through his stage of lament and had had his relationship with God renewed, Job could again turn to the future and believe that justice would prevail. Though he could never again return to the naive outlook of his friends, it is possible for sufferers, like Job, to move back to a hope for God to right the wrongs of the world. Some have called such a transition a "second naiveté," which is similar to the first stage but more profound, deepened by personal struggle and doubts, and often (at least for Christians) containing an eschatological dimension (i.e., not limited in its expectations by the horizon of this world only).

Several Old Testament prophetic books contain sections of oracles against the nations (see Amos 1–2; Isa. 13–23; Jer. 46–51; Ezek. 25–32). They emphasize that God is ruler and judge of all the world, not only the nations of Israel and Judah. God will see that nations that have offended and hurt others will have to be brought to justice. Sometimes God even uses other nations (such as Assyria and Babylon) to punish God's own people.

Nevertheless, those nations are still responsible for the ruthless way they have dealt with their victims, and God will make them pay for that. These oracles are a kind of answer to Habakkuk's question about why God would use nations that are worse than Judah in order to punish Judah (Hab. 1:12-17). These foreign nations cannot excuse themselves from God's judgment because they are not God's special people, have not made a special covenant with the Hebrew God, and have not received a unique revelation on Sinai (or someplace similar). God is God of the whole world. As part of God's creation, they are subject to God's rule and will be judged by their actions. There are certain standards of behavior among nations that they should know even without the laws of Moses.

So, our longing for justice, our hope that it will one day be achieved, sometimes leads to speculation about what God will do to the wicked people. Some of these biblical passages make us a little uncomfortable, however, as they almost seem to enjoy imagining all the horrors that will finally come to those who have caused us grief. The most troublesome are the imprecatory psalms, which call on God to destroy in the most painful way possible all those who have hurt us (e.g., Psalms 58; 69; 137:7-9). Such expressions of a need for revenge sound all too human. Though we want God to be just, we cringe at the hostility expressed here. If justice has not caught up with the wicked people in this life, this reasoning goes, they still will not be able to escape from facing the penalty for their sinful lives. A conclusion of this way of thinking is that such people will be punished in hell. God's justice will pursue them into the grave.

God will send human leaders who will see that justice is done. Justice occurs in the human community when people, from those highest in authority on down, deal justly with one another. And so, as we hope for justice, we ask God for good rulers, wise judges, who will protect those without power against those who would use their power to take advantage of the weak. God need not act only in direct, dramatic ways to achieve justice. God can work behind the scenes in our human endeavors to make this a just world. At this point, our hope for justice corresponds with "messianic" hopes which we surveyed in the last chapter. Like the prophet of Isa. 11, we, too, would like a ruler who judges the poor with righteousness and "decides with equity for the meek of the earth" (Isaiah 11:4). In Psalm 110, God will act through the newly crowned king to "shatter kings on the day of his wrath," to "execute judgment among the nations" (vv. 5b-6a). This royal psalm, as mentioned earlier, becomes a future-oriented hope for a new king who will bring God's justice into the world. It is frequently quoted or alluded to in the New Testament (Matt. 22:44; Acts 2:34; 1 Cor. 15:25; Eph. 1:20; Heb. 1:3, 13; 10:12-13) as a word that has been fulfilled in the coming of King Jesus.

God is the ultimate judge. If our hope for justice in the future is to be more than wishful thinking, a tranquilizer to calm us sufficiently that we can live with the ambiguities of today, then we need to believe in a God who is just and who will one day exercise the power that it takes to make his judgments stick. There are many biblical texts that emphasize this quality of God as that kind of judge. They are used by the worshiping community to remind itself of what God is like and, thus, to provide a basis for hope.

All the nations should be glad and sing for joy because God judges the people with equity and guides all the nations of earth (Ps. 67:4). Since it is a good God who is the ultimate judge, then we have nothing to fear; we can be glad and joyful and hopeful. "Let the heavens be glad, and let the earth rejoice; let the sea roar, and all that fills it; let the field exult, and everything in it! Then shall all the trees of the wood sing for joy before the Lord, for he comes, for he comes to judge the earth. He will judge the world with righteousness, and the peoples with his truth" (Ps. 96:11-13; see also Ps. 98:7-9).

In Isaiah 61 an unnamed prophet says that God has anointed him to bring a word of comfort to the exiles. Their long wait for justice is over. He brings good news to the afflicted, announcing liberty to the captives (v. 1). It will be a day of comfort and vengeance (v. 2). Perhaps a better word than "vengeance" here would be "vindication." That is to say, justice will be done. Those who have suffered at the hands of evil nations will be set free. Their fortunes will be reversed (vv. 3-6). They will receive double portions of what was lost, have respect instead of dishonor, and shall live in everlasting joy (v. 7). The reason that God is bringing all this about is because God loves justice and hates robbery and wrong. "I will faithfully give them their recompense, and I will make an everlasting covenant with them" (v. 8). God's justice is, of course, two-sided. Relief for the oppressed means restraint, maybe even punishment, on those who had been holding them captive. Justice means not only vindication of the innocent but also judgment on the wicked. According to Luke, Jesus chose to preach on this text at the beginning of his ministry in his home town of Nazareth (Luke 4:16-30). Somehow, this text was fulfilled in the coming of Jesus (Luke 4:21). Hopes for justice, both for this world and the world to come, both from earthly kings and from God himself, are all bound up in our expectations for Jesus who will come to judge the world with equity. Though the prophet intended to speak "good news," Jesus was met with hostility (Luke 4:23-30). Apparently there are those who do not want God's rule of justice. They prefer the present state of injustice which works for their own personal gain.

Hope for Justice in the Next Life

Like the other objects of our hope, justice does not always work out within this world. If it is to come, for some of us it will be later, beyond our lifetime, perhaps never in the world as presently constituted but only after a climactic end of the world or in a personal heaven or hell.

Old Testament urgency for justice in this life

Since most of the Old Testament has no clear hope for an individual life after death, there is a great sense of urgency that God's justice come to fruition in this life. If individuals, such as

Job, do not receive justice while they are alive, then the best they can hope for is to be remembered well by those who are left behind. Though one may long to see justice among the nations, return from exile, and judgment on the oppressors, there is some comfort in hoping that God will accomplish those things even though I may be dead and buried and unable to witness it for myself. At least I will be indirectly vindicated through my community, my descendants who live on in God's promise.

Old Testament apocalyptic

Apocalyptic literature seems to originate in times of great persecution. The following ideas are typically included: (*a*) Justice is virtually impossible because all the power is in the hands of evil ones; (*b*) there is no hope for this world; (*c*) God must take direct action to destroy all evil and bring about a new age; (*d*) there is concern for the fate of this world—judgment on the wicked and salvation for the innocent—but apocalyptic literature speaks of this final judgment in cosmic, larger-than-life language in which God and other supernatural beings take an active role. Daniel 7 presents a powerful image of the Ancient of Days assuming his seat on his fiery throne, surrounded by thousands of courtiers, sitting in judgment with his court, and then the books were opened (presumably with the names of who was to be judged) (vv. 9-10). Then came one like a Son of Man before the Ancient of Days, and he was given dominion over all nations— a dominion and kingdom that would never pass away (vv. 13-14). This imagery and language about a Son of Man is picked up in the New Testament to describe the role of Jesus as king and judge of a kingdom that encompasses the whole world and yet is not of this world.

Daniel 12:1-2 is probably the clearest expression of belief in resurrection in the entire Old Testament. There will be a time of judgment after a period of trouble such as the world has never seen. Even those who have already died shall awake to face judgment. For martyrs who have died for their beliefs, this means another chance, a vindication of their stand against evil. They will enter into everlasting life. For the evil ones, there will also be justice. Even though they have already died, seemingly escaping God's judgment, they will be called back to life so that they can be properly punished. Their reward will be shame and everlasting contempt. And so, if justice has not been achieved yet in this world, there is still time. This is, of course, good news to those who have died in the faith. For the evil persons of the world, it is bad news indeed. The evil one who dies in a peaceful old age will still be made to answer to God for his crimes. The Adolf Hitlers of the world cannot escape God's judgment even though they kill themselves.

Jesus' teachings about retribution beyond the grave

In a number of places, Jesus indicated that justice will not always come about in the present world. Life is not always fair, with good rewarded and evil punished. When the disciples asked Jesus why the man was blind (John 9), Jesus dismissed both their options—it was neither because of his own sin nor the sin of his parents. Life does not work so neatly that we can see nice cause and effect relationships between a person's morality or piety and that person's good or bad fortunes. Sometimes the faithful must suffer even more than the wicked. In a world where wicked ones have so much power, you may be in bigger trouble by being faithful than by turning against God. The follower of Jesus should expect persecution and should be willing to take up the cross.

But justice will be done, nonetheless, in the coming judgment. In the parable of poor man Lazarus (Luke 16:19-31), the score will be settled after death when the poor man now lives in bliss while the rich man, who had withheld kindness, now suffers forever in the flame. At several places in the Sermon on the Mount, Jesus pushed morality below the level of outward action to include also secret thoughts and feelings (Matt. 5:17-30). Even to hate is to commit murder; to have lustful urges is to commit adultery. And the consequence of those sins (assuming they remain unforgiven) is to burn in hell (Matt. 5:22, 29, 30).

In several places, Jesus speaks of the Son of man (presumably speaking of himself—see the Daniel 7 passage), who will come in judgment over the world. "For the Son of man is to come with his angels in the glory of his Father, and then he will repay every man for what he has done" (Matt. 16:27). In Matt. 25:31-46, Jesus tells of a great judgment scene "when the Son of man comes in his glory, and all the angels with him, then he will sit on his glorious throne. Before him will be gathered all the nations, and he will separate them one from another as a shepherd separates the sheep from the goats" (Matt. 5:31-32). Both the sheep and the goats are surprised at the judgment that is given to them—some do not know that they have done wrong and others do not realize that they have done what is right. But they will all be judged by what they have done. And, in the end, some "will go away into eternal punishment, but the righteous into eternal life" (Matt. 25:46).

The book of Revelation

There are many similarities between Revelation and Daniel. There will be a great turmoil at the end of time leading to the final judgment on all the evil of the world. Seven bowls of God's wrath are poured out on the earth (Revelation 16; compare the plagues on Egypt in Exodus 7–12). Chapters 17 and 18 describe the fall of Babylon (Rome) and are reminiscent of the prophetic oracles against the nations. Finally, Christ and his heavenly armies win the victory over the beast and all his followers (Rev. 19:11-21). Then there is a judgment on the dead (Rev. 20:11-15). All the dead stand before the throne. Books are opened and the dead are judged by what is written about them in the books. They are judged according to what they have done. "And if any one's name was not found written in the book of life, he was thrown into the lake of fire" (Rev. 20:15). Then follows a wonderful picture of what the new heaven and new earth will be like for those who have received a favorable judgment (Rev. 21:1-7). But, again we are reminded that this glorious new world is not for everyone. There are some whose lot "shall be in the lake that burns with fire and sulphur, which is the second death" (Rev. 21:8).

So, like in Daniel and the words of Jesus, there will be proper justice even for those who have escaped it in this life. That is a comforting word of hope for those who received little or no justice in this world. It is a terrifying word of warning for those who perhaps participated in the injustices done to God's faithful ones.

We are justified, though sinners

Our zeal to paint a picture of ultimate justice, of a time when right will be rewarded and evil punished, can backfire on us. If all are judged according to what they do, then we all have reason to fear. The writers of apocalyptic may so clearly be the victims in a case of injustice that they can easily read the ending of Revelation as a promise, a comforting word that gives them hope even in the darkest of days when the present world offers nothing in which to hope. But it is less clear for many of us. Perhaps we are more the problem than the victim, more the oppressor than the oppressed, more the sinner than the one sinned against. And, therefore, even though we may have had a decent life, a moderate share of the world's goods, relative peace and security and good health, we may be liable to severe punishment in the life to come. How can we be assured that we will not be thrown into hell to burn forever in the lake of fire?

And so many of us in the Protestant tradition, identifying with the experience and theology of Luther and/or Calvin, turn toward other biblical passages to help us keep this in perspective, to maintain hope for God's justice without living in terror of our own culpability. None of us is good enough to get an acquittal from God. We all fall short of the glory of God. But we are justified by God's "grace as a gift, through the redemption that is in Christ Jesus" (Rom. 3:24). God is indeed righteous, but God has passed over former sins with divine forbearance and justifies the one who has faith in Jesus (Rom. 3:19-26; see also Galatians 3). Now we can hope for God's justice to come in its fullness because we are assured that, sinners though we be, God has pronounced us to be just and worthy of being included in the heavenly kingdom.

Theological and Pastoral Observations

The possibility of justice in this world

Is there any truth to the optimism of the deuteronomic historian or the writer of Proverbs or the pastoral advice of Eliphaz? Is there a moral order in the world as we know it? Can we see any evidence of God at work to reward good and punish evil? Another way to raise the question is to wonder if there are not certain laws of cause and effect built into the creation. It is not so much a matter of morality as it is a matter of observation—some acts have certain consequences. We can find out what is good for us and what will hurt us. That is what the scientific approach to medicine and good health is all about. You may or may not think that it is immoral to smoke cigarettes. But there is no doubt that it is a bad idea if you care at all about quality of life and longevity. It may be overstating the case to say that God punishes smokers by giving them lung cancer. But it is becoming ever more certain that smoking is a contributing cause to this and other illnesses. There are observable cause and effect relationships in the world that we would be wise to heed, regardless of how we theologize God's participation in the process.

Where we get into difficulty is when we assume too much, believe that we have explained everything, make our observations into absolutes, and lull ourselves into the pretension that we have the ability to avoid unpleasantness and guarantee happiness merely by making the right decision. What Eliphaz and the others have to suggest for us is still good advice. It may work most of the time. If we listen to them the chances are that our life will be better than if we act with less wisdom and caution. But the nonsmoker may still get lung cancer while the pack-a-day inhaler lives to a ripe old age. The one who has worked hard and faithfully for the company may still lose her job. The health fad zealot may still die of a heart attack. Terrible diseases may strike innocent children. And when such things happen, it is not helpful to be reminded that God is just and the world is a moral place and everything bad that happens must be explained in a way that protects these presuppositions.

We are called to work for justice

We should not assume that justice will work in the world automatically without some effort. We should not be so blindly optimistic that we always submit to the status quo, assuming that God is at work in the rulers of this world or in the economic system making sure that all people receive what is their due. If justice is to be achieved in the affairs of human beings, it may take dedication on our part to see that it happens. We must be alert to injustice when we see it and work to change what is inequity—whether it is an unequal distribution of the world's resources, or an imbalance in the sharing of power, or uneven opportunities for schooling or work, or disproportionate availability of health care. We should not assume that some people have less of these things than others because God has willed it, or they have deserved it, or the system can be relied on to bring the right people to the top. Some people hesitate to work for justice because they are still in stage one and they really believe that the world is working well enough just as it is. To interfere is to disrupt the natural order of things, to mess it up, perhaps even to work against God's will.

Others hesitate to work for justice in this world because they have moved on to stage three. There is no hope for this world. We cannot set up the perfect system that will reward all according to their works. The communists have tried that, and we know what a disaster that has been for the countries who have tried it. Let God worry about settling the balance and bringing justice in the next world. In the meantime, be submissive to God and content with your lot.

God intends justice for people, now and in the future. Those Old Testament prophets demanded it immediately. We have no permission to excuse ourselves from this task—even though we know it will not be fully achieved by our own feeble human efforts. We thank God that even though we fail, that is not the end of the story. God will see that justice is done. That is our hope. In the meantime, God calls us to join in the task.

Difficulty in bringing comfort to one in a different stage of hope

Job's counselors had not yet had their naiveté challenged. They confidently believed that the world is a tidy place where the consequences of a moral or immoral life are easily perceived. This belief served them well, and it was very hard to give it up and plunge into the ambiguity that is inevitable when simple answers are no longer acceptable. Job had no choice. He had to move away from simple answers because his terrible experience no longer fit what he had been taught. So he was now in a different place from his friends. They continued to push the old ideas which now were intellectually unacceptable to Job. When they insisted that what was happening to Job was just, they left Job with few options—either he must admit he was a bad enough person to deserve all this, *or* God must not be good and just (for a time he chooses this option), *or* he must abandon the quest for answers and find some way to believe in a good God anyway (finally he is able to come to this). When people still in the first stage keep pushing their easy answers on those in the second stage, the result is usually something like that between Job and his friends. Like Job, they feel condemned ("they are saying I had this coming"). Their lament is stifled; they are not permitted to complain about the unfairness of it all. They feel alienated from both divine and human support when it is most needed (more of this in the next chapter).

But the problem can also exist when those in stage two try to counsel those in stage one. One can hear complaints about pastors who seem too skeptical, too doubtful, too pessimistic, too "intellectual." They don't preach the simple gospel but rather are always trying to raise all kinds of hard questions. Why don't they just leave well enough alone and quit trying to upset the simple faith of the people? Recently I heard about a person who was sick and asked a certain pastor (from an unidentified church) to pray for her recovery. The pastor replied, "I'm sorry. We don't do that in our church."

Or suppose someone in stage three tries to bring comfort to someone in stage two by stressing what a wonderful place heaven will be and it will be so good to go "home to be with Jesus." Unfortunately, the one who is looking for comfort is not ready to rest easy in those words, true though they may be. She has just heard that her disease is terminal. She doesn't want to die, leave her family, abandon all those plans for what to do with the rest of her life, miss seeing those grandchildren not yet born. It is too soon to find much comfort even in the promises of a glorious life to come.

We cannot help what stage of hope we are in. It would be nice to avoid the struggles of stage two. But some of us are not permitted that luxury. No matter where we are in our personal search for hope, we should be sensitive to other people in their pilgrimage. We should listen to them and try to understand them, and not attach labels to them which may seem pejorative—such as "simple-minded," "skeptic," or "pie-in-the-sky dreamer." At some periods in our life, we may spend time in each of those stages.

Attitude toward the wicked

An unfortunate by-product of our emphasis on the inevitability of God's justice is the expression of hostility toward the wicked. This anger is often expressed even in biblical material. Those who have been hurt greatly and unjustly by an enemy find it hard to be magnanimous and uninvolved as they wait with glee for God finally "to get even." We have heard that we should love our enemies, and though we know we don't do that very well, we probably should feel a little guilt about wishing the worst of earth's pains and hell's fire on those whom we hate. It seems so "unchristian" to take great delight in another's misfortune, deserving though they may be of their torment. After all, doesn't God love sinners? In fact, aren't we all sinners? We hope God will be more merciful toward us than we would be if we were punishing our enemies.

Our human need for justice often leads some of us to a strong sense of revenge. There is a great outcry when a criminal does not receive a severe enough punishment from the court. The protest is often particularly strong from the family of the victim of the crime. Courts or lawyers that are too easy on criminals are attacked viciously for their softness on crime. Capital punishment has become a major issue in much of the United States. Like our biblical ancestors who had a strong sense of justice and a deep feeling of hurt, we sometimes get carried away in our hostility toward the wicked. That is certainly understandable, if not laudable. To be sure, we need to work for justice in this world. Those who hurt others must be prevented from doing so. People must learn that they will be held accountable for their actions. But even justice must be tempered with mercy. And some matters of justice are finally better left in God's hands. Let God be the ultimate judge so that we can let go of grudges and hostilities and bitterness. As Paul says (quoting from Deut. 32:35), "Vengeance is mine, I will repay, says the Lord" (Rom. 12:19b).

Fear of being on the wrong side of the judgment

Insistence on God's final and decisive act of judgment that will sort out good and evil and reward or punish accordingly is a word of hope for the eventual righting of all the inequities of this world. But it does carry dangers with it. As we have said, it could backfire. Since none of us is perfect, we too will face judgment, and the verdict will not be entirely positive. And so, as already mentioned, we take refuge in God's assurances of forgiveness, so profoundly demonstrated in the life and death of Jesus, who gave himself as a ransom for many (Matt. 20:28). However we articulate the work of Jesus on our behalf, it certainly has something to do with insisting on God's justice while maintaining God's mercy toward those who have come seeking forgiveness for their sins.

We have experienced God's love for us but we are limited in our understanding of the immensity of that love. When we fear being on the wrong side of judgment, we need to remember that the Bible abounds with messages of God's grace. "For by grace you have been saved through faith; and this is not your own doing, it is the gift of God" (Eph. 2:8).

5
HOPE
FOR
COMMUNITY

We are meant to live in community—in relationship with God and other human beings. We can be hopeful about the future when our relationships are sound, our communication with others is open, our faults are known but accepted, and we are confident that our future sins will be forgiven and promises to us will not be broken. If we are already profoundly alone, for some reason cut off from the support of a loving God and caring humans, hope will be much more difficult to maintain. Or if we live in constant fear that God or others will remove their love from us (perhaps because of some things we might do or for no good reason at all), then too, hope will be elusive, constantly challenged by our anxiety. If God is on our side, and we know it, we can always hope, even in the midst of the most terrible experiences. Similarly, if surrounded by loving human beings, we can face the future confidently. Their support will be of enormous strength to us, even for those events in our lives which we must endure on our own (the most obvious example being our own death).

Hope and Our Relationship with God

As we have said, hope and trust (or faith) are closely connected. What weakens our faith will diminish our hope. And what increases faith will also strengthen our hope. As we move through different stages of life, our relationship with God will change and, likewise, the way we hope.

How it used to be between God and humans

When a person grows older and life becomes more complex and hurts or disappointments begin to accumulate, he or she may look back to the "good old days" when everything, including one's relationship with God, was much simpler. Somehow, it was easier to believe then. The supernatural seemed more accessible. God was near and God was responsive, and life was good and all things were possible. We hate to leave that stage of life. We often wish we could return to it. But childlike faith is not an easy option for one who is no longer a child. A return to faith will, perhaps, resemble the naiveté of the child, but it will be different, hardened and matured by struggling with the horrible reality of what it would be like to live apart from God.

There are several biblical examples of looking back to a golden time when God was close and communication was easy and all was right between God and human beings. Such expressions of nostalgia for times long past express a belief in the way things ought to be. God and humans are meant to live together in peace and to find joy in each other. And, since that is the way God intended it to be, our hope is that it will again happen.

In the Garden of Eden (Genesis 2). In the creation account beginning in Gen. 2:4b, God takes a very active and personal role in the creation of the world and its creatures. God formed the man from the dust and breathed the breath of life into his nostrils (2:7). God talked personally to the human being and gave advice about what he should and should not do (2:16). The communication was clear and understandable. The problems that soon arose were not because the humans did not know what God wanted from them.

Though God and the human being were close and the world was good, the human being needed a relationship with another creature who was on the same level, with one who was equal to the male (2:18-25). And so, humans are male and female. We are meant to relate both to God and to other humans.

In the beginning, it was good. God walked and talked with the man and woman. God's presence was so close and easily accessible that the story makes God seem almost like a human that we can see and hear. But God is not a human. The story makes that abundantly clear. When the humans were not content with the limits of their humanity and they aspired to know what God knows, they betrayed a lack of trust in their relationship with God, and the idyllic proximity between God and humans was destroyed. And, along with the damage done to that relationship, the humans lost their innocent trust between themselves. The man and woman who were naked and not ashamed that another could see them completely exposed (2:25) now knew that they were naked. And they covered themselves so that neither God nor other humans could see their flaws and imperfections (or what they imagined to be defects) (Gen. 3:7-10).

Those were the good days, the way it was supposed to be, when communication between God and humans was open, when God could be heard and seen and was deeply involved in our daily life. But it didn't last. And we, who were created to be in relationship with God, long for a time when it will be that way again.

Job's memory of his good days with God (Job 10:8-12; 29:1-5). Job had been a good, pious man. His relationship with God had been close. He believed in the value of prayer and sacrifice (Job 1:5). He understood his own good life as evidence that God had been good and kind to him. When his troubles descended on him in such rapid succession, he became confused about his relationship with God. How could the God who had created him with his own hands now turn and destroy him (Job 10:8-9)? Job thought of himself as God's own creation, lovingly formed by God in his mother's womb (10:10-11). Further, all through Job's life, God had cared for him and preserved him with steadfast love (10:12). At other times, Job expressed anger and a deep sense of injustice toward God, but at this point, Job was terribly hurt and bewildered. His relationship with God had been so important to him. He had been so certain about it. And now he felt betrayed.

It just didn't make sense. He could not deny the reality of his earlier experience with God. But that was so different from his present experience that he found it impossible to reconcile them. Could a good God become so cruel? Why?

In his final soliloquy, Job again took up this theme of reminiscing about the good days in his past relationship with God and wishing that he could return to a time like that. Those were the days when God watched over him (29:2b) and gave him a light to walk through darkness (29:3). Those were Job's autumn days, "when the friendship of God was upon my tent; when the Almighty was yet with me" (29:4-5a). Job here presents a poignant expression of what it was like in the first stage of naiveté, before the troubles came, when hope was easy and the future (like the past and present) looked bright. But all that had ended for Job. He told about the first stage from the context of disillusionment, despair, and a sense of betrayal. He longed to return to his former relationship with God. But that was impossible. His first stage of naiveté could not be reentered because it was based on presuppositions about good people being immune from the kind of suffering he had experienced. What had happened to him was now part of his personal history. It could not be cancelled so that he could again be what he once was. If there was still to be hope for him, his renewed hope could not ignore his present difficulties as if they had never happened.

Among all the other suffering that he had endured, surely Job's spiritual distance from God was one of his most difficult burdens to bear. The God who had seemed so close and kind and just seemed now to be distant, cruel and unjust.

God is always present (Psalm 139). The psalmist here speaks of a close relationship with God, in which God knows all that we do and think (vv. 1-4) and is always present with us, no matter where we might be, from highest heaven to deepest Sheol to the "uttermost parts of the sea" (vv. 7-10). Whether we choose to try to remove ourselves from God or whether the distance is brought on by events in our lives, God will always find us and continue to know all about us. With such assurances, one can feel confident in God's guidance and presence no matter what the future might bring. This psalm has brought enormous comfort to many people. No matter what trials they face, God will be with them.

But the psalmist is already speaking as one who knows that life brings its problems. Psalm 139 is a lament. The psalmist had been troubled by malicious people who had hurt him and defied God. The psalm, then, calls on God's omnipresence and omniscience as a reason why God should act to slay the wicked, whom the psalmist hates (139:19-22), and deliver the righteous ones, like the psalmist himself (139:23-24). If God does not do that, then this message of presence and concern may begin to sound rather hollow. What good is God's presence if God will not do anything to help?

Our relationship with God now

The ideal state of the relationship between God and humans has been damaged. No more do we live in a Garden of Eden where God and humans can communicate freely. Often, there is no clear word from God. We are separated from God by guilt and disbelief and human limitations. We are bound to things of this earth and have trouble imagining the supernatural. Further, our individual experiences have made our relationship with God more difficult. Where we had once found a word from God, now there is silence. Where we had felt love and concern, now there is anger. Where we had felt safe in God's promises never to forsake us, now there is a sense of abandonment.

The silence of God. Of course, very few of us actually hear God speak. But God communicates in various ways—through the word of Scripture, through prophets and preachers and teachers, through the love of a friend or family member, through art and music and great literature, through the beauties of creation, through prayers and liturgies and sacraments. But sometimes none of that seems to work very well for us any more, even if it did in the past, and we are left to contemplate the silence of God. We may go back to the old reliable sources—the Bible, hymns,

111

sermons, the sunset by the lake. But there is nothing. It is as if God has gone away and can no more be found.

In certain bleak and stormy historical times, it was as if the whole society had to cope with the silence of God. At the beginning of the story of Samuel's call, we read this cryptic description of such a time—"And the word of the Lord was rare in those days; there was no frequent vision" (1 Sam. 3:1b). Saul had a very difficult time receiving a word from the Lord. The old prophet Samuel often gave Saul a word that he didn't want to hear, but at least it was some line of communication that was open between God and Saul. But then Samuel died, and there was no place to turn. "And when Saul inquired of the Lord, the Lord did not answer him, either by dreams, or by Urim, or by the prophets" (1 Sam. 28:6). Another time when there seemed to be a famine of God's word was in the years from the close of the prophetic age until the coming of John the Baptist and Jesus.

As we have seen, Job remembered a time when God was close and God was his friend. But now there was only silence. Job longed for an audience with God so that he could argue his innocence as before a judge. He was convinced that he would receive a favorable verdict. But, if there was some reason why he was suffering, if he was in fact actually deserving of his fate, then God should tell him. But where do you find God? How do you pin God down and insist on an explanation? "Oh, that I knew where I might find him, that I might come even to his seat! I would lay my case before him and fill my mouth with arguments. I would learn what he would answer me, and understand what he would say to me" (Job 23:3-5). "Behold, I go forward, but he is not there; and backward, but I cannot perceive him" (Job 23:8).

The anger of God. Our relationship with God has been distorted by our guilt and God's anger. God loves human beings. God is concerned for what we do to each other. God's anger, then, is aroused because of God's love. When we choose what is hurtful for ourselves and others, God, who is deeply involved with humans, is angered. The alternative to a God who was never

112

angry would be a God who didn't care. Once we are aware of our sin and God's anger, we see it everywhere. We interpret all sorts of disasters as the manifestation of God's anger. We cause problems for ourselves when we project our own anger and inability to forgive onto God. Then we despair that God will be angry forever, and we think that we are totally unworthy creatures whom God could never love again.

Even words of assurance about God's omnipresence and omniscience (as in Psalm 139) can be heard as words of condemnation. When our relationship with God goes wrong, we are fearful that God knows too much about us. When troubled with a guilty conscience, belief in God's all-knowing presence becomes a warning not to do anything sinful because God, who knows everything, will get you for it. Amos converted this promise of God's constant presence in our lives into an oracle of condemnation for those who mistakenly think that they can do whatever they want and God will never catch up with them (Amos 9:1-4). Job believed that God had a hand in controlling everything that happened to him. That was a comforting word until his world fell apart. Then it became a troubling thought because it meant that God had brought his suffering upon him. And so God had become a hostile judge, giving no peace, constantly hounding him, searching him out to find something to condemn. At times, Job expressed a preference for a God who would keep aloof from humans and their foibles and give them a little breathing space (see Job 7:16-19; 10:20; 14:6).

Forsaken by God. Lament psalms often express a feeling of abandonment, as if God has broken his promises, forgotten his covenants, or refused to play by the rules which God himself had set up. The good, pious person feels let down, perhaps even betrayed. "How long, O Lord? Wilt thou forget me forever? How long wilt thou hide thy face from me?" (Psalm 13:1). "My God, my God, why has thou forsaken me? Why art thou so far from helping me, from the words of my groaning? O my God, I cry by day, but thou dost not answer; and by night, but find no rest" (Ps. 22:1-2).

The book of Lamentations, which lamented over the destruction of Jerusalem, ends with some agonizing questions. Has God completely forgotten and forsaken the people? If so, why? (Lam. 5:20). The lamenter asks for renewal and restoration but then closes with a question—"Or hast thou utterly rejected us? Art thou exceedingly angry with us?" (Lam. 5:22). In the midst of the lament, drowning in grief and despair, it is still an open question. Hope is tentative and guarded. One cannot be absolutely sure how it will all turn out. The great prophet of Isaiah 40–55 spoke to a people in exile who were demoralized, convinced that God had forsaken them forever. He quoted Zion as saying, "The Lord has forsaken me, my Lord has forgotten me" (Isa. 49:14). The prophet came with a word of hope, the good news of a great act of redemption. Even a mother may forget her sucking child before God will forget Israel (Isa. 49:15).

And so, our relationship with God suffers for various reasons. What used to be a close, secure, comforting relationship can turn into one of silence, anger, and apparent neglect. And many of the biblical words of hope are addressed to those who despair over what has been lost and long for a return to the way it was in the past—or perhaps even better.

What are we promised with regard to our relationship with God?

Wait and pray. Hope is mostly a matter of waiting. And in the meantime, while we are waiting, we should talk to God.

One of the Hebrew words that is often translated as "hope" is *yaḥal*. The basic meaning of this verb is "to wait," but by implication, it comes to mean "to hope" or "to be patient." Many times, the best advice that one can receive when one's relationship with God has gone sour is simply to hang in there, tough it out, wait. Things will get better. It may not seem like it now. But others who have been through their own times of doubt and despair have attested that if they can make it through the deepest valleys, there will be an upward slope on the other side. God has not abandoned them, despite all evidence to the contrary.

"But for thee, O Lord, do I wait. It is thou O Lord my God,

who wilt answer" (Ps. 38:15). "Wait for the Lord; be strong and let your heart take courage; yea, wait for the Lord" (Ps. 27:14). "I wait for the Lord, my soul waits, and in his word I hope; my soul waits for the Lord more than watchmen for the morning" (Ps. 130:5-6). The whole creation waits with eager longing for the glory that will one day be revealed to us (Rom. 8:18-19). Even those who have the first fruits of the spirit continue to groan inwardly, waiting for final redemption, hoping patiently for what is not yet seen (Rom. 8:22-25).

There is often nothing else to do but wait. And waiting becomes hope when there is some expectation that the present state of affairs is not the way things are supposed to be nor the way things will remain. Waiting can become hope if there is prayer, if one is still engaged in conversation with God. As long as one continues to talk, rather than withdrawing from God in anger and disbelief, then there is hope that the good relationship with God will be restored. This does not mean that one must be pious and proper and submissive while one waits. The communication should be open and confident that God will listen, even as we lament and express fear and anger and doubts. Better to talk to God about our hostility and skepticism than to refuse to talk at all because we consider such prayers to be inappropriate. In his book, *Hope in Time of Abandonment,* Jacques Ellul says that "without prayer, there is no hope, not the slightest." "Prayer is the sole reason for hope, at the same time that it is its means and expression."[3] Though prayer may be difficult in times of suffering, disillusionment, and doubts about God's mercy and power, God reaches out to help us in our efforts to tell God what we think and feel. According to Paul, "The Spirit helps us in our weakness; for we do not know how to pray as we ought, but the Spirit himself intercedes for us with sighs too deep for words" (Rom. 8:26).

The covenant will not be broken. How are God's people to interpret their present troubles? Has God left them, withdrawn protection, cut off the relationship, taken back the promises? Maybe God has finally reached the breaking point and will not be bothered with humans in general or any specific chosen people (Israel or the Christian church) any longer. God was tempted to give it all up at the time of the flood but then promised never again to destroy the world with a flood. Is the exile perhaps the sign of God's final break with the people? One might get that impression regarding the northern kingdom of Israel from read-ing the book of Amos. The end of Amos (9:11-15), almost surely written by a later hand, speaks to that question and makes it clear that God has not given up yet. Though it may appear from our perspective that God has reneged on his covenants to Abraham, Moses, and David, that is not the case at all. If anyone has broken the covenant, it is we, God's rebellious children.

Other biblical responses to catastrophe also remind us that the covenant has not and will not be broken. Those words of assur-ance to exiles and others can be words of hope to us in our own times of despair over God's faithfulness. Though God may di-vorce Israel for good reason, there will be a reconciliation. As Hosea brings back his wife, so God will restore his relationship with Israel (Hos. 3:1-5). Israel's separation from God is not final. Though Jeremiah had many harsh words of judgment directed toward Judah, once the ax had fallen, the destroyed nation needed to hear that God had not abandoned them forever. There are many references in the book of Jeremiah to a covenant that will never be broken (as in Jer. 31:35-37 and 33:19-26) and the assurance that God will not make a full end of the people (Jer. 30:11; 4:27; 5:10, 18). In the middle of the book of Lamen-tations, we find the strongest words of hope and assurance of God's unfailing love. "But this I call to mind, and therefore I have hope: The steadfast love of the Lord never ceases, his mercies never come to an end; they are new every morning; great is thy faithfulness (Lam. 3:21-23). It was not easy to hang on to that hope in the midst of the terrible tragedies that surrounded the fall of Jerusalem. As we have noted, the end of Lamentations drifts back to questions that evidence a continuing doubt about whether this is indeed the end of God's relationship with Judah. But the prayer goes on in spite of the doubt. There is a core of hope from which the prayer is uttered: "I believe. Help thou my unbelief."

As he hung on the cross, in pain and great distress, Jesus prayed the prayer of Psalm 22, "My God, my God, why have you forsaken me?" And that could also have been the prayer of his followers during those awful days. Was it all over? Had Jesus not come from God after all? Where was God to protect and deliver Jesus from this cruel death? Was not Jesus the Messiah whom God had chosen and sent into the world? Why then would God leave him to die in such a humiliating and painful way? But that was not the end. God had not forgotten. God raised him from the dead. And we Christians have the best and clearest word of all about God's refusal to abandon his promises. Even the death of God's own son is not the end of the story. And, similarly, not even our own death is the end of our relationship with God. If anything, our relationship with God beyond the grave will be even more wonderful than anything we can imagine from our limited human perspective.

God will take the initiative to restore the relationship. When we feel forgotten by God, we don't know what to do. We go to all the old places where we used to find God but meet only silence. Like Job or the psalmist, we look here and there and everywhere but cannot find God. But *God* will find *us*. The restoration of our relationship with God is not dependent on our own ability to find God and patch things up. God takes the initiative. God comes to us, seeking to ease our pain and relieve our discomfort. Job wanted his day in court with God. As it turned out, God did come to Job (Job 38–41), but did not follow Job's agenda. Though there are many ways to interpret the God speeches, most commonly they are understood as the means by which Job's relationship with God was restored. Job had worked himself into a terribly distorted picture of God in which God was an enemy, an unfair judge who did not play by the rules of retribution. By dealing directly with Job and avoiding discussion of who was to blame for Job's troubles, God demonstrated that he still cared for Job and would not leave Job in his state of despair. Perhaps

God had tried to reach Job at several times, but Job was not yet ready to listen, still too absorbed in his lament and his efforts to make intellectual sense out of his suffering. Many have noted that Job came to God seeking an intellectual answer but was given a relational answer.

The process that goes on in the typical lament form is a movement from lament to praise. If one has the resolve to continue to pray, to take one's trouble directly to God because God is God and should care and should be able to help, then eventually (waiting is still important) God will hear and the situation will improve. The person who began the prayer with bitter complaints closed the prayer singing God's praise. That is a process that cannot be fully explained, though modern psychology can help us understand it. Surely, most people don't move dramatically from despair to praise in the time it takes to say a psalm. But the process itself is real. Many have attested to it. The lament form itself is evidence of it. The liturgy reflects the reality of people's experience. In our deepest valleys of pain and doubt, feeling forsaken and sorry for ourselves, God will be there to offer hope through the strength of a renewed relationship with him. It is not even necessary that all our troubles go away. If God will be there with us, if we no more doubt God's faithfulness and love, even terrible trials can be borne.

Throughout the Bible, we read how God acted to take the initiative in reaching out to people who have drifted away from where they belong—from their proper relationship of love and service toward God. And so God sent Abraham and Moses and David and the prophets. And, finally, for us Christians, God came in a new way in the person of Jesus, God's own son, again coming after us to bring us back to God. It is not only that *God* will not break the covenant. God will not allow *us* to do it. God will not rest as long as our relationship with him remains broken.

God will communicate with us. The silence of God can be a great burden. How can we know God is even listening? How can we know what God would have us do? If God would just say something—even a simple admonition to hang in there and be patient. If God won't speak to us directly, maybe he can send a word with someone else. Genuine messengers of God are too few and far between. And even when God sends them we often reject them. And how can we tell the true from the false prophets? Often, it seems, the false prophets are much more appealing and interesting than the ones whom God has sent.

There are specific words of hope in the Bible directed toward this need to hear a clear word from God. God told Moses that "I will raise up for them a prophet like you from among their brethren; and I will put my words in his mouth, and he shall speak to them all that I command him" (Deut. 18:18). In Joel, we read the famous prophecy that "it shall come to pass afterward, that I will pour out my spirit on all flesh; your sons and daughters shall prophesy, your old men shall dream dreams, and your young men shall see visions. Even upon the menservants and maidservants in those days, I will pour out my spirit" (Joel 2:28-29). God's spirit will come on everyone. We will not be dependent on someone else who has the gift of hearing God's word and interpreting God's will. The barriers between God and human will be lowered so that all will be in direct touch with God's spirit and will be able to prophesy. The difficulty of waiting for a word from God and then trying to decide between prophets with conflicting messages will be over. Even the young people and the servants will have the gift of prophecy. The book of Acts records the Pentecost experience where barriers of communication between God and humans, and also among humans were removed and quotes Joel as a prophecy that was now being fulfilled (Acts 2:17-21).

We continue to live in hope for a clear line of communication between God and humans. We Christians believe that we know more now than we did before the coming of Jesus. We believe that God continues to speak to us in many and mysterious ways, both structured and spontaneous. But there are times when we continue to long for something more direct, less ambiguous, uncluttered with the psychological or ideological or theological bias of the messenger.

Sins will be forgiven. Sin is the great aggravation in our relationship with God. It is the primary reason for our broken
relationship with God. God has been hurt and angered by our
lack of faithfulness to God and by our sins committed against
others whom God loves. We have suffered because of what we
have done and because of what others have done. Much of the
suffering of the world can be interpreted as the result of human
sin, our inability to choose what is best for ourselves. We feel
God's anger, we recognize our own guilt, and we are ashamed
and cautious in our approach to God. We try to hide our real
self, as if God will not discover our secret thoughts and desires.
Many of us have had too few examples of a forgiving spirit among
our human relationships, and that makes it hard to believe that
God will forgive and accept us in spite of all that we have done.
Emphasis on God's zeal for justice sometimes overshadows our
image of God as compassionate and forgiving.

There are innumerable biblical texts which could be quoted to
show that God is a God of forgiveness who is hoping that we
will give some indication of recognizing our need for repentance
so that God can forgive. People praying the penitential psalms
(such as Psalms 6, 32, 38, 51, 102, 130, 143) come to God with
the expectation that God will forgive. "If thou, O Lord, shouldst
mark iniquities, Lord, who could stand? But there is forgiveness
with thee, that thou mayest be feared" (Ps. 130:3-4). Job, in a
couple of places (16:18-19 and 19:25-27), spoke of his need for
a mediator or redeemer who could stand between him and an
angry God in order to plead his case.

The fallen nation of Judah had learned from prophets and
historians that they had deserved their fate. But what now? Would
God forgive them or were they forever to be cast off, as a father
might disown a renegade son? Prophets arose who spoke words
of hope that God would forgive. There would be a chance to
begin anew in the relationship between people and God. Some,
like Jeremiah and Ezekiel, who had uttered words of dire catastrophe, now began to speak of hope for the future. God says, "I
will cleanse them from all the guilt of their sin against me, and
I will forgive all the guilt of their sin and rebellion against me"

(Jer. 33:8). Isaiah 40–55 begins with wonderful words of encouragement from a God who is eager to forgive. "Speak tenderly to Jerusalem and cry to her that her warfare is ended, that her iniquity is pardoned, that she has received from the Lord's hand double for all her sins" (Isa. 40:2). And a little later, "O Israel, you will not be forgotten by me. I have swept away your transgressions like a cloud, and your sins like mist; return to me, for I have redeemed you" (Isa. 44:21b-22).

Jesus Christ came teaching a gospel of forgiveness of sins. By words and actions, he demonstrated the message of forgiveness for those who repent. His own life and death became a way in which the world is forgiven, reconciled to God. "Therefore, if any one is in Christ, he is a new creation; the old has passed away, behold, the new has come. All this is from God, who through Christ reconciled us to himself and gave us the ministry of reconciliation; that is, in Christ God was reconciling the world to himself, not counting their trespasses against them" (2 Cor. 5:17-19—see also Col. 1:19-23). No matter what our past has been, there is forgiveness with God through Christ Jesus. The impediment of sin need not keep us separated from God any more. We can start over as if all things were new.

God suffers with us. God is deeply involved in the lives of God's creatures. And so God feels hurt and anger and disappointment. God regrets certain actions he has taken and sometimes changes his mind if moved by an act of repentance or a cry of lament. God, then, is very much present in the ups and downs of our life (cf. Psalm 139), sharing both the good and bad with us. We may have a problem, however, if we focus primarily on God's power to control events. We may find little comfort in knowing God is present but not doing anything when we endure great suffering. Why doesn't God help us out if God is there and knows what we are going through? Assurances of God's presence may be heard as signs of a punishing or cruel or indifferent God if no relief is in sight.

But assurances of God's presence can bring comfort and hope even if our troubles persist. God feels with us, aches for us, understands fully what we are enduring. And that can bring hope because it bridges the gap between God and humans. God has been willing to come down here to know what it is like. God is very receptive when I pray my prayer of abandonment because God, in the person of Jesus, has also said the same prayer. Like a suffering servant led to the slaughter (Isaiah 53), God has not only suffered *with* me but *for* me. Theologians have a hard time making logical sense out of all of this. We will continue to write books about how we can benefit from the death of Jesus. But with regard to our relationship with God, it can have a profound effect on us to know that God is not causing or ignoring my troubles but is sharing them. A God who is willing to do that can be trusted. And to trust in God is to have hope. At other times we can return to other images of God as the powerful one who will see that the suffering will not last forever, who will be victorious over all that is hurtful. But in the midst of trouble, the presence of a God who has also suffered can be a profound source of hope.[4]

Nothing can separate us from God. We have been saying something like this as we have looked at each way that hope for our relationship with God is articulated. "If God is for us, who is against us?" (Rom. 8:31b). Since God justifies, who is there to condemn (Rom. 8:33-34)? No matter what ordeals you have to endure in this life—"tribulation, or distress, or persecution, or famine, or nakedness, or peril, or sword"—nothing will be able to separate us from the love of Christ (Rom. 8:35). "For I am sure that neither death, nor life, nor angels, nor principalities, nor things present, nor things to come, nor powers, nor height, nor depth, nor anything else in all creation, will be able to separate us from the love of God in Christ Jesus our Lord" (Rom. 8:38-39). Not even death, nor supernatural powers, nor any person or creature or natural disaster will be sufficient to break off our relationship with God. If we can truly believe that, there is nothing that can destroy our hope.

Hope and Our Relationship with Other Humans

Our hope for the future is very closely associated with our relationships with other human beings. If we have good relationships with others, the support of loving and caring persons, then we are strengthened in our hope. Further, one of the things for which we hope as we face the future is to have our broken relationships restored. We long for a time when families will love each other, strife and hatred and war will cease, people will know what God wills and they will do it.

How it was

We look back and imagine how the world could have been. If only Adam and Eve had resisted the urge to taste that fruit. The man and the woman were created to be at one with each other. None of the animals were fit partners for the man—and so God created man and woman. They are one flesh, meant to live and work together in love and respect. They were naked and were not ashamed (Gen. 2:25). There are probably many levels of meaning to this curt statement. It probably implies something about their free and natural acceptance of their sexuality. But it could also be symbolic for their total relationship to one another. They had nothing to hide. They were free to be who they were, no need to cover anything up, no fear that they would be found out and love would be withdrawn. That was the way it was intended to be.

Many times we look back and idealize the past as a time when everything, including relationships between human beings, worked better than now. We imagine an idealized past when people got along better with each other. Often we think that the time of the founding of a religion or a nation was the "golden age," a time which is held up as an example to contrast with the present state of the community. We suppose that there was peace, cooperation, mutuality, love and respect back then—in the time of Abraham, or Moses, or David, or Jesus, or the early church, or the Protestant Reformation, or the founders of our own nation. If only we could go back to those good old days when loyalty to family and community and country was so obvious. Never mind the stories of the murmuring in the wilderness or the deterioration of David's family or the arguments between Peter and Paul or between Calvin and Luther.

Sometimes we do the same glorification of the past in our

individual lives too. We remember the days of our youth when life seemed uncomplicated and people loved us and we didn't yet understand all those complicated dynamics that were at work in the relationships among various members of the family. As we look back from a greater distance, negative feelings of hurt and rejection and disappointment are muted somewhat, and nostalgia paints a picture that seems brighter than it really was. Holidays can be a difficult time for many families because they remind us of good times of warmth and togetherness that we never seem to be able to recreate.

In the beginning of the book of Job, three friends came to see Job. They had the best of intentions. They made an appointment to come together to comfort him (Job 2:11). They were genuinely distressed by his appearance. They mourned with him and sat with him in silence for a whole week (2:12-13). They represent the possibilities of humans bringing support and hope to one another in times of trouble. But unfortunately, as we shall note later, they were not able to accomplish what they had set out to do. And so, they also represent the reality of broken human relationships. Even when we come with the best motivation, we can be hurtful to others.

How it is now

Humans were created to live in love and harmony with one another. But obviously, something has gone wrong.

After the fall. When the man and woman knew that they were naked (Gen. 3:7), they hid themselves from each other and from God. The curses that followed indicate that there would be ongoing problems in their relationship to each other (including their sexuality) and with all creation (Gen. 3:16-19). Matters quickly got much worse. The first sons competed against each other for God's favor. When Cain's offering was not accepted, he took Abel out into the field and killed him (Gen. 4:1-8). The first murder was an act committed between the first brothers. It became so bad that God was sorry that he had made human beings (Gen. 6:6). Though tempted to wipe out the human race completely, God decided to save Noah and his family.

124

But the post-flood story is no improvement. Human beings still could not live together in peaceful community. When they tried to work together to build the tower of Babel, God stepped in to thwart their attempts at cooperative enterprise by confusing their language (Gen. 11:1-9). It is hard enough to communicate with others even in our own language. People say one thing and mean another. The same words have different nuances to different people. But the problem of human communication is greatly compounded by the multiplicity of languages. Those who have tried to travel in a land where no one speaks their language know what a barrier that can be. How can you learn to know someone if you can only communicate by waving your hands, pointing to a picture, or trying to pronounce an isolated word or two? The Tower of Babel story represents all those human failures to communicate with others, even in our own language, but most severely across linguistic barriers.

"Enemies" in the lament. The lament psalms speak often of one's "enemies." They clearly show that in times of trouble, when one is looking for support and hope, other people are more often part of the problem rather than a source for hope. Psalm 69 is more hostile than most psalms in its expression of curses on the enemy. The psalmist asks God to deliver him from his enemies (v. 18). "Thou knowest my reproach, and my shame and my dishonor; my foes are all known to thee. Insults have broken my heart, so that I am in despair. I looked for pity, but there was none; and for comforters, but I found none" (vv. 19-20).

There are several reasons why a person may turn hostile toward others in times of trouble. It may be that my trouble is caused by someone else. They have hurt me in a profound way. People do hurt each other. Or it may be only my imagination, my paranoia, my need to blame someone, my urge to strike out against someone in my frustration and anger. Or it may be that people have not been properly comforting to me. They have not come to see me at all. Or they have come but have mouthed platitudes, talked down to me, or condemned me with simpleminded explanations that link my problems with my own sins. Or the enemies may be those who have drawn my envy because they are not suffering like I am. The more I look at them, the more I wonder why I should have to endure all of this while they go on about their lives without any disturbance at all. Surely, I am as good or better than they are. I am angry at them because they prosper and I do not. It isn't fair.

Job and his counselors. As we have said, Job's friends came to him with the idea of comforting him. But it did not work that way at all. They came with their packaged explanations for the presence of suffering in the world. They were determined to fit their "answers" to Job's situation, without regard to Job's past reputation or Job's own arguments. They did not listen to what Job said to them. They insisted that Job, all evidence to the contrary, must be a sinner who was deserving of his trouble. God would not do this to him without some reason. And the most logical reason was that he needed to be punished, or perhaps he needed to be taught, disciplined, or humbled.

Job resisted the explanations of his friends and scolded them for their treatment of him. As he responded in bitterness toward them (not unlike the psalmist who rails against his "enemies"), they became more hostile and condemnatory toward him. And poor Job, who needed the support of friends and family as he faced his future with little or no hope (see Job 7:6), was left completely alone (though his friends were actually there), with no one to listen or understand his situation. He accused his friends of withholding kindness, like rushing streams that dry up when it gets hot (6:14-17). He complained that they had talked down to him (12:2-3; 13:1-2) and have told lies about him in order to protect their theories of divine retribution (13:4, 7-10). They had to make Job look like a sinner in order to maintain their balance between God's power and justice. He called them "miserable comforters" (16:2) and wondered how much longer they would continue to torment him (19:1-4). By the end of the dialog, Job and his friends were scarcely talking to each other. Their conversation had become an abstract, impersonal argument about whether or not the wicked would ever be properly compensated for their behavior.

Job was denied comfort not only from his three friends. He had become a laughingstock to his whole community (12:4; 30:1-10), in sharp contrast to the kind of respect he used to have (see Chap. 29). In 19:13-22, he spoke about all his human relationships that had gone sour because of what God had done to him. He was estranged from everyone—kinsfolk and close friends, even his guests and servants, his wife, young children, and intimate friends. They had all turned against him. And he pleaded for someone to have pity on him (19:21).

Job had become a problem to people. They didn't know what to say to him. He exposed their weak efforts to make sense of his suffering. He looked terrible and he complained all the time. He struck out in anger even toward those who had come to support him. He protested his innocence so long and so vigorously that people suspected he was protesting much too much. It was no wonder that people did not flock around him to bring him comfort.

As is often the case, when we are most in need of other people to help us revive hope, we drive them away with our negative attitude and words when they come. And, from the other side, as would-be comforters, we are often too easily driven away, taking too personally the angry outbursts of one who suffers, too willing to preach worn-out words of good cheer rather than to enter into the depths of feeling with the one who needs to know that there is someone who will listen.

War, destruction and exile. Human history has been the story of conflict, not only on personal levels (as murder or rejection within families) but also on community, tribal, national, and world levels. The biblical story reflects this constant state of conflict. Some of the stories in Genesis show the origin of conflicts that have persisted for centuries—Ishmael and Isaac, Jacob and Esau (Edom), the Egyptians and the Israelites. When the Hebrews came into the promised land, they had to contend with people who were already there. There was a brief respite at the end of David's reign and in the time of Solomon. But at Solomon's death, there was civil war and then innumerable wars with

Syria and others. Finally, the great world empires came sweeping through, one after the other—Assyria, Babylon, Persia, Greece, Rome—bringing horrible destruction and chaos and pain and suffering. One wonders if there can ever be peace in the world. Our history since biblical times has certainly shown no sign of improvement. If humans are meant to live in peace with one another, when will that happen? Or will it ever happen?

Jesus came as the Prince of Peace. But he stirred up much controversy, from his first sermon in his hometown where they tried to lynch him (Luke 4:20-30) to his humiliating execution as a criminal. He was quoted as saying, "Do not think I have come to bring peace to earth; I have not come to bring peace, but a sword. For I have come to set a man against his father, and a daughter against her mother, and a daughter-in-law against her mother-in-law; and man's foes will be those of his own household" (Matt. 10:34-36). Peace there may be one day, but in the meantime, in the here and now, there will continue to be conflict. The kingdom of God will not come without considerable resistance on the part of demonic forces and wicked people. If anything, at least as represented by the more apocalyptic passages (as Matthew 24; Mark 13; Luke 21; 1 Thess. 5:1-11; 2 Thess. 2:1-12; the books of Daniel and Revelation), things will get a lot worse before they get better.

And so we live in a broken world. Brothers turn against brothers. We are unable to communicate openly with one another. When we need comfort, we drive our comforters away. And when we try to bring comfort, we condemn, patronize, intellectualize, and fail to listen. War and fear of war continue to preoccupy our attention as they have for centuries. Will we ever learn to live together in peace?

Hope for the human family

What are the words of hope for our human relationships? What promises can sustain us as we face the future in a world like this?

Hope for human comfort. Job and Jeremiah and the psalmists longed for human support, a friendly ear, someone who would understand and not critique their expressions of pain and anger and bitterness and betrayal. They wanted someone to go with them through their ordeal. But instead they had to face it alone. Human companionship, a good relationship with those who accept and understand, can bring hope.

The future is never so bleak if we can be assured that someone will be with us. We could do better at providing this basis of hope for people. The church should be the kind of community that provides hope not only because it keeps people connected with God but because it also keeps them in loving relationships with other human beings. We can learn much from other groups in our society that have banded together to bring hope to others who have experienced similar difficulties—such as support groups for alcoholics, spouses or parents grieving over the death of a loved one, heart or kidney transplant patients, single parents, and so on. Those who have already been there are better able to understand and transmit hope to others facing similar problems.

Even death seems less of a terror when one is not left to die alone or in a huge, impersonal, antiseptic medical environment. And so we have hospices for those who are dying, that they may be with others whose earthly days are also coming to a close and with their own loved ones. Though it is certainly true that we all must die on our own, still there is much comfort and hope if a loving community surrounds us to send us gently on that journey.

It is not the content of the hope that sustains one in such a situation so much as the relationship with others. If we try to promise too much, speak too glibly, explain what we don't really understand, we may stifle another's lament and give the impression that we have not really been listening to what they have been saying. Thus, it is possible for us to contribute positively to another's hope, even though we have never talked about it. Our respect, love, and acceptance of them has done a work which mere words could not do.

Hope for forgiveness. We have talked about our need and hope for divine forgiveness. But we also need the promise of forgiveness in our human relationships. Without the hope of forgiveness, the possibility that mistakes and hurts inflicted on others can be overcome and left behind, it would be impossible to make commitments to one another. We need to be free to make mistakes, or we are not able to make any decision at all. Though we enter into relationships with the best of motives and make solemn promises to do what is right, we will sometimes fail those with whom we make such covenants. Without forgiveness, that would be the end of it. There would be no hope for any ongoing close relationship. At the slightest provocation, we would take our marbles and go home, nurturing a grudge or resentment for the rest of our lives. Without forgiveness, we would have to be perfect. And since we cannot do that, the future can only be terrifying without forgiveness.

Sometimes our biblical ancestors were capable of admirable acts of forgiveness. Esau, that much maligned elder brother who boorishly gave up his birthright for a mess of pottage, surprises us all (but most of all Jacob) by his gracious act of forgiveness. And by so doing, he became a manifestation of the presence of God. Jacob said, "For truly to see your face is like seeing the face of God, with such favor have you received me" (Gen. 33:10b). Joseph forgave his brothers all the evil that they had intended to do to him and perceived that God had used their sin and his suffering to achieve the purpose of saving many from famine (Gen. 50:15-21).

Jesus taught his disciples, when they pray, to ask for their sins to be forgiven as they forgive those who sin against them. That is rather a scary thought. Is our own forgiveness contingent on our ability and willingness to forgive those who have offended us? At the least, it is very difficult for us to imagine that another could be much more gracious and forgiving than we are capable of being. There is a two-way quality to forgiveness. Those who know how to forgive others are more likely to believe it is true when another says to them, "I forgive you." Jesus says that we should first be reconciled to a brother who has something against us before we come to offer our gift at the altar (Matt. 5:23-24). Reconciliation on the human level opens the way for restoration of our right relationship with God. And the reverse, failure to deal with our broken human relationships, will interfere with our comprehension of God's grace and forgiveness.

The father of the prodigal son is both an image of how God relates to us wayward children and an example of how we should receive those who now come to us asking for forgiveness. We are to be lavish in our willingness to forgive, not counting how many times till we finally refuse. Jesus said to Peter, "I do not say to you seven times (a number suggested by Peter), but seventy times seven" (Matt. 18:21-22).

Hope that people will change. What a wonderful world this would be if people knew in their hearts what they should do and then actually did it. Jeremiah dreamed about such a future in the famous new covenant passage (Jer. 31:31-34). If each individual was obedient to God, then there would be peace on earth. The law would not be an external demand laid on people with the threat of punishment for refusal to comply. Doing what is right would be as natural as breathing. Preachers and teachers would be obsolete because they would be unnecessary. Of course, it would take an act of God to accomplish such a tremendous task. And one wonders what will happen to human freedom in this future where all do exactly as they should. Will we finally all be puppets controlled by God, the end of the noble experiment that God began at creation and decided to continue after the flood? Ezekiel expressed a similar hope for humanity when he proclaimed an oracle from God in which God promised to "give them (the whole house of Israel) one (or a new) heart, and put a new spirit within them; I will take the stony heart out of their flesh and give them a heart of flesh, that they may walk in my statutes and keep my ordinances and obey them; and they shall be my people, and I will be their God" (Ezek. 11:19-20).

Obviously if everyone did what God desired, this world would be a better place. All the hateful things that we do to each other would be a thing of the past. Our relationships with others would be bright and good and wonderful. But is this possible? Has it somehow happened in the coming of Jesus? Jer. 31:31-34 is a popular prophetic word, much loved by Christians and particularly by Protestants who read it for Reformation services. It expresses our conviction that we cannot earn God's favor by keeping the law, that outside coercion will not bring peace on earth, that God acts to renew us and make good works possible. And yet this promise, though begun in the lives of many, has not yet reached fruition. We still live in this world, not the next. We still do not always know what God wants us to do, and even more certain, even when we know, we do not always obey. Spontaneous obedience to God still does not come naturally. This is still a hope for some future time and future place—beyond our experiences with this life.

Hope for peace among the world's peoples. Out of the midst of devastations wrought by war and hostility among nations, biblical prophets arose to speak of a time when there would be peace among the peoples of the earth. Israel is called to be a light to the nations (Isa. 49:6; 42:6; see Luke 2:32). Through the witness of Israel, other nations will learn about the Hebrew God and will come to worship the one true God (see Isa. 42:5-6; 43:9-10; 45:6-7; 49:5-7; 60:1-7; Jer. 3:17 and 33:9; also Isa. 2:2-3 and Mic. 4:1-2). Surely there will be peace on earth when all the world has united in the worship of the one true God. Then God "shall judge between many peoples, and shall decide for strong nations afar off; and they shall beat their swords into plowshares, and their spears into pruning hooks; nation shall not lift up sword against nation, neither shall they learn war any more" (Mic. 4:3; also in Isa. 2:4). What a glorious vision of a world of peace, where the instruments of war are no longer needed. Similarly, the oracle in Isa. 11:6-9 speaks of a time when even the creatures that are natural adversaries shall lie down together in peace—the wolf and the lamb, the leopard and the kid, the calf and the lion, the little child and the poisonous snake. "They shall not hurt or destroy in all my holy mountain; for the earth shall be full of the knowledge of the Lord as the waters cover the sea" (Isa. 11:9).

These texts speak hope to a world torn by war. They promise an end to hostility and conflict and a new age of peace. We live in the hope that one day those words will come true. We know they will be achieved in the next world, in a time following death or in a new era. We struggle to know what we should do now, in this world. Some would have us act as if peace were already a reality if we would just throw down our arms and give our enemies a chance to react positively to our generosity. Others seem to believe that they can achieve peace by stockpiling more and more powerful weapons of destruction, a strategy that seems not to have worked very well throughout history. So what are we to do? Surely we must struggle for peace in the here and now, acting as if it is a possibility. But we are comforted in our struggle by the knowledge that this world is not all that there is, that God intends that his creation will one day live in peace, and that what God wants will finally be accomplished.

Hope for community after death. We will discuss our hope for life after death in more detail in the next chapter. In this context, however, we should make note of our hope that death is not the end of all those relationships that we have made during our earthly life. That hope sustains us as we move to the future. What has been good in our relationships with others will not end. Also, a life consumed by what has been destructive, negative, and unfulfilling, has not been lost forever. There will be other opportunities to do what has not yet been done, or undo what has, unfortunately, been done. The reconciliation that was not achieved, the word of love that was never spoken, the forgiveness that was never sought or never granted, the hurtful word that was not recalled—all that can still be resolved. Even death cannot close the door on our relationships with others. That is a profound word of hope.

6
HOPE
FOR
LIFE AFTER DEATH

If this life is all that there is, then what hope is there? All things of this world will one day pass away. Mighty nations that are able to keep their people secure from outside dangers will one day fall to outside aggression or inner decay. Lands that were once fertile will become deserts. Temperate zones may again be covered by layers of ice, and vast jungles (like the Amazon) may erode into useless wastelands. The rulers who reigned with justice will be replaced by despots. Justice will always be elusive, and peace, whether between persons or among nations, seems always to be short-lived. Communities are constantly breaking up. Close friends move away. The neighborhood changes. The children grow up and leave for other places. And always there is death. Sometimes it surprises, coming suddenly to those who least suspect it. Even when it comes in due season, at the end of a good, long life, it is disruptive and painful, forcing us to reorient ourselves to a community in which some of the most important persons in our lives are no longer there.

And then there is our own life. We, too, must die. At age 20 we may not believe it. By age 30 we suspect that it may also happen to us. By the time we are 40, we know we will not be able to avoid it. What hope is there for us if our future has such an abrupt ending, if there is nothing beyond this life?

The question is particularly acute for those who have waited in vain for the fulfillment of God's promises in this life. They have not received their share of the world's resources (food and land), not been protected from danger (persecution or war or severe health problems), not received justice from this world, and have not been supported by loving human communities. How are they to understand God and God's intentions to work for our good when life has been so bad? There must be more time, some other place, some ongoing future in order for God to make good on his promises.

But even those of us who have had a relatively good life are pained and angered and frightened by the reality of death. We want more time not only because life has not lived up to our expectations (there are, of course, unpleasant parts to everyone's life), but because life has been so good that we do not want it to end. Though I may thank God for the life of a wonderful parent, a life which was long and productive and loving and relatively free of pain and suffering, I will still cry out in anger that such a person must die. Why should anyone die? Why should such a beautiful life end? Why must our loved ones leave us? And why must we someday leave them? Without hope for a life that reaches beyond the chasm of death, our hopes seem incomplete as we bravely try to find comfort in the face of a grim reality that is inevitably going to destroy us. If hope is about the future, how can we hope when, if death is the end, there is no future? Is it possible to resign oneself to a future of nonexistence and still have hope?

What Does the Old Testament Say about Life after Death?

In the Old Testament there is not much explicit hope about a continuing individual existence after death. The Old Testament does not claim too much. The few passages that are more forthright in promising a life after death are in the apocalyptic literature.

Sheol

When people died they went to Sheol. We have no specific doctrine about Sheol, but we can learn something about it by references to it in various parts of the Old Testament, particularly in the Psalms. Sheol was a place where everyone went when they died. There were no distinctions between good and bad, pious and rebellious, rich and poor (e.g., Job 3:11-19; 21:23-26; Eccles. 2:14-16; 3:19-22). Death was the great equalizer. There were no rewards and no punishments, no hell, no levels of status or privilege. This meant there was no fear of punishment (which might be a word of comfort to some), but it also meant that there was no righting of the wrongs done to innocent sufferers or the calling of prosperous evildoers to account.

Sheol was like sleep, with very little consciousness of what was happening or what had happened (e.g., Ps. 88:12 speaks of Sheol as a "land of forgetfulness"). Though not a very appealing place, at least there was rest there from earth's pain (e.g., Job 3:17). In spite of this semiconscious state, there did seem to be an ongoing sense of individual identity. It was possible, for example, to call someone back from this existence to ask them some questions (as was the case with Samuel in 1 Sam. 28:13-15). This is an important point to consider because it lays the foundation for a later belief in the resurrection of the dead. If people lie sleeping in Sheol (called Hades in the New Testament), and they have not lost their identity as persons, then it is possible for God to revive them and bring them back to life (though the Old Testament very rarely takes the next step to promise that).

There are some biblical passages that seem to say that God is not present to those in Sheol. They are separated from God and either cannot praise God or have nothing for which to give praise. Often in lament psalms the psalmist pleads for deliverance from danger (even death) and argues that God must save because if one dies, he or she will no longer be able to give God praise. "For in death there is no remembrance of thee; in Sheol, who can give thee praise?" (Ps. 6:5). The living are contrasted with the dead. It is the ones who are alive who can praise God. But the dust cannot praise God or tell of his faithfulness (Ps. 30:9). "The dead do not praise the Lord, nor do any that go down into silence" (Ps. 115:17). "For Sheol cannot thank thee, death cannot praise thee; those who go down to the pit cannot hope for thy faithfulness" (Isa. 38:18).

One must be careful not to read these passages as if they express the dogmatic beliefs that God could no more help those who have already died, that God's presence had been forever removed from them, and that praise would never again be appropriate or possible on the lips of those who had descended to the grave. Some of these texts no doubt overstate God's absence from those in Sheol because they were desperately pleading with God to act immediately before it was too late, and they would forever be removed from God's presence. In some cases, there might even be a kind of bargaining with God, appealing to God's delight in receiving praise, pointing out that if God's faithful ones were dead, then God would not receive much praise. So, if God wished to be praised, God should attend to the psalmist's predicament.

There are other texts that imply that even Sheol was within God's realm. Not even a descent into Sheol would be able to separate one from God. "If I ascend to heaven, thou art there! If I make my bed in Sheol, thou art there!" (Ps. 139:8). "Even the darkness is not dark to thee, the night is bright as the day; for darkness is as light with thee" (Ps. 139:12). Amos 9:2 presents another implication of this word that God could penetrate even the remoteness and darkness of Sheol. Though Psalm 139 might be a word of comfort to the faithful one who faced death, Amos 9:2 is a warning to the wicked ones who thought that they could do whatever they desired in this life and then safely retire to Sheol for an eternity-long nap without ever having to answer for their misdeeds. Sheol was not out of God's reach. God's presence was also there. Even to die and go to Sheol was not necessarily a hopeless situation as long as God could reach them there.

Sheol was probably located under the earth (e.g., Num. 16:30) in the depths of the cosmic sea (as Jonah 2:5-6). (When people speak of hell, which is not quite the same thing as Sheol, they still talk about it as if it were under the earth.) It was generally considered to be a place from which one could not return, a one-way street (see 2 Sam. 12:23 and Job 16:22). This of course was true to people's experience. No one knew anyone who had been dead and returned to life. We have noted at least one partial exception in the person of Samuel, who reappeared briefly to speak a harsh word of doom upon the unfortunate Saul (1 Sam. 28:13-15).

A sense of community in life and death

Though most of the Old Testament does not explicitly promise life after death for individuals, this lack is not as severe perhaps as it may seem to our Western, highly individualized mentality. We cannot imagine not existing as identifiable, distinct persons. We have been conditioned to think of salvation largely in terms of our own individual passage from this life into heaven after we have died. It is difficult for us to see how a religion that does not promise this can be of much comfort to people.

But there was a corporate sense in Old Testament times that is hard for us to recover and which must have eased the terror of death. They knew that they were part of a community that had an existence before they were born and would still be there after they were gone. God was from the beginning and God would still be there with their descendants when they were gone, keeping promises, remembering the covenants. With this sense of involvement in the ongoing history of the community, death was not quite so bad. There was a sense that one lived on in the lives of one's descendants. Therefore, it was particularly important that one have children. Many biblical stories, from Abraham and Sarah to Rachel and Hannah and Job, show us what a tragedy it was if one died without leaving any children. The laws of levirate marriage, in which a widow was married to her deceased husband's brother to produce an heir, were ways of compensating for this terrible situation (Deut. 25:5-10; Boaz in the book of Ruth; see also Mark 12:18-27).

And so death was not quite such an awful thing if one left children, if one's life was not cut off too early, and if one did not suffer too much. Death was still a tragedy, to be sure, but it was not the end of the community, and therefore, it was not the end of the individual whose life was so bound up in that community. The story of the death of Jacob (Gen. 49:29—50:3) reveals this strong sense of community, even in death. After he had blessed his sons, the dying Jacob spoke some final words regarding his own burial. He referred to his coming death as "being gathered to his people" (Gen. 49:29). He wanted to be buried in the burial plot that had been in the family for several generations. That was where Abraham and Sarah and Isaac and Rebekah and Leah had all been buried (49:31). Having said this, he "drew up his feet into the bed, and breathed his last, and was gathered to his people" (49:33). Then Joseph and the others mourned for him and embalmed him and "wept for him for 70 days" (Gen. 50:1-3). This is a typical example of dealing with death in the Old Testament. There is nothing here about life after death. There is no promise that Jacob would live again and carry on some sort of individual existence in this world or any other. There is genuine grief and mourning when Jacob died. He was no longer with those who were left behind. They would miss him, but they were helped through their grief by the support of the community which joined together in prescribed rituals of mourning. So there was community among those left behind, but there was also community even for the one who had died. To die was to join one's ancestors. There was a bond between the living and the dead, between those who had gone ahead and those who would join them, and among those who were already dead. The place of burial took on significant symbolism. It was very important for Jacob to know that his bones would mingle with those of his ancestors and his wife, Leah.

In modern mobile societies, it is hard to feel the impact of the common burial place, where generations past and present are still in touch with each other, where one can take a stroll through the cemetery and review the family tree and tell stories about the persons who lie there, and where we can feel again the influence of their lives on our own. In our day, even our dead often lie in isolation. One does not even know where to buy a burial plot. Our parents are often buried in another part of the country, we don't know where we will be living when our final time comes, and we surely have no idea where our children will be.

Possible allusions to life after death in the Old Testament

Though the Old Testament, as we have said, promises very little in the way of life after death, there are some passages which give hints in that direction. From the later perspective of a community that has come to believe in the resurrection of the dead, these texts may be reinterpreted to support that belief.

1 Samuel 28. We have already spoken of Samuel's return from the grave to haunt Saul. This text at least implies that people still have their individual identity after death, they are in a place from which return is possible, and they can be summoned back. Though this is a temporary return for Samuel, there is no reason to close off the possibility that a more general resurrection might be possible.

Enoch and Elijah. Enoch and Elijah are the two Old Testament characters who did not die a normal death but went directly to heaven. After Enoch lived 365 years, "Enoch walked with God; and he was not, for God took him" (Gen. 5:24). In our day, we might use that kind of language to describe someone who had died, but tradition came to believe that Enoch was up in heaven (not in Sheol where dead people go, but in heaven where God lives). Elijah went up to heaven in a whirlwind with Elisha looking on (2 Kings 2:11-12). For three days, the sons of the prophets carried out an extensive search to see if Elijah's body was anywhere to be found (2 Kings 2:15-18). The fact that it could not be located reinforced their conviction that he had indeed gone directly to heaven. The unusual situation of both Enoch and Elijah led to an enormous amount of speculation about what they were doing in heaven, what God had in mind for them, what part they might play in God's future plans for the world.

These two are obviously special cases. But they do hold forth some hope for the rest of us who will have to die the death of all human beings. If God can choose some to be with him in heaven, then is it not possible for God to do so with many more of us? In fact, these two characters may play some part in ushering in the new messianic age which will make life after death possible.

Elijah and Elisha miracles. Both Elijah and Elisha performed miracles in which young persons who were dead were returned to life (1 Kings 17:17-24; 2 Kings 4:32-37). This is not a promise of resurrection for all believers. Presumably the boys who were brought back to life grew up, lived a normal life, and then they died. (Like Lazarus in the New Testament, they had to die twice.) At least they did not die too soon, as children, before they had the opportunity to live out their normal span of days. Further, the story is a reminder that God is Lord over both life and death, that any life is a gift from God, that God can breathe new life into us just as surely as God (through the prophets) sent his life-giving spirit into the nostrils of those boys.

Job 14 and 19. At one point, early in his struggle to understand and cope with his terrible misfortunes, Job had wished that he could die (Job 3). His life was so terrible that he saw death as a relief, an escape from the horrors of this life. Even though he understood death as final and complete, it would still be preferable to more of the kind of life that he was now forced to lead. But later on, Job began to ponder the possibility of life after death. Chapter 14 is a poignant statement of his longing for something more than his present life. He compared human hope with hope for a tree that is cut down. A tree can put out new branches with the encouragement of a little water (Job 14:7-9), but a man breathes his last, lies down, "and rises not again; till the heavens are no more he will not awake, or be roused out of his sleep" (14:10-12). Job wanted to believe that there is more. If only God would hide him in Sheol till God's anger had subsided (14:13). "If a man die, shall he live again?" Job asked (14:14). He wanted to say "Yes." He tried to believe. He would find great comfort in that hope. But he could not cross the threshold. Though he seemed to come close to believing that death is not the final word on a human life, in the end he fell back into hopelessness, worn down by the relentless erosion of his personal suffering (14:17-19).

The "Redeemer" passage in Job 19:25-27 is very difficult to translate and open to various interpretations. Many think that it is a place where, perhaps only for a moment, Job was able to surmount the obstacle to belief in life after death. If Job was saying that he would be vindicated after he had died (19:26— this is a debatable point among scholars) and he would see it with his own eyes (19:26-27), then perhaps he hoped to return from the dead, at least long enough to appreciate that his good name had been restored. Though the original intention of the text is very unclear, Christians have found here a word that coincides with our Easter message, and we have borrowed Job's words to sing loud and clear: "I know that my Redeemer lives."

Ezekiel 37:1-14. The Lord showed Ezekiel a field strewn with dry bones. "Can these bones live?" God said to Ezekiel (37:3). Ezekiel wasn't sure what to think, so he deferred to God, "O Lord God, thou knowest" (37:3b). How could life come back to bones that were scattered throughout the valley and were so dried that there was nothing left but bare bone—no flesh, blood, sinew, or skin. Surely it was too late for a return to life. Elijah and Elisha didn't have to perform their miracles on dry bones. Most of us would probably answer God's question with "not likely" or "I doubt it" or "Are you kidding?" or some such response. But with God, all things are possible. No doubt Ezekiel's vision was primarily a message to the exiles that their nation could still be revived. Though it be scattered in exile throughout the nations of the world, though it seem without any life and vitality, yet God could resurrect the people and again make them a nation in their own land (37:14). It is probably a prophecy about the whole people and not about the resurrection of individuals from the grave. Nevertheless, the language, and the message, is consistent with a hope that God will do for individuals what God can do for the whole people. This is a message for us who face the hopelessness of a life that must end in death as it is also a word for a community that faces extinction. God says, "Behold, I will open your graves, and raise you from your graves" (37:12a). Whether or not Ezekiel so intended it, this too has become a wonderful word of assurance for individuals to express their confidence in a God who can overcome even the grave.

The Psalms.   Both psalms of lament and psalms of thanksgiving speak of God delivering persons from the pit, the grave, Sheol, etc. These were probably not intended to be words of hope that God would bring back one who had already died. Most likely, the intent was to ask God for help (in the lament) when one was on the *verge* of death and to give thanks when God has saved someone from falling into the pit from which it is impossible to return and where there is no praise of God (note what we said earlier about Sheol).

None of these passages which we have been reviewing here is a clear, direct promise of life after death. Yet each contains the seed of that hope and will be read by later generations (both Jewish and Christian) as expressions of that hope.

Apocalyptic passages

The clearest statements in the Old Testament about hope for the defeat of death and the revival of the dead are in the apocalyptic passages in Isaiah and in Daniel. The Daniel text is the most forthright of all.

Isaiah 25:6-8; 26:16-19.   As part of the vision of the great end time, the prophet speaks of a wondrous banquet for all people (25:6), the destruction of the veil that covers the people (25:7), and God's wiping away of all tears and removal of the reproach of God's people (25:8). In the midst of this passage we read that "God will swallow up death forever" (25:8a). God will defeat even death. What that means for the individual is not spelled out in detail. This is symbolic language, the big picture, a promise of God's authority and control over even our worst enemy— death. Death will no more be able to defeat us. Speculation about what will happen to the individual who has died or will die is left to the imagination.

God's people have been in distress, like a woman great with child who writhes in pain as she struggles to deliver (Isa. 26:17-18). But after all the labor pains, nothing has happened. There is no deliverance and "the inhabitants of the world have not fallen" (26:18b). And then comes the wonderful word of promise: "Thy dead shall live, their bodies shall rise. O dwellers in the dust, awake and sing for joy! For thy dew is a dew of light, and on the land of the shades thou wilt let it fall" (v. 19). Is this a clear promise of a resurrection for those who are in Sheol (the land of shades)? Some suppose that this, like the dry bones vision of Ezekiel, is more likely a promise of the rebirth of the whole people than a hope for the resurrection of individuals who had died. One could argue that case. But the words of the text speak their own message to one who comes to it with no preconceived notions. It certainly sounds like God is promising to reach into the depths of Sheol, to bring light to lighten the darkness, and dew to initiate new life. The dead will live, their bodies will rise, and they will shout for joy. This, indeed, seems to be one of the clearest expressions of hope for life after death in the whole Old Testament.

Daniel 12:1-2. Apocalyptic literature seems to arise in chaotic, terrible times when God's people are suffering persecution at the hands of evil powers that temporarily rule the world. If justice is to prevail, if God is to bring deliverance, there must be life after death. People have already died because of their perseverance in the faith. There must be a time when they can be rewarded and the perpetrators of evil against them will be punished. Daniel puts it quite directly. There will be a time of greater trouble than the world has ever known (Dan. 12:1a). But then deliverance will come for all God's people who have their name written in the book (12:1b). And justice will also come for those who have already died. "And many of those who sleep in the dust of the earth shall awake, some to everlasting life, and some to shame and everlasting contempt" (Dan. 12:2). The need for justice demands resurrection to complete what has not yet been achieved. Innocent victims will be given another chance—in fact, an everlasting life. Wicked people will not be allowed to sleep on into eternity, oblivious to the pain that they have brought into the lives of others and forever immune from the judgment of God. They will not be pleased to be reawakened because, for them, the prospect is everlasting contempt.

144

Like earlier Old Testament texts, it is assumed that the dead are sleeping in some place from which they can be retrieved. There has been no separation of the dead for judgment. All are in the same place. But now, in the last times, the dead (it is not clear if this text is thinking of *all* the dead; note that 12:2 says "*many* of the dead") will be revived, they will be judged, and they will spend eternity in two radically different situations. The good news is that God's justice cannot be defeated by the grave. The good news is that God's faithful, those whose names are in the book, will go on forever. The bad news is that now we have to fear hell (at least the earlier Old Testament folks were spared that). From this time, much effort will be expended by pious folks trying to insure that they avoid that terrifying destination.

What Does the New Testament Say about Life after Death?

In Jesus' day not all the Jews agreed on what happened to persons after death. The Pharisees, more open to ongoing revelation and the oral tradition, believed that there would be a resurrection of the dead. The Sadducees were more conservative, confining their sacred texts to the first five books of the Law where there are very few words of promise for an afterlife even with a very imaginative reading of the text. And they read their Bible in a quite literal way. Jesus was clearly much closer to the Pharisees in his understanding.

Jesus in the synoptic Gospels

In the first three gospels, Jesus had little to say regarding the specifics of what life after death will be, though it is clear that he did believe that life will not end with death.

Mark 12:18-27 (and parallels in Matthew and Luke). Sadducees came to Jesus and attempted to ridicule the belief that there is a resurrection of the dead. They presented the hypothetical case of a woman whose husband died before she gave birth to an heir. Then each of his brothers dutifully took her as a wife to try to provide an heir for the deceased man. Before it was over, she had been married to all seven of the brothers (one wonders if brothers four through seven might have hesitated on their way to the altar when they saw what had happened to all their siblings). Finally, the woman herself died. The Sadducees then raised the tough question: "In the resurrection whose wife will she be?" (Mark 12:23). If people are called back from sleep and resume life pretty much as it was before, then how can this woman be married to seven men at one time? People in our day ask the same question. Widows and widowers would like to re-marry for companionship, but their true love of 50 years is the one they want to be with in eternity. Will the remarriage complicate their time in heaven? What about the new spouse's former spouse? Will they be forced to go through eternity as a foursome? Such questions can be posed as a way of ridiculing the hopes of a pious person. On the other hand, they may reflect genuine struggles to make sense out of something that is beyond our human comprehension—i.e., what will life be like in the here-after? Generally, interpreters of this text have not given the Sadducees the benefit of the doubt regarding their motivation in asking the question.

Jesus' response did not provide much detail. We are interested in his exegetical method, his effort to force an Old Testament saying about God's relationship to the patriarchs into a proof text for belief in life after death (Mark 12:26-27). We are intrigued by his saying that when people are raised from the dead they will not marry but will be like angels in heaven (Mark 12:25). At first glance, that may seem less than comforting. Many people think of heaven as a place where we can get back together with family members who have gone before us, particularly parents and spouses and children. But Jesus' word is a reminder that we are not to be too literal in our imagining what heaven will be like. We cannot possibly know. Clearly, it is not just a continuation of what we know in this world (that would hardly be heaven, even for those of us who had had a good life and happy relationships with others). If we spend too much time speculating over details and arguing over who has the best understanding of what is basically a mystery, we may be like the Sadducees, more concerned with intellectual jousting than with hanging on to the promises that even death cannot separate us from the love of God.

Luke 16:19-31. In this parable about poor man Lazarus and the rich man, Jesus made an important point that in the life after death our fortunes may be completely reversed. Those who have suffered in this life will be comforted on Abraham's bosom while the rich man who has feasted in the midst of victims of poverty finds himself in torment in the flame. So there is a judgment following this life. Justice will be done. There is more than one destination for all who have died. There are two separate places, with an impassable chasm in between (v. 26). The place of comfort was called "Abraham's bosom." The place of punishment was called Hades (usually in the New Testament, "Hades" is more a neutral term, like "Sheol"), and it is apparently very hot and uncomfortable (16:23-24, 28). We, of course, do not know what content to give to a term like "Abraham's bosom." Is this a synonym for heaven? It seems clear that we should not be too literal in using this as a description of what it will be like in heaven. (Are we all to rest on the lap of Abraham or do we each have our own Abraham?) Probably the main point to be communicated is one of rest and comfort. The text gives the impression that the poor man was carried immediately by angels to Abraham's bosom. The rich man was buried and is in Hades. Unlike other biblical references that we have observed, there seems to be an immediate transition to heaven (Abraham's bosom) without a resting time in Sheol until summoned back to life by God.

Luke 23:42-43. Jesus promised one of the thieves hanging on a cross next to him, "Truly, I say to you, today you will be with me in Paradise" (Luke 23:43). There is life beyond the grave. The faithful person who turns to Jesus will go to paradise. And Jesus will be there. There will be community with God and other humans. Of this much, we can be relatively sure. There are a number of questions about this text, most of them having to do with the word "today." How could Jesus have gone to paradise *today* (Friday) if he was going to be in the grave until Sunday morning? Is this a belief in the resurrection of the dead, the dominant biblical view, or does it resemble some later beliefs about the soul leaving the body at the time of death and going directly to heaven to be with God? Some scholars have tried to solve some of the problems by changing the comma from before "today" to after "today." Then it would read: "I say to you today, you will be with me in Paradise." Another possibility is not to take the word "today" in its literal sense. To God a day is a thousand years. When one is sleeping, the hours go by very quickly. When one awakes, it may seem only a few minutes since going to sleep, though it may be several hours. The thief will perhaps live in the grave for hundreds or thousands of years to be awakened at the final judgment to be with Jesus.

The words from Jesus as recorded in the synoptic Gospels make it clear that Jesus did promise life after death to believers, that there will be judgment after death and that the new life will involve a close relationship with God through Jesus. These are all words of promise to support us in our hope for lives that do not end in the grave. But they are not particularly helpful if we wish precise details about what that wonderful life in heaven will be like. Will we still be married? How will we relate to family members? Where is heaven located? Will we pass immediately to heaven or must we wait for the resurrection? Such questions are beyond our comprehension and we need not know the answers in order to have hope. God will take care of it. We Christians take special comfort because we put our trust in a God who has been through the experience of death, has met it head on and defeated it, and promises to do the same for us.

Jesus in the gospel of John

In the gospel of John, Jesus' promises about eternal life were more direct and more likely to inspire hope in the believer than some of his sayings on this subject from the synoptics. Texts from John are widely used in pastoral work to the sick and dying and grieving, and are often the basis for funeral sermons. "For God so loved the world that he gave his only Son, that whoever believes in him should not perish but have eternal life" (John 3:16). Some have described this verse as a microcosm of the entire gospel message. In John 11, we have the story of the resurrection of Lazarus from the dead. Jesus arrived on the scene after Lazarus had already been in the tomb for four days (11:17). Jesus told Martha that her brother would rise again (11:23). She said that she knew he would rise again at the resurrection of the last day (11:24). Here she reflected the belief of a majority of Jews in Jesus' day that there would be a final day when all the dead who had been sleeping would be brought back to life. But Jesus went on to say, "I am the resurrection and the life; he who believes in me, though he die, yet shall he live, and whoever lives and believes in me shall never die" (11:25-26). And then Jesus demonstrated that this was not just an idle promise by bringing Lazarus back to life (11:38-45). This was not yet the general resurrection of the dead. Lazarus was a special case, symbolically representing God's power over death and demonstrating that Jesus is the one who makes that power available to us. Lazarus would have to die again, just as those little boys who were revived by Elijah and Elisha. But their stories inspire hope in us because they show what God has done and has promised to do for us in the future.

The fourteenth chapter of John begins with wonderful words from Jesus. We are not to be troubled. Jesus has gone to prepare a place for us in his Father's house. And after he has gone to prepare a place for us, he will come again to gather us to be with him (John 14:1-3).

These are wonderful words of comfort from the gospel of John. Again, Jesus did not provide many details of what that life beyond the grave will be like. It is enough to know that we are promised an eternal life in close relationship with him if we but put our trust in him. His power to overcome death was demonstrated by a few incidents such as the miraculous emergence of Lazarus from the tomb, and even more so, by his own resurrection on that first Easter Sunday.

149

Epistles and Revelation

1 Corinthians 15. The fifteenth chapter of 1 Corinthians is probably the most detailed and interesting discussion of this subject in the whole Bible. Paul insisted that there is a close relationship between the resurrection of Jesus and the resurrection of the dead. To deny one is to deny the other, and either way, there is no hope (vv. 12-18). "If for this life only we have hoped in Christ, we are of all men most to be pitied" (15:19). Later in the chapter, he engaged in a long discussion of what kind of body people will have when they are raised from the dead (15:35-50). There must be some kind of body, but it cannot be merely a continuation of the same kind of perishable and sinful body that identifies us in this world. It will be a "spiritual body" (v. 44), which seems at first to be a contradiction of terms, but was a way for Paul to conjecture about what humans will be like in the world after the resurrection. When the last trumpet sounds, the dead will be raised and will be changed from a perishable nature to one that is imperishable (15:51-54). Death will be swallowed up in victory (cf. Isa. 25:8) and will forever lose its sting (15:54-55).

1 Thessalonians 4:13-18. This passage is a word of comfort for those early Christians who were grieving because some of their community had already died before the messianic age had arrived. They were not to be ignorant and grieve as those who have no hope (v. 13). "For since we believe that Jesus died and rose again, even so, through Jesus, God will bring with him those who have fallen asleep" (v. 14). When Christ returns from heaven, with the sound of the trumpet, the dead will be raised first, and then those who are still alive will follow, "caught up together in the clouds to meet the Lord in the air; and so we shall always be with the Lord. Therefore, comfort one another with these words" (1 Thess. 4:17-18). Again, there is the promise that death is not the end. Do not grieve for those who have died as if they are lost forever. They too will be revived and we will all be back together and we will all be with God. Community that has been broken will be restored, humans with humans and humans with

God. These events did not occur as soon as the writer thought. The Lord did not reappear in the lifetime of any of the recipients of this letter. But the promise is still there for all who have died, whether in the first generation after Christ or the many centuries that have followed.

Philippians 1:20-26. In this beautiful passage, Paul was so little terrified by death that he was hard-pressed which he preferred—whether to die and be with Christ (v. 23) or to remain in the flesh and continue his work with other Christians (1:22, 24-26). He was content to be alive and to serve God and the church. When death came, it would be a good time of closer fellowship with Christ. He would not seek death because there were still tasks to do. But when it came, it would be nothing to fear. This was not a morbid fascination with death as an improvement over life. Rather, it was almost a matter of indifference. Living or dead we are the Lord's. It really isn't that big a deal when we die since that will only enhance the relationship with God that already exists.

1 Peter 1:3-9. The recipients of this letter would be facing some severe trials. But even though they had to suffer for a time, they would find the strength and hope to continue by remembering that they had been "born anew to a living hope through the resurrection of Jesus Christ from the dead, and to an inheritance which is imperishable, undefiled, and unfading, kept in heaven for you, who by God's power are guarded through faith for a salvation ready to be revealed in the last time" (1:3b-5). No matter what troubles this life may bring, there is still hope for those who remember Jesus' resurrection and his promises to work the same in all those who believe.

Revelation 20:11-15; 21:1-4. Toward the end of this great apocalyptic vision, the seer beheld a great, white throne with all the dead gathered before it for judgment. The sea and Death and Hades all gave up the dead that were in them and "all were judged by what they had done" (v. 13). Then Death and Hades were thrown into the lake of fire (the second death), along with anyone whose name was not written in the book of life (vv. 14-15). Similar to Dan. 12:2, this passage says the dead will be brought to life and subject to judgment. The wicked will be cast into the lake of fire. The good people will be citizens of the new holy city where God himself will be with them and will wipe away their tears and there will be no more death, mourning, crying, or pain (21:3-4). If one can be assured that his or her name is in the book, this is a wonderful word of hope and comfort. If one worries that the final judgment might be a negative one, then this text can instill fear rather than hope.

Punishment in hell

The earlier biblical idea of Sheol did not allow for a judgment after death. Therefore it was very important that justice be achieved in this life. Otherwise, there was no recourse for an innocent sufferer like Job, and no opportunity for the wicked to be punished (so the urgency of many psalms that protest the prosperity of the wicked). Eventually, at least by the time of Daniel and clearly in the New Testament, there develops the belief that there will be a final judgment in which all will be held accountable for what they have done with their lives. In a number of places, Jesus taught that there will be a punishment for those who have escaped justice in this world (e.g., Matt. 5:27-30; 25:30-46). The apocalyptic literature (e.g., Dan. 12:2 and Rev. 20:13-15; 22:12) was particularly insistent that there must be fitting punishment for those who have done wicked and hurtful things to other people, especially to God's faithful ones.

One of the problems of a belief in life after death as a place of ultimate judgment is the fear of hell. How can we be saved from the inexpressible horror of suffering forever? Better to die and sleep through eternity in the semiconscious state of Sheol than to come back to life only to be tormented forever. The promise of life after death can become a curse for those who fear that God may not forgive, for those who scrupulously rehearse their sins and know their inability to live up to God's expectations. Those persons need to know that there is forgiveness, that Jesus has taken care of their sins for them, that if they let Jesus go with them into death and through death, they have nothing to fear. On the contrary, they have hope for a wonderful new relationship with God that far exceeds anything that our human intellects can imagine. Far from being a God who delights in punishing, our God seeks out the lost, refusing to let them perish, and takes great pleasure in their return (as with the lost sheep, coins, and sons of Luke 15).

Theological and Pastoral Observations

Seeds of later belief in earlier texts

Clearly there is a transition within the Bible in the way that belief in life after death is articulated. There are very few places in the Old Testament which promise that there will be an afterlife for individual human beings. By the end of the New Testament, this becomes a primary hope for the followers of Jesus Christ. Later biblical writers build on what their predecessors had believed and written. If dead people are asleep in Sheol, if God's presence reaches even into the gloomy darkness of the land of the dead, if there is a continuing individual identity there (as with Samuel), if there is some sort of community (one joins one's ancestors in death), if God is a God of justice and mercy, if God can take Enoch and Elijah with him to heaven, if God's messengers can bring the dead back to life, then it is not inconsistent, illogical, or impossible to believe that God can and will bring us back from the dead. Belief in resurrection is not such a radical new idea for those with a background in the traditions of the Old Testament. Rather, the old tradition simply did not feel the need to push on to make more specific promises about individual life after death.

Once a belief in the resurrection of the dead had become more widely accepted (by Pharisees and Christians), many Old Testament passages (such as Psalms, Ezekiel 37, Job 19) were read in that new light and were thought to give support to this belief.

Why the need to become more specific about an afterlife?

Apparently Old Testament religion served the people well for many centuries without promising anything very precise in the way of an individual afterlife. Probably the two most important reasons for the transition to a belief in the resurrection were the loss of a sense of corporateness and the failure to achieve justice in this world.

As long as one could feel one's own identity in the ongoing community that was still in relationship with God, then one could have a sense of immortality as one's life continued on in the life of the community. If I do not receive justice in my lifetime, that is too bad for me, but it does not negate God's promises because God will eventually fulfill all his promises. I may not be there to see it, but the community will, and to know that will bring some comfort. But with the loss of the community feeling and the rise of a strong sense of individualism, we become much more concerned for our own individual identity, apart from our identification with any community. We want to continue to exist forever, just as we are (only better), not melting into some great amorphous and abstract entity. "I want to be me," we say. We don't want a time when we will no longer exist as the individuals we are now.

Further, if one has a heightened sense of individuality, it becomes very difficult to see justice at work in the world. Many of those things that God promised have not happened. The good people suffer and wicked persons prosper. Many individuals, even faithful ones, have not received the basic necessities of life, protection from danger, fair and just treatment, or a strong sense of community with God and other humans. If God's promises are to be kept for each individual, then there must be an afterlife because they surely are not now being kept for each and every person. This is particularly true during times of persecution, famine, severe illnesses, or other disasters. What is one to hope if this life is miserable and one is finally destroyed by such forces? It is not surprising that the clearest expressions of hope for life after death emerge in the apocalyptic times.

The impact of the resurrection of Jesus

For the early Christians, the resurrection of Jesus was a powerful symbol and source of hope for their own resurrection. Many of the Jews had already come to such a belief (as we have noted), but the powerful impact of the resurrected Christ both validated Jesus' office and also gave his followers hope for themselves even in the face of severe persecution and what might appear to be earthly failure. Jesus' resurrection was at the heart of Christian preaching. His resurrection and hope for the resurrection of the dead were closely bound together (e.g., 1 Corinthians 15). To believe one was to believe the other and, therefore, to have hope.

Resurrection or an immediate transition to heaven?

When the Bible speaks of life after death, this hope most often takes the form of a call back to life from sleep in Sheol (Hades) at the last days. At that time, there will be a general judgment, and some will live on in everlasting joy while others will be tormented forever. This is the most consistent biblical position, beginning with Old Testament ideas about Sheol and building on them. The New Testament writers expected that final day of judgment to come rather soon. As we well know, it did not. Does that mean then that all those who have died in the ensuing centuries are still waiting for the final trumpets on the day of resurrection? Many Christians speak of heaven (and occasionally of hell) as places (or states of existence) to which people go immediately when they die. Some have even split the human person into body and soul and have assumed that the soul goes to be with God whereas the body decays in the grave. Such conjectures about body/soul splits seem not to have much support in Scripture. There are a few texts, such as Luke 16:19-31 and Luke 23:42-43, which could be read in such a way as to support an immediate transition at death to the next world (angels carry Lazarus to Abraham's bosom; Jesus promises the thief that they will be in paradise *today*).

There are theological and pastoral reasons to support one view or the other. But it seems that the biblical writers, when they speak of life after death, almost always talk about a resurrection from the dead and not an immediate passage to another existence, and surely not an eternal soul that has an inherent quality of immortality within it. It is God who brings the dead back to life. We humans have no right to immortality. All life is a gift from God.

How much can we say about life after death?

Perhaps we can learn something from our Old Testament ancestors by noting their modesty, humility, and reluctance to say too much about the afterlife. They had not been there. They had not heard from anyone who had gone to the land of the dead and returned. They had some strong statements to say about who God was and about God's power and mercy. But they did not try to say too much about things they did not know. They were content, for the most part, to leave it in the hands of God.

Even in the New Testament, even from the mouth of Jesus, we do not have much detailed description of what life will be like in the "sweet bye-and-bye." There will be community, but we won't marry. There will be comfort for some, but punishment for others. God and Jesus will be there. Paul tried to imagine what a spiritual, imperishable body will be. And beyond that, there is not much that we can say. Poets and hymnwriters and artists have shared with us some pictures of what heaven will be like (and hell, too), but these are all, obviously, metaphors, images, imaginings, and are not meant to be taken literally. To argue over specifics about such unknowns is to commit the sin of the Sadducees, who tried to ridicule the hopes of those who believed in an afterlife by projecting earthly details onto a heavenly scene.

Trust (faith) in God is the starting point

As with all our discussion about hope, we return again to the basic point: Do we trust God? Do we have confidence in God even in the face of the deepest mysteries, even when confronted with that most fearsome unknown of them all—death? Can we trust that God will be with us to bring good even out of death? Can we believe this, even as we fear we may be deluding ourselves, hypothesizing an afterlife to make some sense out of all the nonsense of life, to ease our fear of death, and to give God time to make good on his promises? As Christians, the resurrection of Jesus is still the strongest symbol we have to remind us that our hope is not illusory, not mere wishful thinking, but based solidly on the defeat of death, once and for all, by God's own son.

7

HOPE
FOR
THIS WORLD
AND THE NEXT

We all need hope in order to live lives that are not consumed by dread or deadened by meaninglessness. We need direction, purpose, confidence that there will be an ultimate resolution to all of life's ambiguities. Hope for this world and the next can never be completely separated. Though we may come to realize that all our hopes will not be fulfilled in our own lifetime, we still desire some assurance that God is being faithful to his promises in the here and now. Signs of God's justice and mercy in our community and our individual lives strengthens our hope for those expectations not yet realized. We know of God by what God has done and continues to do in human history. From what we have learned about God, we dare to hope for what we cannot see.

And, from the other direction, our confidence in a final realization of all God's promises gives us reason to hope, though the present is sometimes difficult, painful, fearful, or anxious. Belief in a world beyond this one, a vindication in the end time or after our death, is not necessarily (though it can be) a flight from the world's problems, a willingness to tolerate evil and suffering because better things are coming. Rather, belief that God's promises will finally be achieved, even though the world gives much evidence to the contrary, can give us the motivation to work for those purposes in the here and now. Though we cannot achieve them completely in our own lifetime, we need not lose heart. Someday, God's will will be done, and whatever small contribution we can make will be incorporated into God's intention for the world. In this concluding chapter, let us draw together some of the biblical themes of hope into three categories: the corporate quality of hope, Jesus as fulfillment of past hopes and the basis for future hopes, and some comments on how we might convey hope to others.

The Corporate Quality of Hope

Our biblical ancestors saw themselves always as part of larger communities and knew that their own personal hopes were closely bound with the hopes of others. We in the highly individualized West have often lost this sense of corporateness and tend to separate hopes for ourselves and hopes for our society as if they were two distinct categories.

In this world, there can be no isolated hope

If a person wishes to have a life in which he or she receives the basic necessities of life, protection from danger, justice, and a supportive community, it is clear that such things are not possible in isolation from what is happening with other members of the human race.

We have noted briefly the long-running disputes about possession of land in various parts of the world—as in South Africa, the American frontier, Palestine, Northern Ireland. An individual cannot hope for land unless there is peace and settlement of issues that involve many persons. It is shameful that the world produces enough food for all to eat—but in some areas the crops rot in storage bins while in other places people starve to death. If God's promises to provide food for all are to be accomplished, then societies, nations, and corporate bodies of human beings must devise some way to distribute the earth's bounty. Further, if the world's resources are squandered by reckless exploitation, all individuals will reap the consequences.

A person cannot be protected from danger unless there is law and order in the whole community and peace among nations. I cannot build a fence high enough or an air raid shelter deep enough to protect me from all harm if the people as a whole have not produced a just and stable world in which peace is possible. If ancient Israel, or any other nation, is destroyed by corruption within or enemies from without, there is no way that even the most God-fearing and law-abiding citizen can be shielded from the horrors that follow.

If there is not equal justice for all in our society, then there is always the possibility that we, too, will one day be the victims of injustice. We may think that we are in a favored position with the law tilting in our favor. But injustice nurtures rebellion and strife and turmoil from which none in the society will be immune.

Even our ability to hope is often a gift from others. We learn through their faith and their example. Their presence with us, in some intangible way, is hope-producing.

And so our hope as individuals can never be separated from the future of our family, our community, our nation, our world. To repeat a quote in which God spoke to Baruch, through Jeremiah, after Baruch had complained about what a painful life he had led: "Behold, what I have built I am breaking down, and what I have planted I am plucking up—that is, the whole land. And do you seek great things for yourself? Seek them not; for behold, I am bringing evil upon all flesh, says the Lord" (Jer. 45:4b-5a).

This means that if we are to have hope as individuals, we need to work to make a better society. We are not to be isolated and passive recipients of hope, dreaming and praying for a better life for ourselves without accepting the responsibility to work to achieve that for which we hope. God may well use us to answer our own prayer. On the human level of history, it is clear that hopes will be fulfilled only if people work toward those ends.

The community and hope for the next world

Regarding our worldly hope, the intertwining of individual and corporate expectations seems rather clear. But when we speak of hope for life after death, for a new day when all will be made right, we often slip into very individualistic categories of thought. Death is, of course, the one thing that we must do entirely on our own (even birth is a little different because of our mother's involvement with us in that process). But even in death, the corporate nature of hope is very important. We have noted that even though they had no highly developed sense of an individual life after death, early Old Testament traditions did speak of a kind of community in death. While lying asleep in Sheol, one was with others, those ancestors and family members who had gone before. Further, the assurance that God would remain in covenant relationship with the community that was left behind was a word of comfort and hope. One need not see complete vindication or experience a personal eternal life if one knew that God was still at work and justice would one day be done and God's people would again flourish. There is an admirable quality of unselfishness in this attitude toward one's own death and one's community. We, too, might find death somewhat less awesome and terrifying if we could recover a little of this corporate sense.

Further, the sense of community was terribly important for the mourners grieving the loss of a loved one. At such times, we need other human beings to love us and remind us that life goes on, that it is a gift from God, and that we will eventually need to move beyond grief in order to make full use of the life that God gives to those of us who remain. In our day, we are learning again what many people have known instinctively for ages—that the one who dies needs the support of a loving community as he or she lets go of this life and moves into the ultimate unknown, *and* those who are left behind also need others to renew their spirit and bring back hope. Those in the latter category may need that strength from others for a long time, not just for the few days or weeks following the funeral.

As we dream about what the next life will be, one of our most common expectations has to do with community—restoring relationships that have been broken by death and repairing ones that remained damaged at the time of death. Whatever heaven might be, most of us envision a time of renewed and restored relationships. There is a strong corporate quality to our image of heaven. It is not a place for isolated individuals floating around on their own clouds, but rather a multitude of saints, singing and laughing and talking and praising God.

Jesus as Fulfillment of Past Hopes and the Basis of Future Hopes

For Christians, Jesus is the fulfillment of earlier promises made by God to God's faithful people. Further, Jesus becomes the primary reason for hope as we face the future.

The coming of Jesus demonstrates that God keeps promises

The New Testament often speaks of Jesus as the one who has come to meet all the earlier expectations. Old Testament words of promise and hope are examined thoroughly to find those passages which point toward a person like Jesus. God keeps promises. Though there were many hard times for the people of Israel as they struggled through the centuries, particularly during and after the exile, God had never abandoned them. God's purpose was never thwarted, even though the people continually turned away in rebellion. Looking back on the promises from the vantage point of seeing and knowing Jesus, we Christians can speak of God's plan, a purpose and intention that has been there from the beginning.

As we face our own times of disillusionment when it is hard to see the working of God in the world, we can take heart from what God has done in Jesus Christ. What God promised, God did. As Jesus fulfilled the hopes of our Old Testament ancestors, so we can be assured that God will again accomplish what he has promised. God will provide for our needs, protect us from danger, execute justice and restore community.

How Jesus fulfills God's promises

Jesus was not recognized as the fulfillment of God's promises by every person who was familiar with Old Testament hopes. Some believed, but others did not. Since the world continued without the end of violence and hatred, since many still suffered

162

the deprivation of land and food, since tyrants still ruled the land and justice was impossible for most citizens, it seemed strange for some to believe that God had fulfilled our human hopes in the person of Jesus. Is this all there is? Don't we still hope for more? Part of the difficulty lies in the tension between hopes for this life and hopes that will come only in the next age. If we see Jesus' work only within this world, if we limit his activity to what has been accomplished up to this time in world history, then those who disagree that the messianic age has already begun have a good point. Certainly there is more for which to hope than has already been accomplished.

Jesus does meet the needs of the real world. We must not spiritualize or eschatologize the work of Jesus too soon. He did cure real people of real diseases. He did cast out demons and provide food and revive from the dead and reconcile relationships among humans and between humans and God. Those were real accomplishments and the fulfillment of human hopes, and they occurred in the here and now. There is no legitimacy in our refusal to allow such inbreaking of Christ's spirit into our present lives. We need not wait till we die. There can be healing of mind and body and spirit, the replacement of hatred with love and violence with peace. Such things have happened, and they continue to happen this side of the eschaton (end times).

Symbolic fulfillment of our hope. Clearly, the messianic age has not arrived in all its splendor. This world is not God's kingdom, even though we see glimpses of that kingdom here and there. Though we may believe that Jesus is the long-expected Messiah, much more remains to be done. Many of the hopes that we have been examining have not been met. Sometimes the earthbound Old Testament hopes are reinterpreted by Christians so that they speak symbolically of a hope that transcends the immediate situation, which is met in Jesus even though, in a strictly literal and earthly sense, it still remains to be fulfilled. And so we speak of our heavenly home by expanding the promises to possess a land, a place to belong, a homeland to which to return. Jerusalem becomes a place for all Christians, even after death, and not only a city on the highlands between the Mediterranean Sea and the Jordan valley. The fruit of the vine and the wheat of the field become the Lord's Supper, which nourishes not only the body but also gives strength for spiritual battles and assures us of our oneness with others and with Christ. We project our needs for protection from harm, for justice, and for restored community onto a heavenly plane. In short, though God's kingdom has begun in the person of Jesus, though we have seen enough to believe that and to hope for more, it is still true that the kingdom has not yet been consummated. What has occurred up till now has often been on the spiritual level coming in small and subtle signs that are often invisible to those with little faith.

Christ's second coming

And so Jesus must come again to complete the task. Though Jesus has fulfilled some of our earthly hopes and has fed us with heavenly food, there is still more to be done to bring reconciliation, peace, comfort, justice, community. We are grateful for what has been done, for the inbreaking of God's kingdom. And, on the basis of that work already begun, we hope for the final victory over all that can hurt us. Whether it will come in our own lifetime, at the time of our death, or at a final end of the age, we cannot know. But we know enough to live in hope that God, through Christ, will one day fulfill all that God has promised.

On Speaking a Word of Hope

Life becomes tragic if there is no hope. When those we know and love begin to lose hope, we are pained by what we see and we want to say or do something to inspire new hope in them. As Christians we know we are called to comfort one another, to share our own hopes, to speak good news to those who are in despair. But how do you bring back hope to one who has lost hope? One must remain humble and modest in the face of human hopelessness, but there are a few things that we should remember that might assist us in our efforts to be comforters in such situations.

Remember that people are in different stages of hope

We must be sensitive to the face that we are not all in the same place in our personal pilgrimages through life. We have tried to recognize this by hypothesizing three stages as one goes through life—a simple faith that all will work out as God has promised, a disillusionment and confusion in the face of failed hopes, and a realization that the only sure thing is to hope in the next world because everything in this life will one day pass away. We do not move directly from one stage to another, though there is a kind of chronological generality to these stages. The first stage is most characteristic of youth, the second to the struggles of midlife, the third to old age as we contemplate death or that of our loved ones. Sometimes we may, after a period of struggle, return to a new naiveté, similar to the first stage but now tested and shaped by experiences that make us less susceptible to the disillusionment that often results from the first loss of naiveté. Sometimes people will keep various parts of their life in separate compartments. They may be quite realistic, even sophisticated, almost cynical, about some of their hopes. But others will still remain quite unsophisticated, uncomplicated, perhaps even simplistic.

Many times we fail to communicate comfort to another because we have not understood and accepted that they are in a different stage of hope than we are. A person in stage two will not be comforted by a friend in stage one who insists that God acts quite directly in the world, that there is a good reason even for the terrible things that happen to us, that God can heal us if we have enough faith, that we should stop complaining and be more submissive to what God has in mind for us. Like Job, such a person will feel unheard, patronized, and condemned by platitude-quoting friends. On the other hand, the person who is still in stage one, or perhaps has returned to a new naiveté, will be distressed by the spiritual advisor who seems to have lost nerve, who is quick to admit struggle and personal vulnerability and moments of doubt but seems to choke on the possibility that

165

God might be able to do something to help us in this world. Also, even the liberating word that there can be hope beyond what this world can give may not be heard as comfort. For the person who wants freedom now, a postponement of death, a cessation to the endless pain, a loving relationship with some other human being, it is not enough (at least not yet) to dangle hopes for an eternal life. "Sure, I want eternal life," such a person might say. "But not yet. Let me have some more enjoyment in this one first. Later on you can tell me about what comes next."

Obviously, we cannot be what we are not. We cannot be all things to all people. If we are no longer (if we ever were) the bubbly optimist, we cannot fake it. If we have not suffered deep disillusionment and personal spiritual struggle, we cannot completely put ourselves in the shoes of one who has. But at least we can listen and try to understand the context out of which another speaks. Then, perhaps, we will not speak to them a word that is entirely inappropriate to their efforts to be honest and to keep hope alive.

The question of trust in God is basic to hope

If we desire to help someone in their struggle to hope, we should remember that the primary question is one of trust. Is God on my side or not? Will God keep those promises that God has made throughout the centuries, especially as conveyed to us by a believing community in Scripture and tradition and liturgies? And so, the question of hope becomes a matter of faith. If one's faith is strong, then hope is easy. But when faith falters, then hope, too, is less assured. So, whatever we can do to bolster one's faith will also help them to hope.

Repeat the past. One way to hang on to faith (and thus to hope) in times of struggle is to recite over and over the evidence of God's care and love and power and justice in the past. Our religious community does this for us on a regular basis through worship, Bible readings, sermons, and sacraments. What God did for the ancient Hebrews or the first Christians is told again and again to remind us what kind of God this is and how we can

166

continue to put our trust in him. Television programs that are most successful are those in which "happy ending" stories are told again and again. Books which tell of victory over dark and powerful forces that once controlled a person's life are read with interest by those who identify with the struggle of the author and hope for the same success. We also look to our own personal life for those occasions when God has been with us in dark times and has brought us safely to better days. Having been there once, we know that we can make it again, though the path will not be easy.

No method of inspiring faith is fool-proof. Faith is an elusive thing, not to be grasped even by the one who seeks it and surely not to be given by a third party. Everyone must do their own believing. Faith, when it comes, is a precious gift, something for which we can only be thankful. Though we may recite all the stories of God's mighty acts in the past, both remote and more recent, both in our community's past and our personal past, the listener may still lack faith and despair of hope. "All that is fine and good," one may say. "But why doesn't God do something for me now?" We continue to tell the story of what God has done. And we share in the anguish of one who tries but cannot believe. We cannot create faith in another. That is the Holy Spirit's work. It is not our business to force faith commitments from another. We are only called to present as best we can, both by word and by deed, our story about a loving God who can be trusted. Then we should step back and let a person's struggle with God continue. The God whom we know will not rest while a beloved child continues in the painful situation of hopelessness.

The effort to find meaning. Since the basic problem for hope is whether to trust God, one of the first things that comforters try to do is find an explanation for our problems which will not tarnish God's image. When terrible things happen to people, when hopes based on God's promises are dashed, people wonder how God, who is supposed to rule the world with power and justice, could allow it to happen. And so intellectualizations, rationalizations, and attempts at theodicy emerge. God's justice and power must be defended to show that God is still trustworthy. The most common result of such efforts is to push hard for explanations which make humans look bad. It is human sin, not God's cruelty or injustice or indifference, that has caused our problem. On one level, this helps us to hope because God is still reliable. If we can just do what is right from here on, we can be assured that things will go better. But there are also dangers in this quest for meaning, especially as we try to be precise in connecting specific sins to specific examples of suffering. Other efforts to make sense of our human situation (in which hope is a necessity because things will have to get better) have taught that God can bring good out of even the most hopeless situation. And some theories have toyed with the inconsistency between God's justice and power in a world where terrible things happen even to good people. Perhaps God is not as powerful as one might think (humans or demonic powers, for example, seem to act often without being restricted by God). Therefore, we can hope in a good God because God has not caused our troubles. But one may be left with doubts about what God can finally do to make a better future for us if we have stripped God of most of his power.

There comes a time when our efforts to find a rational explanation for all human pain and suffering will fall short of inspiring hope in one who is struggling mightily in stage two. Though the motive is to paint a picture of God which can renew our confidence in God, the negative effects of such explanations may outweigh the positive ones. If our goal is to inspire faith and hope in another, the best method is not to persist in intellectual efforts to legitimize even what is clearly hurtful. That is what Job's counselors did. Instead of ministering to a human being who needed their presence and support, they treated Job as a problem, a tough case which required an intellectual solution. In the end, Job felt condemned and alone and, in spite of their best efforts, God still seemed like an enemy who could not be trusted. It is no wonder that Job felt hopeless.

Whether or not one returns to a stance of hope is not dependent on success in finding meaning, an explanation for all that has happened. Hope, as faith, is not simply a matter of intellectual assent. Hope is a relationship restored, and that can happen even though huge gaps of mystery and uncertainty persist. By the end of the book, Job again lived in hope, though he never did understand why all those terrible things happened to him.

Our relationship may be at least as important as what we say. If we truly desire to help another recover hope, we may, often to our own surprise, be more effective in ways that are subtle, relational, intangible, than by the best arguments we can present for God's goodness and our best rationalizations for why God's promises seem to be missing in a person's life. Intellectual struggle is part of the effort to bring back hope, to be sure. And we should be open to share in that struggle with someone. But what is important is that it be a *shared* effort and not pronouncements, platitudes, wise sayings, easy answers that we proclaim as if they were absolute and eternal truth. If we listen to another, do not stifle their lament, enter with them into their pain, modestly share how we have dealt with difficulties in our own life (but do not impose our answers on them), there is at least a chance that we will not hinder God's spirit from reaching out to inspire new hope. God will be there, at any rate, no matter what we do. But some ways of communicating hope are clearly better than others. Who we are is certainly as important in such a process as what we say.

We close with a word that has now been repeated several times. The primary obstacle to hope is our inability to trust God to do what is best for us as we move to the future. If we are in a relationship with God that is based on God's great love for us, then we can be confident and hopeful both for our earthly life and for the life to come. We are best advised to pay attention first to our relationship with God and not to get bogged down either in theories of theodicy or in despair over specific hopes that may or may not be fulfilled this side of the grave. The foundation of our hope is the love of God. As we come to know how much God loves us, we are able to claim the promises of God. Seek first God's kingdom "and his righteousness and all these things shall be yours as well" (Matt. 6:33).

NOTES

1. See Walther Zimmerli, *Man and His Hope in the Old Testament* (Naperville, Ill.: Alec Allenson, Inc., 1968), p. 9, and Zimmerli, "Hope in the Old Testament," *IDB Supplement* (Nashville: Abingdon, 1976), p. 417.
2. See Donald Capps, *Biblical Approaches to Pastoral Counseling* (Philadelphia: Westminster Press, 1981).
3. Jacques Ellul, *Hope in Time of Abandonment* (New York: Seabury Press, 1973), p. 272.
4. For further discussion of a God who feels, and even suffers, with us, see Abraham Heschel, *The Prophets* (New York: Harper & Row, 1962) and Terence Fretheim, *The Suffering of God* (Philadelphia: Fortress, 1984).

SELECTED BIBLIOGRAPHY

Donfried, Karl Paul. "Hope," *Harper's Dictionary*. San Francisco: Harper & Row, 1985, pp. 402-4.

Ellul, Jacques. *Hope in Time of Abandonment*. New York: Seabury Press, 1973.

Fairchild, Roy W. *Finding Hope Again*. San Francisco: Harper & Row, 1980.

Hebblethwaite, Brian. *The Christian Hope*. Grand Rapids: Eerdmans, 1984.

Keen, Sam. *Gabriel Marcel*. Richmond: John Knox Press, 1967.

Lynch, William F. *Images of Hope: Imagination as Healer of the Hopeless*. Notre Dame: University of Notre Dame Press, 1974.

Marcel, Gabriel. *Homo Viator: Introduction to a Metaphysics of Hope*. Chicago: Henry Regnery, 1951.

Minear, P. S. "Hope," *Interpreter's Dictionary of the Bible*. Nashville: Abingdon, 1962, vol. 2, pp. 640-643.

Moltmann, Jurgen. *Theology of Hope*. New York: Harper & Row, 1967.

Moule, C. F. D. *The Meaning of Hope*. Philadelphia: Fortress (Facet Books), 1963.

Schwarz, Hans. *On the Way to the Future*. Minneapolis: Augsburg, 1979.

Sherman, Franklin, ed. *Christian Hope and the Future of Humanity*. Minneapolis: Augsburg, 1969.

Williams, Daniel Day. *God's Grace and Man's Hope*. New York: Harper & Bros., 1949.

Zimmerli, Walther. "Hope in the Old Testament," *IDB Supplement*. Nashville: Abingdon, 1976, pp. 417-19.

Zimmerli, Walther. *Man and His Hope in the Old Testament*. Naperville: Alec R. Allenson, Inc., 1968.

INDEX OF BIBLICAL PASSAGES

OLD TESTAMENT

NEW TESTAMENT

Dere's Demons

A Regency Romance

by Tara Manderino

Copyright © 2008

ISBN: 978-1-58749-690-5

Earthling Press ~ United States of America

Editors: Kathryn Struck and Dick Claassen
Cover Art: Delle Jacobs

Dedication

Thanks to Tracy T for her knowledge of the 19th century
and finding me the answer to my plot problem, and to Tina
H for her tireless critiques.
And as always, thanks to my very own heroes, Anthony, Chris
and Aaron, for putting up with old maps on the floor and
odd questions. I love you guys!

Author's Note:

I truly enjoyed writing Brayden and Jane's story. Much of it
takes place in Manchester, which was one the largest cities of
the time. An interesting bit about Lancashire is that it is
home to one of the two royal duchies in the United
Kingdom. The Duchy of Lancaster was and is a hereditary
estate. It's holdings are kept within the royal family, and it
exercises the right of the Crown in the County Palatine of
Lancaster.
Factories were becoming more prevalent at the time as the
United Kingdom entered the industrial age. The life of the
factory worker was not an easy one, and I wanted to portray a
little of that in my story, although it is highly unlikely that a
true lady would have resorted to working in a factory. Also,
through my research, I did not find any reference to such
things as late in days. Factory workers were treated the same
as the machines, but much more dispensable.

Prologue

1813:

"I don't have time for this nonsense, Brayd!" Nigel said, tapping his riding crop against his booted foot.

Brayden resisted the urge to jump to his feet. He forced himself to remain seated behind the estate desk in the Earl of Raby's office. Said earl, his older half-brother, had no problem relinquishing his estate duties to him. They were duties Brayden gladly accepted. It was beyond him how Nigel could have no interest. From all accounts, the man inherited his wild streak from his mother.

Brayden leaned forward; his hands held a death grip on the edge of the wooden desk. "Then you had best make time, Nigel. These are your lands and your people. You have to—"

"I am Raby. I don't *have* to do anything." Nigel leaned forward, resting his hands on the desk, staring Brayden in the eye.

Brayden took a deep breath and tried to keep his voice reasonable, although dealing with Nigel when he was in one of his moods was nearly impossible. "Listen, Nigel, I understand—maybe better than anyone—that you don't want to be tied down with estate matters, but these are your responsibilities."

Nigel started to turn away, forcing Brayden to come to his feet and grasp his brother's arm, turning him to face him.

"What are you doing?" Nigel's eyes blazed.

"Making you listen. If you do nothing else, you have to listen to the villagers. They want you to hear their cases. As the largest landowner, as earl, you are the magistrate."

"Bah!" Nigel waved his hand in the air. "What do I care

if John Sawyer poaches?"

Brayden ran his hand through his hair. He wanted to tear it out. His brother just did not seem to understand that it was a matter of honor, not just the actual poaching involved.

"Don't we hire gamesmen?"

"Yes, and they're the ones who caught the poachers. You have to deal with them."

"Isn't that what I hire you for?"

Brayden could feel his nostrils flare at the slight. "No, Nigel. They expect the earl, no one else." No matter what it cost him to say those words, it was the truth.

"All right," Nigel said. "I will deal with the issue after I return."

Brayden tossed his hands in the air and slapped them on his sides. Nigel waved him away. "I already promised Morris we would meet this morning."

"Morris!"

Nigel raised his eyebrows at Brayden's tone, but answered in a calm voice. "I know you don't approve of Morris, but he's not a bad sort."

"It's more a matter that I don't trust the man," Brayden said. He watched his brother's neck grow red around his cravat, and his lips tighten. A glare in Brayden's direction and Nigel strode from the room.

After his brother left, Brayden removed his coat and loosened his cravat. He had devoted several days to dealing with the estate books but kept being interrupted with other matters. For now, he knew that Nigel would be occupied longer than just the morning and it would be several hours before Heston, the estate secretary, made his appearance.

Instead of working, he spent most of the time contemplating Nigel's behavior. It was definitely worse of late, but so far he had found nothing in the books that indicated it had any bearing on the estate in any way. Whatever it was, he was certain Morris—Lord Hawke—was involved. The man was an out an out bounder as far as he could tell, yet his sort appealed to Nigel. If he hadn't the niggling feeling that his brother was holding something back, he might be inclined to let the other matters go, but this morning's row had been building for many weeks.

Shaking off all thoughts but those of the estate, Brayden bent his head to the task, at least until there was a commotion in the hall that drew him there, along with the butler calling his name.

Running into the hall, he saw Morris, his face drained completely of color, issuing orders. As soon as the other man saw Brayden, he grabbed his arm.

"Thank God, Brayd! It's Nigel. He took a jump over the west hedge—"

Brayden didn't wait for the man to finish, but immediately ran to the stables, where one of the stable lads already had a horse ready. Ignoring the mounting block, he threw himself on the beast's back. Morris was already mounted, as were several of the other groomsmen.

"Lead," he barked at Morris, pushing his mount to an all out speed. He knew that his face was as white as Morris's. If Nigel could have been moved, he would have been here. He glanced at a few of the other riders and noted that they were well prepared and had a stretcher with them. He set his mouth in a grim line, and forced his horse to a faster pace, quickly outdistancing Morris and the others.

He heard the weak whinny of the horse before he spotted his half-brother lying partially in the ditch on the side of the hedge. He detected no movement.

"Nigel!" he screamed. Sliding from the saddle, he fell on his knees next to his brother, fearing that he was already too late. Extending a trembling hand, he laid it against Nigel's neck. The pulse was weak, but there.

He patted his brother's cheek, looking for response. Finally Nigel opened his eyes the merest slit.

"Good ride, Brayd," he said weakly.

"Listen to me! The men are coming, they have a

stretcher. We're going to—"

"No...time..." His eyes drifted closed, but opened again when Brayden called his name. "Safe...not Morris..." His voice was growing weaker so that Brayden practically had to hold his ear to his brother's lips.

He moved away now to look at him. "Nigel, I need to know. What is in the safe? What do I need to do?" When there was no answer, he put his hand to Nigel's pulse again. Even weaker, but present.

"Mis..sive...attend..." Again, his voice drifted off, then suddenly his eyes opened wider and his voice was stronger. He shifted his gaze to Brayden. "Good sort, Brayd. You'll do right. Always do."

Brayden watched in despair as Nigel's eyes rolled back and his breath came in a gasp. He knew without checking his brother's pulse that he was gone.

The ride back was a somber one, but even that paled in comparison to a few days later when Brayden recalled all of Nigel's words and checked the safe in the study and withdrew the missive Nigel mentioned, with the Prince of Wales' seal on it. Brayden didn't even want to touch it, let alone read it. Opening it, he began to read.

Still holding the papers, he sank into one of the chairs in the study and let his head fall back. Saddling him with the earldom was something Brayden could handle, but for Nigel to leave this the possibility of forfeiting his lands if he did not return the artifact Nigel was practically accused of stealing... Brayden sat up and looked through the paragraphs again. He had one month, at the most, to settle the matter. Oh God, what if he hadn't even been with Nigel? He would have lost his lands and known nothing.

Chapter One

Brayden Derrington, Earl of Raby, looked at his cards from under heavy lidded eyes. He fanned them slightly, then gathered them in a neat pile and laid them face down.

"I say, Brayden, you're not out, are you?"

"Don't be absurd," the man on the left said, his voice sharp. "Derrington is waiting for everyone else to decide their play." Edmund Morris, Lord Hawke, gave a snort. "Damn puppies."

There was a time when Brayden might have been inclined to agree with the man, but not tonight. Now, he would not agree with anything that passed Morris's lips. He would choke on the words.

There were one or two titters, but they abruptly died when Brayden cast his steely gray gaze on them.

As the night wore on, several of the men left the table, but few chose to take their place. The stakes got higher. Brayden willed Collin to leave the table, but the demme man insisted on staying. As long as he stayed, Brayden knew he would have to. He could smell the desperation on Morris; he wanted that pot. Desperate men make mistakes, Brayden reminded himself, keeping his eyes on his cards. Collin, Lord Worsley, was the one who should have been desperate, but he held his ground. Brayden tried not to look in his direction.

Morris threw in his last hand. "That's it. Dere. Done up for the night."

Brayden lounged back in his chair, letting the edge of the card mutely tap the baize covered table. "I could advance you." He didn't raise his voice, just stated the offer in a matter of fact tone.

For a fleeting moment, Brayden watched the potential

greed flicker in Morris's eyes. The card did a steady tap against the table, one edge, then another. He could see the battle Morris was waging with himself before he finally gave in. Shrugging his shoulders, he once again seated himself at the table. "One more hand."

Brayden looked at the man his eyes tired. He knew damn well he had practically cleaned the man out. He really didn't have much interest in the game itself. He was there to trounce Morris—to keep him from winning heavily against Worsley. He had heard Worsley often gambled more than he could afford. Tonight he seemed bent on proving it. If there had been another way to catch the man's attention without gambling, Brayden would have used it. From all accounts, games of chance were stamped on the Worsley family birth records.

Several years younger in age and eons younger in experience than most of the other men at the table, Worsley had managed to hold his own for most of the night, at least until Morris stepped in. When Morris moved in, Brayden did too. The man was not to be trusted.

He looked over at Worsley. "Figured you were done up for the night too."

"No sir, a few more good hands and my luck could change."

Brayden gave a nearly silent sigh and nodded to the dealer to start the play. It was going to be a long night. If it weren't for the fact there was a connection between Worsley and his half-brother Nigel, he'd have very little interest in the man. But Brayden wanted, no needed, to know what that connection was. He planned to talk to the man—informally, of course—as soon as he could cut him out of the pack. But with Morris always about, that was damn near impossible.

Brayden took his cards as they were dealt and the play began. It went quickly, and the others swiftly folded, leaving himself, Morris and Worsley. He could see that Worsley's pile of chips was rapidly dwindling. Blessedly, the hand ended and

Brayden hoped to God that Worsley would pull out.

Neither God nor luck appeared to be with him. The betting became heavier than Brayden liked. If the game were not soon called, the losses would be heavy indeed. He could practically feel Morris bristling with the anticipation of winning. The stakes were upped, and the tension climbed in the room. With nothing left to ante, Worsley called one of the waiters for pen and paper and wrote his vowels for his house and its contents.

Brayden pushed down the bile in his throat. What was the man thinking? Didn't anything work in that brain-box? For the first time, he really looked at the other men who were standing about, no doubt wishing they were still in the play. They were practically licking their lips over the pot. These had been his half-brother's friends! With friends like these, he doubted that Nigel needed enemies. He knew he would have to win this hand and the house before the man did something even more stupid. What a dunderhead.

To Nigel's credit, he had not included Collin in his circle, although the man had wanted to be. Collin was too young in years, and certainly in experience, to keep pace with Nigel or his cronies.

Brayden was the last to turn his hand and when he flipped the cards on the table, he stared. He had lost! He had been wool gathering instead of counting cards. It was one thing for him to lose, but in doing so, he lost his chance to bargain with Worsley.

Worsley was the first to rise. "You have my vowels, my lord," he said to Morris, and quit the room. Brayden fought the inclination to follow to be certain the man did nothing else stupid and watched as his source of information disappear. He could hardly say what he wanted with a roomful of onlookers.

Morris reached out his hand to gather his chips and vowels.

"Another hand, Morris?" Brayden asked lazily.

"I think not. I'm quite content with my winnings."

Seeing that the play was finished, one of the waiters appeared, offering to take the chips to the cashier for the gentlemen.

Brayden stretched his legs out in front of him and settled back in his chair, inviting Morris to join him for a drink, then issuing the order to one of the waiters. If he was going to be denied Collin's company and information, then he would see what Morris had to offer. It might be the only thing he could salvage of the night. "Worsley looked pretty well trounced tonight, Dere," Morris said.

"That he did." He took his drink from the tray the waiter presented to him. "I hadn't expected him to bet the house."

Morris took his own drink before answering. "Demme puppy. Finished off what his father started. Had to happen." He turned his half empty tumbler, letting the light catch on the amber liquid within. "Would have been a damn sight easier if your brother had just let him into the group."

Brayden felt his heart thump against his chest. This is what he wanted. He raised his glass to his lips, not looking at Morris. "He must have had his reasons," he said. He just wished he knew what they had been!

"Nigel always had a reason for what he did." Morris heaved a sigh, then put his glass down on the nearby table. "Not quite the way I was planning to search Worsley's house, but...," he shrugged. "...it will do."

Was it possible he would learn what he needed without Worsley? "Why search Worsley's?"

Morris gave a small laugh. "Come Brayd, you have to know that Nigel gave the man goods for keeping."

Brayden ignored the man's careless use of his shortened name that only his closest friends used. While Morris had been one of Nigel's closest friends, he certainly was not one of Brayden's. "I can't imagine what that would be," he said, sipping his own drink, thoughts running rampant through his mind. Could it be possible that Nigel had given Worsley the artifact mentioned in the missive? It seemed highly unlikely. He couldn't see Nigel entrusting valuable pieces with Collin, but what if he had? The only one who could answer now was Worsley.

Morris shook his head. "And Nigel always claimed you knew everything that happened." His voice took a sharper note, "If you don't know, it's going to be even harder to control the Riders."

"I think I can manage," he said dryly. He didn't have a choice, but did Morris know that? It seemed that his instincts were right again. Worsley was definitely involved, whether knowingly or as an innocent accomplice still remained to be seen. The trick would be to see him before Morris did, for he had no doubt Morris would be there the next day to make sure Worsley vacated the property. He willed his distaste not to show on his face.

Morris put his glass on the table and rose. "Thanks to you, I have enough ready blunt to get me through a few more games, and thanks to Worsley, I don't need to worry overmuch about it tonight." He sketched a brief bow to Brayden and headed off.

Brayden studied the amber liquid in his glass, wishing that Nigel were still around. The two men had not been particularly close, their ages alone precluded that. But for Nigel to have created this mess, intentionally or otherwise, irked Brayden immeasurably.

"Heard tell Morris won from Worsley," Kit Landford, Viscount Hulton, said as he dropped into the chair Morris had just vacated

At six foot, Kit was close to the same height as Brayden, His sandy-colored hair and deep blue eyes were a striking combination. Along with his pleasant disposition, it always made him a favorite guest.

"You heard right."

"You had a reason for it, I take."

Brayden snorted in response. "I was wool-gathering!"

Kit shook his head in amusement and ordered his own drink. "We're drowning our sorrows here instead of at your place where we could do it in comfort and with decent drinks because..."

"Because I'm tired, Kit."

The other man sputtered, then quickly coughed when Brayden turned and arched one brow in his direction.

Brayden didn't think his friend would believe him, but he was tired. Of course, he was blistering angry too.

"Saw Morris leaving when I came in."

Brayden tossed back the rest of his drink. "I almost had him," he nearly growled.

"So I heard. Why did you let him go?"

"Let him? No, he refused to play any more. Probably headed to some hell to fleece some green behind the ears lordling."

"I suppose you'll go after him tomorrow."

Brayden held the glass to the light, and looked at the remaining liquid pooled in the bottom of the glass. "Won't do for him to amass too much blunt. He's comfortable with what he has now."

"There's nothing you can get out of this, Brayden. It's not going to bring Nigel back or change the past."

He gave him a wry smile. "No, it won't change the past, Kit, but it will curtail future events."

Saying goodnight in a clipped voice, Brayden gathered his cane, gloves, hat and overcoat from the major-domo and headed out the club doors. What in God's name had Collin been thinking? Clearly the man had been in his cups, no doubt of that. He shook his head in disgust—still to wager the Town house—or in Worsley's case, the only house. The man must have been mad as well as in his cups. He refused to think of the men who had watched him make that bet with no intent of stopping him. These men were honorable? He couldn't see it; hadn't seen it. His real friends should have led him out—forbade him from making that wager.

He climbed into the coach, refusing to think about it anymore for the night. Or morning, as it might be. Later this morning he would head to Worsley's and try to see what they could salvage of this mess.

* * *

Brayden had just finished pouring his coffee when his sister entered the breakfast room. Dressed in a pale yellow walking dress, trimmed in white, Arabella was a picture of maidenly modesty, which he knew was a great disguise. Not that she wasn't proper. She was just known—at least to him—for getting her own way. Very effective disguise though.

"Oh, don't get up, Brayden," she said, sailing past him toward the sideboard.

He looked at her over the top of his paper and grinned. He had no intention of moving and the chit knew it. "Had a good night at the ball, I take it," he said, laying his paper aside.

She didn't answer until she was seated. "It was boring, Brayden. Although I did hear some interesting gossip later in the night."

He took a sip of his coffee, watching her and waiting. "Do tell," he said in a drawl.

"About you." She took a dainty bite of her toast.

He put his coffee cup down. She wanted to play it out, then let her.

Finally, she gave a little huff, and said, "If you must know, that dreadful Mr. Edwards—William," she clarified, "stopped by after playing at his club. He said that you won a Town house. What in heavens name are you going to do with it. You did win, didn't you?"

"I didn't win, Arabella, so it's nothing to be concerned about."

She relaxed against the back of her chair for a moment before resuming her correct posture. "I couldn't picture you being responsible for throwing someone out of their home."

He resisted the urge to shudder. He couldn't see it either. And in that light, he didn't wonder if fate had dealt him the kinder hand in not being the one to have to deal with Worsley and that issue. Instead, he now had a bigger bargaining chip. One he hoped the man would consider, if for no other reason than his options were seriously limited. Collin could help him locate the artifact, and Brayden would work to keep Collin out of jail and in his own home.

Brayden's personal pockets were deep. As a younger son, he would not have the earldom. In its place he had his mother's lesser property combined with his keen business sense. Now he had the wealth of the earldom behind him too. Granted, his was the deeper pocket, but titles and land carried their weight! He only hoped it would work with Worsley and Morris. Morris was the type that would do something to his detriment if it meant keeping someone else from their goals. Right spiteful, his nanny would have said.

Taking a last sip of his coffee, he excused himself. He'd better head over to Worsley's and get this mess straightened out before anyone else got any hare-brained ideas. Especially if William *had* been spreading tales.

Riding there on his gelding, Nelson, he began to wonder at his own ideas. If Collin agreed to help him, he was certain he could keep the man out of Newgate, especially since the Prince Regent was the one who wanted the artifact. And even if the Regent went back on his word, he would see there wasn't enough evidence to convict Collin. He was sure he could manage that much.

If Nigel hadn't started the idiotic Dere's Demons he wouldn't have to worry about a missing artifact, Collin wouldn't have been trying to desperately ingratiate himself with the group, and Brayden would not have the whole bloody mess to deal with. Absolutely typical of Nigel to leave it all on his shoulders.

Once he dismounted in front of the house, he looked about. It was fairly well kept—white, the same as its neighbors. The small wrought iron fence stood on either side of the stairs. As there didn't seem to be any grooms about, he looked around for a tying ring, where he could leave Nelson. He glanced up at the house again. It did look dark; could Collins have already left? He didn't think that would have been possible.

Not seeing a doorknocker in place, he became a little more concerned. Thumping on the door, he waited for it to be opened. When there was no reaction, he thumped again. Slowly, the door opened, but no one was there.

"Are you lost?" A light voice came from somewhere below his chest.

Looking down, he took an abrupt step back. He was wrong, someone was there. A moppet with golden curls looked up at him.

"Um...No..." Would the child even know Collin? Her simple gray gown with the frayed sleeves declared that she must be one of the servant's children.

"Emily!" he heard a frantic voice float in the hall. "Close that door at once." This was followed by the sound of scurrying feet, and then another face, identical to the first one, peering out at him. He looked down into two pairs of bright blue eyes.

"No," the first girl said over her shoulder. "Someone is lost. Can you help him, Jane?"

Great, he was going to be greeted by every servant Collin hired before he could even get his question out.

An unseen feminine hand whisked the two children out of his sight before he was greeted by a rather plain looking woman. She wore an outdated gray gown of linsey-woolsey and had her hair pulled so severely back from her face that it was difficult to determine its true color. It could have been anywhere from brown to gray. But when she focused her eyes

on him, he nearly lost his breath. Never had he seen such
clear, piercing green, eyes, magnificently framed by thick dark
lashes. He hastily revised his opinion. She must be much
younger than she looked.

"May I help you?" She had to repeat the question before
he could pay attention to what she really said. And that was a
mistake because now he had to focus on her pink lips,
perhaps slightly too wide, but the bottom lip, fuller than the
top caused its own distraction.

He dragged his gaze away when he noticed that the two
little girls were trying to peer around the woman's skirt. He
quickly looked away. No denying the poppets were adorable.

"I have business with Lord Worsley."

The woman looked him over, and he noted the wariness
that came into her eyes as she moved closer to the door,
clearly intending to close it on him. "I'm sorry, he's not at
home now."

"I assure you, it is most urgent that I speak to him." It
was urgent if he didn't want the demme puppy to do
something truly stupid. Though at the moment, it was
difficult to decide what could be more stupid than
wagering—and losing—your only home.

"I'm sorry," she repeated, "but he's not at home." She
started to close the door, but he could hear the little imps in
the background.

"Collin left this morning," one whispered in a voice sure
to carry across the street.

"No, it was night, I saw him when I came downstairs,"
the other insisted.

Brayden looked at the woman in front of him, and was
surprised to see that she was blushing. Why? She hadn't lied,
evidently.

"Perhaps later would be a better time?" he inquired
politely. Perhaps he would catch the man out at his club.

"I don't think so," the woman said.

One of the girls stepped around the woman and looked

at him. "Collin packed his valise," she said, "and took Henry with him."

Who was Henry? Glancing at the woman showed that she looked mortified. He had no doubt she would like to slam the door in his face. Looking up and down the street before addressing her, he said, "I think it would be best if I came in." He suited action to words and entered the house. At first, she held the door firm, but when he put his gloved palm against it and pushed, she easily yielded, albeit with a loud sigh.

Once inside, Brayden looked around. The hall was well proportioned, but the floor looked as if it could use a good polishing.

He removed his hat. When she didn't offer to take it, he tucked it under his arm as he removed his gloves. Reaching inside his coat, he removed his case and handed her a card. She had to take it in her hand since she did not present him with a tray. "Could you please leave that for Lord Worsley when he returns," he instructed her. She didn't bother looking at the card.

"I'm sure you heard the girls," she said wryly. "Collin is not at home, and I do not expect him any time soon."

Brayden's irritation grew. When he caught up with the man, he was going to throttle him with his bare hands.

Brayden slapped his gloves against the palm of his other hand, unsure of what to do next. Seeming to come to a decision, he abruptly stopped.

"Perhaps I could speak to the major-domo," he said. The woman in front of him must be the housekeeper, but why she was answering the door, with the young girls yet, was beyond him.

She seemed to draw herself up so that she stood a few inches taller. "I'm afraid that won't be possible."

He scowled. He knew it, but couldn't stop himself. He noticed that the two younger girls took a step closer to the woman, and he forced himself to smooth his brow.

"Then, whom *can* I speak to?"

"Perhaps if I knew your business..." She looked down at the card and he swore she tried not to let her own eyebrows raise... "My lord."

Lord Raby! What in heaven's name was Collin mixed up in now? Ever since he had come into his title it had been one thing, then another. Even she had to admit that they were getting increasingly worse. She had done her best to keep a close watch on her brother, but even though she was the elder by four years, she was female, as he so often reminded her. As far as she was concerned, the absolute worst of Collin's escapades began when he first met Lord Dere and his nefarious band of riders. She certainly wanted nothing to do with them, but that was neither here nor there. Right now, she had to deal with Lord Raby..

"I am Lady Jane Worsley, Collin's sister. Perhaps you could talk to me in his place." She leaned down to speak to the twins in a low voice before sending them on their way with a gentle push to their shoulders. They turned to look at him once, but did as they were bid.

His sister! Collin has a sister? Never heard of her. She must be older than he. Perhaps those were her children. That make sense.

Then she leveled her gaze on him again, and he felt the full effect of her heavily fringed green eyes. They would be lovely if they didn't hold such scorn. He blinked. Perhaps Collin had told her what had transpired. And where the devil was the man anyway?

"If you would follow me, my lord, we can speak in Collin's study." She led the way past several doorways before entering a dark room.

Evidently, the darkness held little appeal for her because she immediately moved to push the heavy velvet curtains aside after indicating that he should take a seat in front of the desk. When she finished her task, she turned to join him in the second chair. He rather expected her to take Collin's seat, but she left it empty.

"Now, my lord," she said, turning to him, "how may I help you?"

Where to start? He was still reeling from the fact that the man had a sister, but that was no concern of his. Presumably, she would go back to her husband—he hoped. His concern was finding Collin.

He looked at her, finding it difficult to meet her eyes. He would bet that she didn't look at her husband the way she was looking at him—as if she would like to see his head at the Tower of London.

"First, it would be best if you were to tell me exactly where Collin is. I truly need to speak with him before he does something foolish."

A slight, humorless smile played on her lips. "Why do I fear that is too late?"

He watched her smoothing the front of her dress. It was well worn. Perhaps she was cleaning, though he would have thought servants would have done that. Then he looked at her hands. They were rough looking and red, as if such work were not uncommon to her.

Sensing his attention, and following his gaze to her hands, she quickly folded them on her lap and waited for his attention to again focus on her face.

"I believe my sisters have told you—"

"Your sisters!" he interrupted her.

"Is that a problem, my lord?"

"No, of course not." And with a very sinking feeling in the pit of his stomach, he realized that might be a very large problem indeed! How could that be? He peered at her harder, trying to gauge her age. She could be anywhere between nineteen and thirty!

"My apologies," he said. "You were saying..."

"Merely that my sisters already answered you. He left here in the very early hours of the morning. What those two were doing up, I have no idea."

"And Henry is...?"

"His valet, of course." She moved her hands to the sides of the chair. She wanted to stand, but if she did, then he would follow suit and she wasn't sure that she liked him standing so far above her. She had immediately noticed the way he towered over her five foot, two inch frame.

"Now that we established that Collin is not here, what did you need to discuss?" There was no need to tell him that she was the more level headed of the pair and Collin often left any business matters up to her—discretely so, of course. She watched him shift in his seat, not quite meeting her eyes.

"I'm quite familiar with Collin's foibles, you know. I can't imagine that anything you have to say to me will come as a surprise."

Her voice was low and soothing, though at the moment it seemed to hold a tinge of humor. He wondered if she would think the whole situation a lark? Mentally, he brushed away the thought. She didn't look as if she would see humor in anything. He briefly wondered why she dressed the way she did if she were Collin's sister.

"How familiar are you with your brother's affairs, Lady Jane?"

"Quite, I assure you. Since you are not a tradesperson, I am to suppose you did not come to settle accounts." She tilted her head to one side, studying him. "And since you do not appear to be angry, I am to guess that you have not come about his latest d'amour." He felt his cheeks heat. "Since you *are* a gentleman, I can only assume that it is a debt of honor." She gave him a rueful smile. "The problem is that Collin appears to have taken everything with him, so I am afraid I cannot immediately settle the account." Waving one hand toward the desk, she told him, "But if you care to leave a note with the amount owed to you, I will see that you get it as quickly as possible."

Dere looked at her, his eyes hidden by half-raised lids. He did not want her to readily see the surprise there. Evidently, she knew quite a bit about her brother; she had not lied about that. Perhaps, though, she did not know him quite well enough.

Chapter Two

He turned various words and phrases over in his head, trying to decide the best way to approach the subject. There was no best way, damn it. He opened his mouth to speak, then closed it again. What the devil was he going to do about the woman and the girls? This was not his responsibility, he reminded himself. He thought back. There was nothing in Collin's words or demeanor that indicated he would not be here.

She watched him, waiting, and no doubt wondering, what the problem was. He could hardly tell her that they were homeless, thanks to Morris. Well, thanks to her brother, but that was neither here nor there at the moment. He was not the one who should be delivering the news.

Finally, his decision clear, he leveled his gaze on her. "Your brother does not owe me money," he finally told her. It nearly pained him to see the relief on her face. He raised one of his hands to forestall anything she might say. "However, we did play last night."

"Then if you owe him money, please feel free to leave it," she told him, waving toward the desk.

There was no masking the excitement in her voice. He frowned at that. Was Collin so mean-fisted that he didn't give his sisters any funds? He looked at her dress in a new light and drew his lips into a thin line. She must have mistaken his reaction for anger, for she hastily spoke up.

"There's no need," she hastily assured him. "I was merely making a suggestion."

"I am aware of that. You have no idea when he will return?"

It was her turn to drop her gaze.

"Look, he left before we could get matters settled."

He was trying to be honest with her, she could sense that. Shouldn't she return the courtesy? "If you must know, Collin does not plan to return anytime soon." She tried to keep the bitterness from her voice.

Dere started at that. "What the deuce do you mean? Forgive my language."

She gave him a weak smile. She certainly had heard a lot worse! "I spoke to him very briefly before he left," she admitted. "He said that we should see him when he returned."

"Which will be when?" This is where his conversation had started some time ago.

She spread her hands wide and let them drop to her side, and shrugged her shoulders. "I'm afraid I really couldn't tell you that. I really do not know," she added hastily in case he should think that she merely did not want to share that information with him.

Now what? As a gentleman, and aware of the situation, one he helped precipitate, he could hardly leave her and her sisters here to fend for themselves, even if she did look old enough and capable enough. "How old are you?" he asked abruptly.

"Twenty-four, my lord." She kept her gaze steady on his.

"And your sisters? They are twins, are they not?"

Her features softened as she indulged in a slight smile. "Yes, they are. They just celebrated their ninth birthdays."

The tall case clock in the room struck the hour, and Dere knew that he had already overstayed his welcome. Still, he had not done what he needed to do. Not that he knew what that was now that Collin was gone. Hadn't the man even told his sister? He looked at her sharply. She didn't look as if Morris had been by. She didn't look distraught enough. He felt his own lips tighten. If neither man had yet told her, was it his responsibility to do so? Dere never shirked his responsibilities. If he had, perhaps he would not be in this predicament to begin with. He nearly shuddered at the thought of Morris meeting the sisters. He would not want that reprobate anywhere near those young girls. Or the older one for that matter! Taking a deep breath, he started.

"There was a game last night," Dere repeated, his voice brisk now that he knew what he needed to do. "Your brother was in his cups and lost more than he should have."

"How much?" she interrupted, her voice breathy, as if all of the air had been knocked from her person. Her hand had instinctively gone to her throat as if the words were choking her. She took a deep breath. "How much?" she repeated in a stronger voice.

"Rather a lot, but that is not the concern at the moment." He waved his hand as if dismissing the problem entirely.

"Then what is?" Jane felt her voice climbing higher, but she couldn't stop it. There was simply nothing left. She had sold the little bit of jewelry that she had. The few close-to-valuable paintings had been sold long ago. The only servants left were Grace and Samuel, but only because they had absolutely refused to leave. They would have to leave now; she could not even afford to feed them. She would have to find employment for herself just to be able to pay their pension, let alone care for her sisters. She closed her eyes at the thought. Damn Collin! They were too young to have to face this. Surely some relative could take them in. She raised dulled eyes to his, wanting to listen to whatever else he had to say. At least they had the house for now. It would be a place to return to, even if they couldn't afford to live there.

"As I understand it, Collin lost quite a bit of money last night before I ever got to the club. Then his luck seemed to change." Quickly, he went over the evening's events, finishing with the fact that Collin had literally bet his home and its contents.

"That is ludicrous," she said.

"My thoughts exactly," he said. "The problem remains

that we need to locate Collin."

"So...what? You can return the house to him?" she asked, her voice bitter.

"I did not win," he said quietly. "Morris—Lord Hawke—won." He was rather surprised that Morris had not been to the house yet. If he had, the girls would already be gone; he was sure of it.

"Even Collin could not have bet the house," she declared. But she knew he very well could have. The house wasn't in a prime area, but she knew it was still a fashionable one. She raised her hand to her forehead, trying not to shake her head. What in heaven's name had her brother been thinking? She let her hand slide down to her mouth to cover its trembling. Not a moment ago she was certain they had the house, their home, for security, now they didn't even have that.

Composing herself, she let her hand fall to her lap. She resisted grasping them tightly. Instead, she focused her gaze on Lord Raby. His face had hard planes and angles, and his chin was squared and very solid looking. *He* was very solid looking. She was sure he did not have to pad the shoulders of his jacket the way Collin did. His mouth was compressed into a tight line, but when she looked into his eyes, they did not seem as hard as the rest of him. Perhaps he could tell them what to do. Perhaps it would not be so bad if they could live here—paying rent, of course.

She hadn't realized that she had spoken aloud until she saw his lips moving. Even then, it took her a moment for his voice to register. "That is impossible, nor will Morris permit it."

Jane literally felt all the blood drain from her head. She didn't know that one could feel it, but she did. She wanted to just continue to sink to the floor. She could feel herself moving. Good lord, was she swaying? She was never overcome. From a seeming distance, she noticed the alarm flare in his eyes as he quickly came to his feet, and a moment later he pressed a cool glass in her hand. She could smell the spirits Collin favored.

"Drink this," he said, his voice insistent.

She couldn't look at him, but with trembling hands, she raised the glass, with his help, to her lips and took a sip. When she would have placed the glass on the desk, she felt him push it firmly to her lips, and tip! She gasped as she drank more of the liquid than she wanted, then immediately began to cough and sputter. She pushed the glass away, and this time, he let her, taking an appreciative sniff of the liquor before placing the glass on the end of the desk.

When she made to rise, he let her, continuing to talk to her. "Much better. I'm sorry Collin's news has distressed you, but there may be a way to set it all right as soon as we find him."

"It...it wasn't just Collin's news," she admitted. "I just had expected that we would still be able to live here." She gave a shrug, elegant in spite of the coarse gown that she wore.

"That is impossible."

"So you said. But you are not Lord Hawke."

"No, but I know the man well. He is eager to take possession." He watched her closely.

She winced at his words, but her voice was steady. "Why would he be eager? Even I know the house needs some work."

'Even she?' Who better than she? And why hadn't any upkeep been done. He mentally waved that away, that was not his concern. "He seems to think that Collin has something valuable hidden here."

A genuine smile tugged at the corners of her mouth. "I assure you that anything of value, Collin used long ago."

He felt his own hopes sink. "He may not have known of its value."

"I assure you, there is nothing of value in this house."

He gave her a quick glance before settling his gaze on the wall in front of him. *She* was of value. And to someone like

Morris, her sisters would be of great value.

She looked down at her fingers twisted together in anxiety. Where in Heaven's name would they go? She took a deep breath, telling herself to remain calm. A few more moments and Lord Raby would leave. Once he was gone, she could give in to hysterics. For her sisters, she would ask. She would have to. "I wondered if it were possible if you could care for my sisters—just for a few days," she said.

Seeing the dark look on his face, she hurriedly assured him that she would send for them as soon as she found a place to stay. As soon as she found employment, but she didn't tell him that part. He might not take them if it took longer than a few days. "No more than two days," she assured him.

"That is impossible."

She gave him a genuine smile then, albeit a tired one. "You do not have to care for them, exactly! They are old enough to care for and amuse themselves. They are even quite helpful." This was not really working, she reasoned. Besides, they did help her. "I will tell them to be extra good; they will not disturb your wife or family."

"I do not have a wife," he declared.

She stopped speaking and closed her mouth abruptly. "I see." She let her hand trail over the back of the chair and realized that it was his chair. She stopped. "Williams, the butler, and Mrs. Parker have been here a long time," she said. She couldn't look at him. Didn't want to see what he was thinking or feeling, if anything. "They will be pensioned off, but they need time to make arrangements as to where they are to go. Should I tell them that they can stay here until those arrangements are made?"

He must have moved closer because his voice practically sounded in her ear. "That will be up to Morris."

She gave him a tremulous smile because she could see that was what he wanted. Fairness dictated that she not hold him solely responsible for her brother's actions. He was gentleman enough to come by, to talk to Collin; if only they knew where he was.

"If you hear from your brother, you will tell him that I wish to speak to him?"

"Of course, my lord." She looked at him then, standing tall, said, "Williams will see you to the door."

She didn't wait for a response, but left the room, hoping that Williams would be nearby. Quickly, she asked him to see Lord Raby to the door, then meet with her and Mrs. Parker in the kitchen.

She leaned against the wall, her hands covering her face for a moment. Lord, what was she going to do. And who was this Lord Hawke? Lord Raby didn't say anything against the man, but his inflection of voice clearly stated it was not someone he cared for. Taking a shuddering breath, she stood straight and let her hands fall to her side. For now, she had to meet with Grace and Samuel. She would deal with her sisters later. She leaned against the door frame, holding her hands to her cheeks, willing herself to stay calm. It was difficult with so many emotions swirling through her, rage and fear warring for supremacy.

"That one's real quality," Williams said, when he came back into the kitchen.

Jane scowled in his direction, but knew he spoke the truth. Lord Raby had been nothing but kind and reasonable when they spoke. She could not fault him for being the messenger and delivering the news that her brother should have done.

Without going into the detail that Collin had lost their home in wager, she informed the elderly servants that Lord Hawke was the new owner and would be taking possession shortly.

"When do we have to leave, Miss Jane?"

Jane warned herself not to let her smile slip. "Actually, the girls and I are leaving today." She ignored the gasp from the housekeeper. "You and Williams will be staying here until further notice. That will be up to Lord Hawke."

"Now that's just not right, Miss Jane," Williams said. "It'll be a scramble, but I'm sure Grace and I could be ready when you are."

"No, no." She smiled at the servants who were as dear to her as her own family; were her own family, basically. Although her father had outlived her mother by a few years, she could barely remember him since he spent so little time at home, and even less after her mother died. She reached out and patted Grace on the arm. "It's very possible Lord Hawke will have need of your services for a while." She crossed her fingers in the folds of her gown. That relieved the worry she could see gathering on Grace's face. "And of course, as soon as the pension starts, it will be easier for you when it is time to leave."

Samuel's face cleared this time.

"You didn't think I would forget, did you, Williams?" she admonished him.

He gave her a sheepish smile. "You hadn't said anything, Miss Jane."

She caught the glance he gave to Grace. So, they had been worried, but they had never said anything to her.

"Everything's fine," Jane told them. She heaved a sigh of relief. "Now that's settled, I guess we better get back to business. Right now, I have to go find Emily and Evangeline." She headed for the door quickly in an effort to avoid any questions she couldn't answer or didn't want to answer. She nearly made it out of the door before Grace stopped her.

"What about you, Miss Jane? Why aren't you staying here too?"

Taking a deep breath, she forced herself to smile as she faced them, and calmly told one of the biggest lies of her life. "Oh, arrangements have been made with Lady Brooke's." On that note she quickly left the room, calling for her sisters before she had time to think of what really was to become of them. She could hardly say that based on the unvoiced opinion of a man she barely knew, she did not want to stay and meet the new owner.

To their credit, the girls came rather quickly when she called. Then she hastily ushered them up the stairs to their rooms and explained that they would be leaving the only home the girls had known.

"How will Collin find us?"

"Where will we go?"

Two different questions at the same time; typical of their behavior. She assured them that Collin would find them. If she didn't find him first, she amended to herself. Of course, if Lord Raby were looking for him too, she had no doubt that Collin would be found no matter what his wish.

"We're going to go stay with a friend of mine," Jane told them. She explained to them that they would each have one valise and what items must be put into them. If there was any room left, then they could add something else.

She looked around the room. The items were all familiar to her. Indeed they had come from her room once the girls were old enough to appreciate nice surroundings. She had had to supplement them with extra fabric, but in all it was quite pleasing. Jane was rather proud that she had managed to fashion the counterpanes, draperies and even the few cushions about the room, from the materials from her own room. The combination of blue toile from her room, and the old blue counterpane from her mother's room worked well together. Her mother would have been pleased, she thought. Now the twins would have to leave that too.

"I want to take Sarah," Evangeline said, referring to her favorite doll. To make her point, she went and sat beside her on her bed.

"That will be fine," Jane said, "as long as you pack everything else." Even if the contents of the entire house belonged to Lord Raby. She didn't think he would miss the appearance of one doll that he would never know even existed. She felt somewhat guilty, but not enough to deprive her little sister of the only joy she might have for some time.

"I want to bring Lord Henry," Emily insisted.

"Absolutely not," Jane told her. "We cannot bring a live animal to someone else's home." She tried to ignore the tears welling up in Emily's eyes but stood firm. She had no idea where they were going to end up, and the last thing she needed to worry about was an animal. Softening, she stooped down in front of Emily, and wrapped her arms around her, then put her hands on her shoulders so that she could look her in the eye. "I'm sorry we can't take Lord Henry, sweetling, but I promise that as soon as we can, we'll come and visit him."

Both girls looked at her in astonishment.

"What do you mean, visit, Jane," Evangeline asked. She left the bed and came to join her sisters.

Jane looked from one small face twisted with concern to the other. God, she was going to have to find some place for the girls to live, even if it were away from her.

She swallowed past the lump in her throat. "The house has been sold." She blinked to keep her own tears at bay.

"So, we're moving?" Emily asked.

She ran her hand down the silky smoothness of her sister's hair. "Yes, we are. Just the three of us."

There was no mistaking the worried expressions on the girls' faces, so she forced a brightness that she was far from feeling. She hugged each of them, and stood up. "This will be a great adventure, girls!"

"Like *Pilgrim's Progress?*" Evangeline, the great reader, asked.

"Exactly!" Clapping her hands, she encouraged the girls to start gathering items while she retrieved their valises from the attic.

Once she was in the attics, Jane made her way to the small window and sat on the floor in front of it. She wouldn't cry. There was no time for tears. She would do that later. She swallowed the lump in her throat. It seemed to be getting larger. She wiped her cheeks with the back of her hand. She would not cry.

Taking a deep breath, she looked around the section of the attic that she could clearly see. Surely there had to be something up here that she could sell. She had a total of several pounds. Hardly enough to keep her and the girls with a roof over their heads and food in their stomachs. She could certainly do without, but the girls could not, would not. She would find work because she was desperate, and she was a good worker. She knew that, but how quickly would be the question.

With a renewed sense of purpose, and knowing that time was not on her side, she began looking through the trunks in the attic. She supposed in reality that they belonged to Lord Hawke now. But these were *her* things given to her by her parents in what seemed another lifetime now. Before her mother had given her the locket she presently wore, she had given her a smaller one. She hadn't been much older than the twins. It had been her first real jewelry. Selling it wouldn't bring much, she was quite certain, but it might be enough for another day's food or lodging.

It wasn't in the first trunk she looked through, but finally she did find it in the third. She hardened her heart to any sentimentality she felt looking through the clothes and keepsakes. However, she did pull out several dresses she hardly remembered. They looked as if they would fit the twins. They were a little outdated, but she was sure she could fix them to be more fashionable.

Slipping the locket into her apron pocket, she gathered up the dresses, found the valises and made her way down the stairs. She stopped in her room before checking on the girls. She didn't want them to see the dresses just yet. She wanted it to be a surprise for them. Good thing she had very little that needed packing, she thought as the dresses took up a fair amount of space. Packing was more a matter of gathering and putting things in the valise rather than having to pick and choose. In spite of the bulk of the dresses, she had some room left over.

Which was a godsend, she thought, when she made it to the girls' room. She handed them each a valise and in a short time they had them filled with clothing. While they had done remarkably well, she thought, they still had not packed their undergarments or shoes. Fortunately, it was cool enough that they could wear their winter wraps without anyone thinking it odd, and save room in the valises that way. Praising them, she encouraged them to take their cases downstairs; she would add their forgotten items to her case and join them.

"Are you certain I can't call a hackney for you, Miss Jane," Samuel said.

"I'm certain. Lady Brooke lives a very short distance from here and we shall be there in no time."

"Time for tea?" Emily asked.

"Oh dear, yes." It nearly killed Jane to lie to her sisters, but there was nothing else she could say with Samuel present. She didn't even know if she could give them supper tonight, let alone tea!

"There's no problem, is there, Miss Jane? You seem sad."

She stayed the girls while she turned to face the butler. Putting her case down, she gave him a quick hug. "I can't hide anything from you, Samuel. It is somewhat sad, but we'll be fine."

* * *

"Jane, where does Lady Brooke live?"

They had been walking for some time, but the girls said nothing about their surroundings, though Jane was sure they had to notice that they were no longer in the neighborhoods they were used to. The fact that both of the girls now walked much closer to Jane was proof of that.

Jane gave Emily's hand a slight squeeze. "I'm afraid I told

a fib earlier."

"You never did, Jane!" Evangeline said.

In spite of their situation, Jane was hard pressed not to laugh at the outrage in her young sister's voice.

"I'm afraid I did. Lady Brooke is away this week and her house is closed so we can't stay there."

"Then where are we going to stay?"

Trust Emily to ask the one question she desperately wanted to answer, but could not. "We're going to see a woman who has another house. I thought we could stay there." She peered down the street. She had never been in this section of town, but she had heard some of the other women talking, saying that some of their daily maids lived in boarding houses. Mrs. Beetle's was one of the names she remembered.

The houses were quite close together, and the neighborhood was not terribly well kept, but the people they passed seemed pleasant enough. People who worked for an honest day's wage, she guessed. If she were lucky, she would be able to join their ranks.

Stopping in front of the house, she looked up at the narrow flight of stairs to the front door. It did not look especially welcoming, but looks could be deceiving, she reminded herself.

Chapter Three

Instructing the girls to stay quietly at the bottom of the stairs, Jane briskly climbed the wooden steps and knocked at the stout wooden door. When the woman answered, Jane quickly told her that she was in need of a place to stay. Jane was relieved to see that the woman was dressed cleanly and neatly. Her gray gown looked thick and warm, and the apron she wore was free of spots.

The woman looked at Jane and then down to the twins standing close together at the bottom of the stairs. The young girls wore dresses that were a bit outdated, but were quality all the same.

"Yer not runnin' away with the wee ones, are you?"

Jane suppressed the flare of anger, but answered the woman calmly. "No. They're my younger sisters." It was good that the woman was concerned, she told herself.

The woman looked pointedly at Jane's serviceable brown dress, then down to the younger girls. Her words couldn't have been plainer. Still, Jane lifted her chin. There was something lowering when a common woman who ran a boarding home dressed better than she could.

She gave Jane the price. "More if you want separate rooms."

Jane felt her stomach drop. She knew she hadn't enough money to stay anywhere for long, but she thought it would be enough for a few weeks. At this rate, it wouldn't last her but two. One, if she calculated in their meals. She did not have to eat much, but the girls were young, they needed nourishing food. She swallowed past the lump in her throat and readily agreed. At least they would have a place to sleep tonight.

"Come along then."

Hastily, Jane encouraged the girls to bring their valises and they followed their new landlady up the stairs. There didn't seem to be anyone else around; for that Jane was thankful.

"When you're all settled, you come down and I can tell you the rules of the house."

Once the woman had left, Jane closed the door and moved her valise near the tallboy. She encouraged the girls to do the same. She would unpack things shortly. Right now, she needed to hold her sisters close and study this room that would be their home for the next week. Longer if she could manage it.

"I don't like it here," Emily said, a slight wobble in her voice.

Jane dropped to her knees in front of the young girl and hugged her, then opened her arms to include Evangeline. Although the other twin made no sound, Jane could feel her shoulders shake as she buried her nose in Jane's neck.

Jane let her hand run down both of their heads. "I don't like it much myself, darlings. We won't stay here any longer than we have to." She closed her eyes, sending a quick, fervent prayer that they could at least stay as long as they had to, whether she liked it or not beside the point.

"How will Collin find us?"

Her sister's voice brought her attention back to the girls. She pushed herself a little away from them so that they could see her face. "Why, we will leave him direction, of course, silly." She gave them a big smile. Emily matched it with a watery smile and Evangeline followed suit. She gave them hugs, then stood.

"Besides, think of what stories we can tell him about our adventures!"

"What kind of adventures, Jane? Will they be fun?"

Grabbing each of their hands, she sat on the bed and encouraged them to hop up close to her. "The first thing we are going to do is take a good look at this room! We want to be able to tell Collin everything."

The girls solemnly looked about, studying the white walls and the large fireplace. Jane leaned past Emily and moved one of the curtain panels to let more light in.

The room was clean, and for that Jane was immensely thankful. The water pitcher was in one piece, as was the bowl. The mirror above the stand had some spots around the edges, but the center of it was clear so it was quite useable.

A set of straight-backed wooden chairs stood near the window, with a small table between them. She was glad to see it, since it would be a good place for the girls to do their schoolwork, as well as a place to eat whatever meals she could find for them. The bed was far from plump, but it appeared to be comfortable—at least for sitting. They would know after they spent a night on it. It was covered with some type of patched together quilt. It didn't look too thick, and there appeared to be no other cover in the room, so Jane again was glad it was not terribly cold yet.

* * *

By the next afternoon, Jane knew she was going to have to sell the small locket. The landlady was very kind, but not too helpful when it came to suggestions for employment. As the twins walked about the minute garden in the back, the two women enjoyed a cup of weak tea, courtesy of her landlady.

"A strong lass like you should be able to find work in the factories right enough," the woman said, looking at Jane across the table.

"I hadn't really thought about the factories," Jane said. Frankly, she was appalled at the idea. She didn't know much about them, but they were dirty, dangerous places. Even a few miles away, one could see the dirt spewing into the air. "I was hoping more for a governess post, something where I can bring my sisters along." She tried to keep the desperation out

of her voice, but Mrs. Beetly had truly shocked her when she
mentioned factories. Gentlemen might accept working in
factories, for she understood that they did make a good
return, but *ladies* certainly never worked in them. She did not
want to be resentful of Collin, but it was his actions that had
brought her to this point. She was almost glad that Collin was
out of her reach, even if Lord Raby didn't appear of the same
mind. Just thinking the man's name brought his face
immediately to mind. In spite of his abrupt manner, he had
seemed kind.

It took a moment for Mrs. Beetly's voice to penetrate her
thoughts. "Ah'm afeart there's no call for any of that here.
That's for them fine folks and lords." She looked at Jane more
closely, then must have come to some conclusion, because she
nodded her head as if finally understanding something. "Had
to leave your last job, did you?"

Seemed the woman had no problem believing Jane was a
governess. Of course, she thought, there was little else that
would account for her straitened circumstances, *and* her
educated speech. She was debating how to best answer, when
the woman started talking again and there was no need.
"Tim, that's my boy, he can take you down to meet the
foreman at the factory where he works. If he don't have
something, the next one will. They all need people."

A factory! How could she ever consider such a job?

"They'll be glad of your sisters too," Mrs. Beetly
continued.

Jane found her voice by then. "No, my sisters will not go
into the factories."

"Ain't much else for the young ones, you know. Besides
that, think you can earn enough in the factories yourself to
take care of them?"

Jane wanted to tell the woman to mind her own
business, but realized that the older woman thought she was
being helpful. She took a deep breath before speaking. She
even managed to give her a small smile, showing that she

knew the woman meant well.

"It's kind of you to be worried, but I only have to watch my sisters for a short while. Someone else is to care for them."

Mrs. Beetly looked relieved. "That's all right, then. They'll be fine. Nice little girls like that." She took another sip of her tea. "I'll tell Tim to wait for you in the morning, shall I?" She rose to tend to the bread making she was about.

"That would be kind."

"He leaves here four o'clock sharp. You won't be late, will ye? He won't wait." She turned back to Jane and gave her a sharp look.

Four o'clock in the morning. She didn't know if she was strong enough to do this. She gave herself a mental shake. It wasn't as if she had a choice. Right now, she would get this settled, then talk with the girls a bit. Perhaps they would even walk to the park today.

"Mrs. Beetly, one other thing, please." Jane stood and moved next to the older woman before pulling the locket from her pocket and showing it to her. "I need to sell this."

The woman gave her a sharp look.

Jane ignored the look that said the woman clearly believed she had stolen the jewelry. "I have the rent for this week, but I think the locket would provide for next week, and for food."

Mrs. Beetly closed Jane's hand over the locket. "You hold on to it, dearie. We'll see what happens when you go with Tim tomorrow."

Smiling her appreciation, Jane called the girls in and headed for their room. The air had done her sisters some good, but they were still restless. She would get them started on their afternoon lessons to give them something to think about.

While they worked on the geography lesson she assigned to them, she had a few more moments to think. She tried to tell herself that it was good that she had some type of work she could do, even if it were a factory. Hundreds of people did it every day, she reminded herself. But the thought of her younger sisters doing the same was beyond the pale. They were not brought up to be trades people, let alone *workers!* Neither was she, but she could do it. Surely she could make enough at the factories to keep a roof over their heads for a short while. She would have to write to some of her old friends. She nearly laughed at that. She had no old friends. Since Collin had come into his title over seven years ago, she had essentially ceased to become a lady. She knew he saw her as little more than a drudge, but someone had to be there to care for the twins. Perhaps if she had some claim to beauty Collin would have made sure she married, but with no beauty, and certainly no funds, she was of little use to him in that way, Gradually, the few friends she had ceased to come around as the difference in their life styles grew. They were all young women of breeding preparing themselves for a season; they did not overly care about raising children at this point. Not that she had been either, but there had been no choice. First her father insisted that she would care for the babies, then her brother expected it. She had not regretted her choice, but she had regretted her loss of friends. No, she would write to some of her mother's old friends and ask for help—for the girls. Someone, somewhere surely needed a governess. If there had been one relative left, she would certainly have approached them, and thrown herself on their mercy, but there wasn't. Both of her parents had been only children. The Worsley line was not a prolific one.

Recognizing that she was growing maudlin, she stopped her pacing about the room and stood in front of the girls, neither of whom seemed particularly interested in completing their lesson. She knew they felt as unsettled as herself. "What do you say to a walk in the park?"

Both of the girls whipped their heads about so quickly, their braids flew straight out from their heads.

"Really?" Evangeline asked. "Can we go to Aston Park? We have not been there in weeks."

"Has it really been that long?" Jane asked, teasing the young girl. "Then I suppose that we must indeed. Though I have to tell you it will be a long walk."

Evangeline's face dropped. "Can't we ride?"

Jane reached out and caressed the girl's head. "I'm afraid not, sweetling. But it's sunny out and we'll have fun."

"Will this be part of the adventure?"

"Of course it will! And I will bring my sketch book and we will have something to show Collin."

It didn't take much more urging for the girls to put on their coats and prepare for the outing. Jane scooped up a few of her precious coins. The girls would be hungry and it would be a treat for them to buy some hot chestnuts or an apple from the vendor. She slipped some drawing charcoal into her coat pocket and picked up her sketchpad.

By the time they arrived at the park, the girls were ready to sit near the pond and watch the ducks. Encouraging them to do just that, Jane opened her sketchbook, flipped to a blank page and quickly caught the scene. With the girls, she *knew* she had to be quick. And sure enough, before she was finished, Evangeline had wandered over to see the outcome.

Jane waved the girl to come and look over her shoulder. "See, I'm adding the shading to Emily's dress."

"That looks just like Emily, Jane."

Jane hid a smile at that. Only the two of them could immediately tell who was who. There were times she even had difficulty.

"Could you teach me to sketch as well as you?" the girl continued.

Jane felt a moment of guilt. Why had she not taught them? That there was precious little time for such things was not an excuse. "I can certainly try! When do you want to start?"

Evangeline's eyes lit up with pleasure and she came around her sister to sit next to her on the grass, leaning her head against her shoulder. "Is it too late today?"

Jane swiftly added a few more strokes, then turned to a blank page. This actually could work quite well. If she showed Evangeline the basics, the child would be busy all day tomorrow when she went with Tim to the factories.

The girl had a natural talent that far surpassed Jane's when she had been that age, and she told her so.

"Maybe Em does too."

"Somehow, I doubt it! She can't sit still long enough," Jane said wryly.

As if she heard her name, the other twin came loping over from her spot near the ducks and sat on the ground near her twin. "I say, that's good, Evan! I can practically hear those ducks."

"You can hear the ducks, Em, because they're following you." She pointed behind her sister to where the ducks were waddling their way out of the pond.

Emily giggled, then looked at Jane. "I'm getting hungry."

Jane stood, and motioned for the twins to do the same. "Then I suggest that we stop and get some hot chestnuts and start to walk back to the lodging house. It will be dark soon."

Taking her sketchbook from Evangeline and tucking it under her arm, she led the girls to where the chestnut vendor was tending his wares.

With the girls munching happily, Jane told them her plan for the next day and what she expected of them. "It will only be for a short while," she told them.

"Will we go to Lady Brooke's then?" Evangeline asked.

"Not there, but somewhere different." She didn't tell them they would be separated from her just yet. Perhaps one of her mother's relatives really would need a governess. She would be happy to go. She kept her thoughts to herself.

* * *

Brayden spent the next several days trying to locate Collin. The man apparently did not want to be found. If he were hiding anywhere in Manchester, he would have been discovered by now. Before digging any deeper into the unsavory parts of town, Brayden planned to meet with Morris. He heard that the man had already taken up residence in Worsley House, so he at least should be easy to find, he thought darkly.

As he climbed the steps to the house, he recalled his first visit and the way the two little girls had greeted him. Oddly enough, it wasn't their faces that came to mind, but their sister's. He hadn't thought her eyes could have gotten any larger but when he told her of Collin's wager, they had. And the mouth, a shade too wide, but made for smiling, had quivered. He had wanted to hold her and comfort her the way he did with his own sister; tell her everything would be all right. But he couldn't. All he could do was hand her a glass of spirits. Frowning at where his thoughts were taking him, he knocked briskly on the door.

He was relieved to see that Collin's butler greeted him. At least Morris must have found some use for him. "Have you any word form Lord Worsley?" he asked the man.

"No, my lord. Nor Henry."

Henry? The valet, he recalled after a moment. "What of Lady Jane? Is she settled?"

The butler looked unsure of how he was to answer. It could not be that complicated. "I would like to pay my respects," he said.

"We have not heard anything, but perhaps Lord Hawke has heard something."

Apparently he had not.

Refusing any refreshment, Brayden got to the heart of the matter. "I'd like to buy the house," he said as the men sat in the parlor. Brayden was glad it wasn't Collin's study for surely he would spend time picturing Jane there instead of concentrating on the matter at hand.

"Why?" Morris sat back in his chair, watching Brayden. "You have several houses, you don't need this one. I, on the other hand, am in need of a house."

"I can give you enough to find one in a more fashionable section of town."

Morris smiled at him. "You must want something here very badly." He looked around the shabby room. "Although I cannot imagine what."

Brayden leaned back in his own chair. He simply did not have time to play Morris's games. "What I need are answers."

"I wouldn't think this house could talk."

"True," Brayden gave him a tight smile. "But I believe that Collin could." There it was in the open. Now Morris would know that he was aware of Collin's activities or at least aspirations to join the riders.

"About the Demons?" Morris shook his head. "I don't think so. Nigel never wanted him in the group, you know that."

"I never understood why. Nor do I understand why Collin was so intent to join."

Morris chuckled at that. "He is twenty, Brayd. If he's not joining the military, where else could he find such tame excitement? You know that society turns a blind eye to Dere's Demons."

"For how long?" He kept his voice neutral, as if he were unaware that there was already a change in the ton's thinking.

Morris shrugged. "Until we tire of it."

"I would have thought that Nigel's death would have been a good time to end it."

"But you so kindly stepped in, Brayd. Se we now have another Dere to lead the Demons." Morris smile at him. "What could be better?"

Brayden could think of quite a few things, but nothing he could voice here. He took out his card and left it with Morris. "If you hear from Collin or his sister, do give them my card so that they know to contact me."

Morris's eyes narrowed. "His sister?"

Demme! He was not usually so clumsy. Didn't the man

know?

"Did she live here?" Morris asked.

Brayden's eyes opened at that. Not that the words alone weren't chilling, but the way Morris said them reminded Brayden that all of the contents of the house also belonged to the other man. That would not include his sisters, would it?

Brayden shrugged. "I do not know. I know that she exists, but I do not know where. I was hoping you could tell me."

"Since I only learned of her existence..." he let the sentence trail off.

Brayden stood before the man could quiz him more about Jane. "We will meet at the same time and ride?"

Morris stood and walked him to the door. "Absolutely. The others are ready. We do have two newer members, you know."

* * *

Brayden was still mulling that over as he drank coffee at his club. First Worsley disappeared, then his sister—sisters, he corrected himself. No one had ever claimed the family had such talents. That aspect of Collin's talents should have made him very attractive to Nigel and the Demons. He wondered why Nigel did not want the boy to belong. He let his coffee cool as he rested his head against the back of his chair. The whole Demon episode was a mess as far as he was concerned. The only good thing about him being in charge, thanks to Nigel's untimely death and the fact that he bore the same last name, was that he would be aware of their happenings.

"Why so brown?" Kit's voice floated down to where Brayden was sitting.

He lifted one eyelid to make sure it was indeed his friend, though he would have recognized the voice in the dark. "Not brown. Just thinking," Brayden said, using his foot to nudge one of the chairs near his, indicating that Kit should have a seat. Once he was seated, Brayden opened both eyes and sat up straighter, and requested the waiter bring coffee for Kit and a fresh cup for himself.

"Do you know that Collin has not resurfaced?"

Kit raised his eyebrows at that. "He can't have gone far. Don't imagine there's much he can do."

Brayden gave a bark of laughter. "My thoughts exactly. Yet, when I went to his house—"

"Morris's house," Kit interrupted.

Brayden waved his hand at such a negligible point. "I discovered that Collin had not told his sister the situation."

Kit accepted the coffee from the waiter and stared at Brayden. "His sister? Never knew the man had a sister."

Brayden held up three fingers.

"Three sisters? Good God, what is the problem with them? I have never heard of them."

"That does not surprise me in the least. It doesn't appear that they were out of the house much. I would say that the question is what to do with them, but it seems they have also disappeared!"

"Well, it seems the problem has resolved itself," Kit replied.

"Perhaps." Brayden prepared to take a sip of his coffee, and stopped. "By the way, Kit, that information goes nowhere else."

"Wouldn't dream of it, Dere." He sipped his own coffee and settled back in his chair.

The girls might be gone, but Brayden did not feel comfortable about it. He was aware that he had an overly moral streak as far as the ton was concerned. He learned to deal with it some time ago. He always rather suspected it was in reaction to his step-brother's wilder behavior.

* * *

After leaving his club and spending the day making

discreet inquiries to Collin's affairs, he headed home. If
nothing else, he learned that the man was expert at
disappearing.

Deciding that the issue of Collin and his estate and
disappearing family could wait, Brayden turned his attention
to what mattered. The reason he was really in this
godforsaken town to begin with was determining who really
stole the artifact from the Indian prince, or was it stolen from
the Crown? He wasn't clear on the issue, but he knew the
Crown wanted it back; he just wanted it over. He wasn't sure
how his step-brother ever became involved in the entire affair,
but he wasn't happy to learn he was bearing the blame.
Neither was the prince regent—at least according to the PM,
Lord Liverpool. Thanks to what he had been able to piece
together from Nigel's friends, Brayden did know that they
believed Collin was involved somehow, which is why he even
got close to the man to begin with. What a mess!

Even so, Brayden knew there had to be more at stake
than the artifact. It wouldn't please him to discover he was
right.

* * *

Four o'clock came rather quickly, Jane thought as she
slipped on her most serviceable dress. Planting a quick kiss on
each of the girl's cheeks she left the room and met Tim Beetly
downstairs. He glanced at the kitchen door as if he would
bolt the moment she appeared, or even if she didn't, she
thought wryly.

"Thank you for waiting, Tim. I'm ready to leave," she
told him so that he wouldn't think they had to wait around
for anything else.

Using his chin, he pointed to the table where there were
two wrapped packages. "Ma thought to give us some cheese
and bread for breakfast. But we best be goin'. It's nearly two
miles to the factory."

Following the boy's lead, she picked up the packet of cheese and bread, and walked behind him. Like the short distance between her home and the lodging house, the nearly two miles between the lodging house and the factory brought her to another world, one she was totally unfamiliar with. This was a Manchester even less than her sheltered upbringing had prepared her for.

As they came to the edge of the factory section, brick monstrosities belched black smoke. There were few windows that she could detect, and those that she could see were covered with so much grime she doubted that they could let any light in.

"Com'on," Tim told her, grasping her by the arm and leading her into one of the nearby buildings. "If you want to see the overseer, ya gotta look right smart."

She let him pull her behind him until they reached what she supposed was his destination. It was a grimy office door. She could still hardly believe that she was actually here! She was out of people she could decently appeal to for assistance, or she would never be here. She made a new resolve to search harder. As soon as she had coin, one way or another, she would place an ad in the papers.

She brought her mind back to the present when a paunchy, balding man appeared and led them further into his filthy office. Quickly Tim told him that she wanted a job.

She never thought she would be thankful to have the younger man by her side, but she was. He managed to say all of the right things leaving her with "yes" and "no."

The overseer quickly sent Tim on his way, and when one of the other girls came in, put Jane in her care.

"You're going to be a doffer," he told her. "You get forty-five minutes for your meal, and you better be on time. Mabel here will tell you the rules as you go." He waved both women out the door.

Mabel was some years older than Jane. At least she looked to be so. Her hair was thin and straight. It was hard to tell if it was clean or not because there was so much lint in it. She had a strange limping gait. The further into the dark mill they progressed, Jane saw this appeared to be the norm among the women there. Was it something they were born with or was it something that happened to them as they worked in the factories? She swallowed the lump of fear in her throat. The noise and the dirt alone were enough to give her nightmares. She had known such situations existed, but certainly had not intended to find herself in such a place.

"It ain't so bad when we're not thronged," Mabel said, calling her attention to the present. "Then quittin' time is seven o'clock."

"What do you mean, thronged? And what time is quitting time now?"

Mabel looked at her. "Don't you know nothin' about the factories? We're busy now so everyone, well most everyone, works until nine o'clock. We're almost through so in maybe a sennight we'll be back to seven o'clock."

Jane tried to keep the horror from her face. She had not anticipated such long hours. Not for her, but for her sisters. She didn't know if she would be comfortable leaving her sisters on their own for that amount of time. She had always thought the people exaggerated the hours worked.

"And you best not be late in the morning or after dinner," Mabel continued. "Ol' Jack don't mind takin' a strap to anyone."

"For being late?"

"Not one minute late," Mabel reinforced.

No wonder Tim looked anxious to get here in the morning.

"But that ain't the bad part. It's when they quarter you that it really hurts." Seeing the puzzled look on Jane's face she sighed, then quickly explained the process. "If you're a quarter of an hour too late, Ol' Jack takes off half an hour; we only got a penny an hour, and they would take a halfpenny more."

"I won't be late," she assured the other woman. She couldn't afford to be!

Once they were in the frame room where the women would be working, Jane fell silent. She almost had no choice, the noise was overpowering. She watched the women working whenever Mabel pointed them out, studying what they were doing. After a few moments, Mabel indicated that she should try her hand at it.

As soon as one of the frames was full, Mabel stopped the frame, and instructed Jane to take the flyers off, then the full bobbins. She had to carry them to the roller on the other side of the floor, and reload empty bobbins on the frame and get it in motion again. It didn't seem too bad, until she realized how many frames there were and how quickly they operated.

By nine o'clock that night she was relieved to see that she had made it through the day, then recalled that she would have to walk back to the lodging house. She was glad to see that Tim had waited for her as he said he would. The walk home was much more silent than the one had been in the morning. She had to save what energy she could.

The girls were waiting for her when she entered the room. It was long past their bed time, but she felt mean telling them so. Instead, she listened to Emily tell how she played with Evangeline's doll and sat for Evangeline as the girl sketched, then she had to inspect Evangeline's sketches, praising her for her efforts. That at least was easy, she thought. The girl was frightfully good. Though she realized that at the rate Evangeline was going she was going to have to purchase sketchbooks and more charcoal. She wondered how she could do that. Perhaps tomorrow there would be a letter from one of her mother's friends.

Chapter Four

The week was interminably long, and Jane could see no solution in sight. The only good thing was that they had a roof over their heads. One that appeared safe enough. She realized that the girls were getting restless and tired of being cooped up in the same room with no release for their energy. Tomorrow she would not have to go into the factory so she promised the girls a trip to the park.

The day out was delightful for all of them. The only sad part, as far as Jane was concerned, was that she still had no response from any of the messages she had sent for employment, nor any from her mother's friends in regard to keeping the girls with them. Any hope she had of sending the girls to live somewhere was quickly dwindling. She had hoped they would not have to work. She did not want them to work, but there was no denying that her meager resources would not last much longer. She absolutely refused to consider that her beautiful sisters should work in a factory. If Collin were here she would make him answerable! Since he was not, she would have to think of something else. She knew as a governess, there would be little difficulty in bringing her young sisters. But as a maid, work she had also considered, it would not be so well looked upon. In fact, it was likely that the girls would be pressed into service with no additional pay. It was something to think about though. She shuddered to think of what type of household they could apply to. There were those among the upper class who would love to be able to order their equals about, or even those above them. That was not for her sisters. Her sisters deserved to be given the life they were born to, and she desperately wanted to give it to them. She watched them now. They managed to find a few other children and were all busy playing a game. How could she take this away from them?

* * *

Two more days of work, and she returned to find a letter from Lady Hughly. Practically holding her breath, she tore open the missive only to find that the lady would be unable to help them. Jane threw it in the fire.

"Why did you do that?" Emily asked. "It was nice paper and Evangeline could have done my picture on the back."

"So, she could have! But don't you have enough pictures of you?" she asked, summoning a teasing note to her voice.

Emily grinned at her. "Yes. That's why we pretend that some of them are Evangeline!"

"I see," Jane said solemnly, then giggled with the girls. How could she give them up? But the next words from Evangeline's mouth convinced her that she would have to.

Evangeline played with her doll's hair, seeming unsure of herself. Jane pulled her closer to her and gently brushed the girl's hair back from her face. "What is the trouble, Evan?"

The girl looked to Emily, then back to Jane. "Living here is all right, Jane," Evangeline assured her. "But I don't like the way that man looks at me." She bit her lip and looked away from her sister. "I'm sorry, Jane." Her voice was practically a whisper. "I know I have to be brave, but sometimes he scares me."

"What man?" Jane was perplexed. The only man she had seen around the premises was Tim and he was at work all day.

"The one across the road," Emily told her as she came to stand near her sisters. "He comes over here all the time. He talks to Mrs. Beetly, but he looks at me and Evangeline. He squints when he looks at us."

"And he runs his tongue over his lips," Evangeline said, suiting action to words.

Jane felt ill. Physically ill. "Has he ever talked to you?"

Her voice was sharper than she intended. But they had her complete attention and she sat straight up in her chair, looking at each of their faces in turn, but both of them shook their heads.

"He doesn't say *anything,*" Evangeline said. "He just stares. Hard." She gave an unblinking stare to Jane.

"I understand," she told the girls. "I don't *ever* want you talking to him. If you see him I want you to come upstairs and lock the door."

"Is he a bad man?"

"I honestly don't know, Em," she told her. "But until I do know, we'd best take care."

"Not tomorrow," she told the girls, "but the day after, I don't have to work until one o'clock."

"Does that mean we can go to the park again?" Evangeline asked.

"No, we're going to have another adventure," Jane told them, before she insisted they get ready for bed.

Lady Hughly's letter had been a blow, but after her sisters told her about the man, she decided something would have to be done immediately. She could not wait to see if anyone else would respond. If she could not have them with her all of the time, then she would have to make sure they were protected somehow. She heaved a deep sigh. Since it seemed that they were going to have to work sooner or later, there was no sense in putting off the inevitable. If they could be in a safe environment, they would be better off than with anything she could do for them at this point. So she told them.

While they were lying there in the dark, Jane wrapped her arms around each of them and told them how their circumstances would change. It was easier not to have to look into their eyes. She had not wanted it to come to this, but she could see no help for it. They would have to work, but not in the factory. Never that. Since it appeared that she had no other options, she would appeal to Lord Raby. He might know of who could take the girls on, or even do it in his own household. She trusted him. She had nothing to base it on, but there it was. She smiled to herself realizing how odd it was that she should feel that way. For the most part, anyone who had dealings with Collin she stayed away from.

She wasn't sure what she expected, but certainly not their relatively easy acceptance of the situation. "It will only be for the shortest time," she told them. "As soon as Collin comes back, or I find us another place to live, then we'll all be together again."

"Working will be more fun than staying in this room all day," Evangeline said. And Emily agreed, though not as whole heartedly.

"I don't know what that means," she admitted.

Jane gave her a squeeze. "It means that you will have to do some of the same chores that you did when we lived with Collin." She felt Emily's body relax as she snuggled against her.

"I can do that!"

Jane planted a kiss on top of her head, then on Evangeline's. "I'm sure you can, sweetlings."

In what seemed like moments, the girls drifted off to sleep. Jane only wished that she could, especially since she would have to awake in several more hours. This was not the life she had envisioned for her sisters. Collin was to make sure it wouldn't happen and instead he hastened it on its way. He had been gone for weeks now, where was he?

* * *

The next morning, Jane dressed the girls with extra care for their outing. She had not had a chance to cut down the dresses she had for them, which she supposed was just as well. They needed to be neat and clean, not necessarily prosperous looking. She wasn't sure the dresses could have done that anyway.

"This is the way back to our house, Jane," Emily said.

Jane knew what the child was asking. "There are lots of houses here, Em. We're going to visit Lord Raby. He came to visit us, remember? I did mention that you might be able to do some work for him."

Both of the girls solemnly nodded. "You too, Jane? You'll be there, right?" Emily said.

Somehow they had managed not to talk about this for the past day and a half. Jane would have preferred never to talk about it. She shook her head. "I have a job, remember," she said brightly. Never had she thought that she would be reduced to working for wages. A governess, perhaps, that would not have been so bad, but she needed coins *now,* not several weeks from now. She squeezed each girl's hand in reassurance. "This will only be for a little while, and then we'll be together again."

"With Collin too," Evangeline stated.

Jane didn't even bother to try and answer that. What could she possibly say? She was relieved to see they were approaching the street where Lord Raby lived. Instantly her feet slowed their pace. All the time they were walking she tried to think of what to say, and she still drew a blank.

She had even considered that he would not be in!

"Perhaps I might leave a message," she said and was rather glad when the major domo looked down his nose at her. What could she possibly say? She would try to come on her own some evening. It would be difficult, but the factory would soon only be working until seven. That would give her time to get back to the lodging house and have a few hours of sleep before going to work. That was a much better plan to begin with and she wondered why she had not thought of it before. There was no need to subject her sisters to this. Saying her thanks, she ignored the insistent tugging on her arm from Emily. She noticed that the major domo stood a shade taller.

"Lady Jane."

She heard his voice close behind her now. It slid like

velvet over her senses. She had not imagined that part. She whipped around to look at him. "We were just leaving, my lord." Since she was on the step above him, they were nearly eye level. The planes of his face were as sharp as she remembered, but his eyes were even more welcoming. How could that be? He had not known they would be coming.

She turned fully on the stairs and would have walked past him had he not stopped her.

"I have been looking for you," he said. "Please come in and have some refreshment."

The younger girls looked up at him as he led them into the house and waited for them to discard their outer wraps.

"Tea, in the blue salon, please," he addressed the housekeeper when she appeared.

Emily's eyes grew huge. "Tea?" she whispered the word reverently.

"With cakes?" her sister asked, echoing her tone.

Brayden looked up at Jane, amusement on his face, to share the moment with her. He could remember as a young child where tea ranked very high on his list too. But Jane was not amused. He could have sworn that she wore the same expression of anticipation as her sisters, but much more quietly. His eyes narrowed as he studied her while she shushed her sisters. Was it possible that she could have grown thinner since he had he last seen her? She was still plain, but he had to admit that her eyes were remarkable and her mouth as mobile. Why did he keep thinking that?

When the tea arrived, Brayden insisted that she pour, which she did with a natural grace. Taking his cup from her, he noticed her hands were unduly red. If she had been in her home then he would have suspected she was doing the cleaning herself, but she was not.

"To what do I owe this pleasure?" he asked once they were all settled and the servants had gone.

Jane considered how to best frame her words. Finally, she opted out and decided to let him answer first. "You were looking for me?"

"I wondered if you have any news of your brother. Surely he would have sent word by now."

She gave him a tired grin. "Obviously, you do not know Collin all that well if you believe that." She took a sip of her tea. Real tea. Something she had not had in years. She closed her eyes for a moment to savor the taste. It was much richer than anything she could recall.

He watched her drinking and her reactions. "Is there something wrong with the tea?"

Her eyes snapped open. "Heavens, no! It's lovely." She gave him a reserved smile. "Was there anything else, my lord?" That did not seem much of a reason. Still, she was glad for it had got them inside and this delightful tea.

"I had not expected you to leave your home so quickly."

"It seemed the best thing to do, my lord. I have not heard from Samuel, so I can only assume that Lord Hawke has taken possession."

"He has. I am puzzled about something. He seems to think that Collin is in possession of some items."

Jane set her tea carefully on the table. "I did not remove anything of import," she said thinking guiltily of Evangeline's doll.

"May I have another cake, Jane," one of the twins interrupted in a whisper. At least he assumed it was to be a whisper; it was rather loud.

Jane looked at the plate in front of them. She could see why her sister was tempted. She was herself. With true regret, she gave an almost imperceptible shake of her head. She had to remember why they were here.

"Please, Jane." That came from the other twin.

Before she could answer this time, Brayden did. "Of course you may," he told them. Turning to Jane he said, "It is far enough to dinner that it will not spoil their appetite."

Jane couldn't even answer. She was sure of that! It also served as a reminder of why she was here. She sat up a bit straighter in the chair and placed her cup on the table. "I have some business I would like to discuss with you, my lord."

Now that was intriguing. "If you think we can trust the moppets with the rest of the cakes, we can go to my study."

She raised stricken eyes to his. She had not wanted them to take more, and certainly she needed him to think well of them. "They will not touch any others," she assured him, and stood.

"It was a jest," he said, standing also, and guiding her to the room across the hall. He couldn't help but notice that she did not smile in return. Whatever was bothering her was weighing heavily indeed.

Ushering her into the room, he gave her a seat in front of his desk. Rather than sitting behind it, he hitched one hip on the edge, so that he was fairly close to her. He noticed her rough hands again as she twisted them together.

"Come," he told her, "it can't be that bad. What can I do for you?"

She gazed around the room before letting her eyes rest on his waistcoat. It was blue, and from the fit she knew it had cost the earth. She didn't think she could look him in the eye. It was one thing for her to lower herself to work in a *factory*, but to have to ask this for her sisters was galling. Knowing the alternative would be for her sisters to join her, she plunged ahead.

"I do not approve of what Collin has done," she began, "but my sisters know no other life. They were born to be ladies, and I have tried to teach them what they need to know." She dared to glance at his face, then quickly down again.

"Yes, I understand that your sisters, and you, are ladies. There is no question. Perhaps this has something to do with the business you wish to discuss?"

She nodded and tried not to be dismayed at his cool tone of voice. She didn't even know if it was to her benefit or not that he deemed them quality. She gave him another glance and a wavering smile. "No, I don't believe that it does." This time she did raise her eyes to his. It was difficult to meet that cool gray gaze, but she thought if she did so it might also be more difficult for him to refuse. "I wondered if perhaps you, or someone you know, could take my sisters in for training as housemaids."

Oh, God! He didn't even blink. He was going to refuse. She could see that immediately. Swallowing, she dropped her gaze and stood, dropping a polite curtsey without looking at him. "Thank you for seeing us, and for the wonderful tea."

"Sit down." He bit the words, each one snapping in the air.

Jane raised her chin. "No, thank you. I see your answer."

"You see *nothing.*" He stood on both feet, towering over her. He shoved his hand through his hair, grasping it as if he wanted to tear it out. "What maggot has got into your head that you should even suggest such a thing?"

She wasn't sure if he really wanted an answer.

Evidently he did.

"My sisters are ladies," she began.

"We've established that fact. So, pray tell how does them working as housemaids—housemaids!—fit in with that lifestyle?"

She felt the tightness in her chest ease. He was going to talk about it at least, even if he didn't seem to hold housemaids in high esteem.

"They are used to living in large houses, visiting large houses," she said. "They are quite comfortable with them. If they become housemaids that is where they will work. It will be the same surroundings for them."

"Housemaids."

She waved her hand now. "I know they are too young right now, but not by much so. If they could train in a grand house, they would have a better chance of getting a position in a grand house later." She didn't think his silence was ominous.

"Do they have any idea what you are planning for them?"

"We discussed it," she assured him. "They are old enough to follow directions."

"And what will you get from this? I assume you mean for me to pay you for this privilege."

He was going to agree! "Of course not. I know that training will not be the same as them being very productive workers."

Brayden shook his head. How could he have been so horribly wrong? He thought that she was innocent, but here she was practically selling her sisters into slavery. He wanted to know why. Perhaps she was not so different from her brother after all.

"They are agreeable to this?"

Jane nodded. "You may ask them if you wish."

"I fully intend to do so. Later."

"You are going to keep them, then?"

He gave her a curt nod. It hurt to look at her, but he insisted on being polite and walking her to the door.

"May I see them before I go?"

"I'm afraid not."

Jane bit her lip, but gave a brisk nod. "I understand. They do have a few things; should I bring them here."

"Perhaps later."

His voice was even colder.

"When...when may I see them?"

"You may check back a week from today."

Thanking him, she left. She was glad that she would be going straight to the factory. She did not think that she could bear to go back to their lodgings and look at their things. Later she would be too tired.

She was tired, but not too tired to notice that the bed was empty without the girls to share it with, or that the room was extremely quiet without their subdued chatter. It was better for them, she reminded herself. She could not bear it if they had to work in a factory and aged beyond their years. She saw the other children and it broke her heart. And now that she knew about the man across the street, she would never feel safe leaving them. The good thing, if there was any good to come of this, was that now she would save her wages more quickly. Soon she would have enough funds that she could look for a governess position—one that would allow the girls to live with her. And if they were already trained maids, it would be easier.

* * *

Brayden could not recall the last time he was so angry. The worst part was that he knew he was angry without reason. Well, he did have a reason, but it should not have bothered him. What did it matter that Lady Jane was not the person he thought? He scowled as he replayed their conversation. One thing that stood out was that she never did give him a reason as to why she truly desired this life for her sisters.

After watching the door close behind Jane he sought her sisters, still sitting in the room where he left them. True to Jane's word, they had not touched another thing. That didn't mean they didn't still gaze at the remaining cakes with longing.

"You may have another one," he told them kindly, as he sat in the chair across from them.

One of them shook her head. "Jane said we're not to."

"Where is Jane?" the other asked.

"She left." He tried to take the edge off his voice, but by the startled looks from the girls he could see that he did not succeed.

"Without saying goodbye?"

"I'm afraid she was in a hurry."

The one who asked for her nodded her head wisely. "Remember, Em, she had to get to work on time."

The other girl brightened. "I forgot."

Brayden hid his surprise. Work? What did a lady work at? Before he could follow that line of questioning, the one—Em, he thought—started asking him questions.

"Are we to work for you now, Lord Raby? I'm not sure what a housemaid does, but Jane says that we dust and sweep very well."

"We do," the other one piped in. "I know how to fold clothes too." She leaned toward him as if imparting a secret. "Sometimes I even ironed Collin's cravats when Jane was too busy."

"Being a housemaid is hard work," Brayden told them. "You must get up early in the morning and do all of your chores before you can go to bed."

"Will we have real tea?" the one asked.

"Evangeline! You can't ask that!"

Brayden suppressed a smile. He supposed that was another whisper. "I have been thinking," he told them. "I'm not sure that I need any other housemaids."

He watched the expression on their faces fall. What had their sister told them to make them think being a housemaid was the best thing for them? Not that he needed another Worsley mystery to solve just yet.

"Jane will be so disappointed."

"It's okay, Evangeline." Her sister patted her on the shoulder. "Jane said she will find something else."

"But how will we get back?"

Brayden leaned forward in his seat. "I could take you back, but I want you to know that while I don't need any housemaids, I might need some little girls about."

"You do?" Emily asked.

"Why would you?" Evangeline asked suspiciously. Her voice and expression were as solemn as Jane's. Why did he have to notice that?

"I have a sister and some nieces," Brayden said. And wasn't she going to be surprised when he insisted that they come down a few days early, he thought. "I know that my nieces would love to have some playmates stay at the house. They are a little younger than you, I believe."

The girls looked at each other and then back to Brayden. "Would we only work as housemaids for part of the day?"

"I was thinking as none of the day. My nieces do like company."

"That would be wonderful," Em said. "But we would not have any money to save."

"You will have everything, you need," he told them, "and some pin money besides."

"What is pin money?" Evangeline asked.

He already had her pegged for the practical one as he quickly explained.

"See, we will have money to give Jane," Emily told her twin. Another whisper.

"No, you will not." Brayden was quite forceful about that. "This is your money to spend for you." He mentally shook his head. This was getting too complex by far. For now, he'd better just turn the girls over to the housekeeper and hope that Arabella planned on staying in for the day, whenever she got back from her morning rounds, that was.

Chapter Five

"Why do we have these girls here?"

Brayden opened his mouth to explain, but Arabella waved away his explanation before he got one syllable out of his mouth.

"I know what you are saying, Brayden, and I agree, they'll be wonderful little companions for the brats, but *why* are they here now? Who do they belong to?"

Brayden looked at his sister, considering how much to tell her. If it were his older sister, Anne, he knew he could tell her nothing, but he never had secrets from Arabella and he doubted that he could start now. So he told her the truth.

Arabella sat perfectly still. One did have admire what a perfect picture of English womanhood she made. Her blonde hair curled just so, and her pink cheeks and blue eyes were set off by her blue striped day dress. Her daintiness often led people to believe that she was helpless. Brayden knew her too well.

She opened her mouth, then closed it again, as if not quite sure what she needed to say.

"She *sold* those darling little girls, Brayden! That was unconscionable of her."

He stood straight, pushing away from the doorframe and clasped his hands behind his back, pacing. "It is. I cannot fathom why she would think this is good. Collin is a bounder, no doubt about it, but his title is an old one. Surely she would have some sense of duty."

"So you would think." She stood and shook out her skirts. "Do you plan to write to Anne, or should I?"

He unclasped his hand and waved away the question. "It's already done." He gave her a wry smile. "I couldn't picture you playing nursemaid!"

"True." She sent a dimpled smile his way. "Hopefully it won't matter if she arrives a few days earlier than she planned. You know, this could be fun," she said, cocking her head to one side.

"Hold your tongue!" he told her. "The thought of two brats was enough to send me running, now there will be four." He stopped his pacing when he was in front of her again. "I will leave the girls in your care for the rest of the afternoon, Bella. I want to see what news there is in the clubs. Do you have an engagement this evening?"

"Yes. And so do you."

"Demme, I forgot. I will be home early enough to escort you," he promised. When facing some members of society, it was much better to do so in pairs, as he had learned. Even if the other half was his sister, it offered some protection. Some thought he was overprotective of his sister, not realizing it was himself he was protecting! Too many marriage-minded women out there for his peace of mind, even in the wilds of Lancashire.

* * *

A week was not long, Jane told herself. Indeed, in spite of the never-ending days, they did manage to pass. One more day, she thought as she let herself out into the night air. As usual, it was dark when she was leaving the factory, but tonight she would not have Tim's company. Tomorrow was his day off and he had promised his uncle that he would help him on the farm which was several miles away from the factories in the opposite direction of his home. She found that she missed his comforting bulk. Even if his conversation was somewhat limited, he offered protection. Normally, it was not something she thought about, but for some reason tonight she found that being alone made her uncomfortable.

It wasn't until she was less than a quarter of a mile from

Mrs. Beetly's that she became aware of someone following her. Putting the sensation down to her overly active imagination she nevertheless started walking faster. If it were daylight, she would be able to see Mrs. Beetly's steps from where she was she assured herself, all the while, increasing the tempo of her walk. Soon she would be running.

Fixed on her goal, it took her a moment to realize that the footsteps had stopped. The man now stood in front of her. As soon as she realized it she stopped, and darted to the right, only to have her arm grabbed and she was jerked to the man's side. She opened her mouth to scream, but a grimy hand clasped itself over her mouth, not allowing any sound to escape.

"Don't be so cratchy," the voice ground in her ear. She wanted to get away from the foul smelling breath, but couldn't. "A gentry sort just wants to talk to ye."

She certainly didn't know many 'gentry sort.' Perhaps there was some reason he could not yet show his face. That she could easily believe. She quit her struggles and her captor heaved a sigh of relief.

"Sez he just wants to talk. Now ye'll not scream if I move my hand, will ye?"

She shook her head.

He released her cautiously. He pointed to the trees beside Mrs. Beetly's garden. She looked at him suspiciously. "He's right there."

Nodding her head, she started in the general direction. Surely it would only be a matter of switching courses and she could head directly up the stairs. She wouldn't yell for Mrs. Beetly until she was closer and sure the woman could hear her. Sad to say, but someone screaming in this neighborhood did not necessarily mean someone would offer aid. The man stayed close to her side, but he didn't touch her. That reassured her somewhat. It had to be Collin in the trees. A mere dozen steps.

She had gone three when a form separated from the

shadows. Her steps slowed, but the man at her side grasped her arm now and urged her forward. "Collin?" she queried as she got closer. Then she was directly in front of him and she could see it definitely was not her brother. She had never seen the man before. Her abductor was correct about one thing though, he was a gentleman.

"So sorry," the man said. His voice was smooth and ran along her senses like oil. "Were you expecting him?" Now he sounded hopeful. "Come, come, my lady. I don't intend to hurt you. I'm looking for answers."

"Is that why you have gone through all of this?" She pointed to her abductor with her chin.

"Not at all." He turned toward the other man and started speaking in a low voice. Jane didn't need that entire second to dash around him and toward the stairs. She was neatly caught, one hand around her waist and the other over her mouth. It was the gentleman this time. "You could invite me in," he said into her ear. She shook her head as far as she could without hurting herself.

"Now, I am going to release you, but no screaming, please." When he got no response he continued holding her and talking. He was not much taller than herself so his breath whispered along her jaw as he spoke. "My name is Lord Hawke." She stiffened and he chuckled. "I see the name means something to you, as it should. I am looking for your brother. Where is he?"

When she didn't respond, he gave her a little shake. She tried to bite his hand that was clasped over her mouth. "Bitch," he snarled.

"If you won't tell me where your brother is, then *you* will have to help me."

She shook her head in denial. In response, he pulled her closer so that she could feel every tightly coiled muscle in his body.

"I went through a lot of trouble to find you. Now I know that Collin has something hidden in that house. I can't find it. I have been through everything." He gave her a shake for good measure. "Either you tell me where your brother is or you will have to come and show me the hidden places in the house."

Was he demented? What was the man talking about?

"I am going to move my hand long enough for you to answer. Do you understand?"

At her nod, he cautiously moved his hand over her mouth. He still held her close.

"There are no hidden places," she said. She took a deep breath of air.

"That is not the correct answer. Where is Collin?"

Seemingly convinced that she would stand and talk to him, he moved slightly away from her.

"I do not know where my brother is. I thought you were he when that man told me someone was here." She did not struggle to move. She didn't want him aware of her actions. "If Collin had anything worth hiding in the house do you think that he would have wagered the house?" Her voice was incredulous.

He stopped at that, seeming to consider it.

That was all the time she needed. She lifted one foot and ground her heel into his instep, causing him to slacken his hold on her. It was enough that she was able to leap for the stairs, calling the landlady's name. The door was open before she reached the top of the stairs. Thankfully, she was alone. She could hardly explain it all to the landlady, merely that she was sure someone was following her.

* * *

Sleep eluded her that night. Long before the first pale fingers of dawn made their arrival she was up and dressed, sitting in one of the chairs, staring out the window. It would be several hours before she could visit her sisters yet.

What could Lord Hawke have been speaking of? She

knew there was nothing of value in the house. If there had been Collin would have surely used it rather than gamble his meager inheritance. She knew he wouldn't have gambled the Curse, would he? She had totally forgotten to check it before she left. The only reassurance was that no one would stumble on it. It was Collin's by right, but would he take it? She gave a mental shrug. It really would not mean anything to her, one way or another. But what could Lord Hawke be referring to? And where *had* Collin got to this time.

As soon as she heard Mrs. Beetly moving around downstairs, she went down to join the woman for a cup of weak tea and a piece of toast. She skimmed over the incident the night before, putting it down to the fact that she had been nervous without Tim's company, an excuse the woman seemed to believe. As soon as she was done and it was a decent time to leave for Lord Raby's house, she did so.

Finally, she could see her sisters. She hoped things had gone well with them for the week. She pocketed a few of her coins. There would be enough to buy them some chestnuts. She debated if she should buy them on the way or if she should hope to take them out. Practicality won and she bought them on the way. As it was, she would be fortunate to get a visit in before she had to get back to the factory. With these late-in days one dare not be late. To be late on any day was a cardinal sin, but on a late-in day, it would be a guaranteed punishment. She had seen it already.

Walking as quickly as she could, she stopped at the chestnut vendor for her two cones of nuts and hurried to Lord Raby's house. She savored the warmth from the nuts in her cold hands.

Scurrying around to the servant's entrance, her knock was answered by a kind looking woman she learned was the cook.

"What ya got there, Dearie?" she asked, eyeing the packages of nuts.

Quickly, Jane realized the woman thought she was selling

something and she lowered her hands. "I'm here to see Emily and Evangeline."

The woman scowled at her, and Jane instinctively took a step back.

"Lord Raby said that I might visit them today." She showed the woman the cones. "I brought these for them."

Still the woman made no move, as if she couldn't quite decide what to make of it all.

"If I may see them for a moment..." Her heart nearly stopped. She had never thought that she wouldn't see them! Lord Raby had appeared to be a fair person. Perhaps he was not home. She calmed a bit. That would explain it. "If his lordship is not at home, perhaps I could leave a message, and give these to my...the girls."

"He's home." She heaved a sigh, and looked over Jane's dress. "If you stay here, I'll see if the little ladies can receive you."

Jane bit back a smile as she watched the woman leave the room. She could see the girls still being ladies. She knew it would make it harder for them among the servants to be seen as ladies, but that's what they were.

She did not expect them to be dressed that way.

"Jane!" Emily squealed as she launched herself at her sister.

Jane wrapped her tight and then held out her arm for Evangeline to join them. They felt wonderful. She released them, and straightened up, handing them each a package of nuts, which they cheerfully took. Then she looked at them, really looked at them.

She swore they looked taller. They looked well fed, which she expected. They were also dressed better than they had ever been before, which she had not expected.

They each took one of her hands and dragged her into the kitchen to sit near the fire, talking the whole time. They pushed her into the wooden rocker near the hearth, and pulled up stools to sit next to her. "We're not housemaids,

Jane," Emily said. "We're companions."

"Companions? To who? I don't understand."

"Uncle Brayden—"

"Who?"

Evangeline giggled. "You sound like an owl, Jane! Lord Raby said that we might as well call him Uncle Brayden since everyone else seemed to."

"We keep his nieces company," Emily told her. "It's so much fun, Jane. We do everything they do." She peeled a nut and popped it in her mouth.

Jane felt a sense of relief, but still felt compelled to correct the girls. "I am so happy for you, sweetlings! I could never have dreamed about something so wonderful. But you must be careful," she warned them. "You are companions. That means whenever Lord Raby's nieces need something, you are to get it. You need to be mindful of what they want.." To think her sisters had landed the type of position she could only dream of, she thought wryly.

Emily vigorously shook her head. "No, we don't. Uncle Brayden said we are to be treated the same."

Jane tried to keep the puzzled look off her face, but wasn't sure she succeeded.

Evangeline grasped her hand. "It would be perfect if you would stay too, Jane. Please stay."

Jane stood up on wobbly legs. This was not what she expected. She had not even dared to ask for this when she learned that Lord Raby agreed to take the girls in. Now she knew she was right to have done so. Certainly, they were a little too familiar, but she trusted they would outgrow that. "I'm afraid I can't, but if I am allowed I will come and visit you again."

"I will ask Uncle Brayden," Emily said, preparing to run out of the kitchen.

Jane stopped her in time. "Listen to me, girls. He is not Uncle Brayden to you. Please call him Lord Raby. It is proper."

Evangeline shook her head. "But he told us, Jane." She wrapped her arm around her sister and gave a hug. "Come and see us next week, Jane. We will have so much to tell you!"

A little disappointed that they seemed in a hurry to get back to wherever they came from, she gave them each a kiss on the cheek, and a last hug before going on her way. She was happy for her sisters, so why did her heart feel so heavy? She did her best to keep the tears from falling as she briskly walked the three miles to the factory. She was delighted for her sisters; it went beyond her wildest imaginings. But she couldn't help but feel sorry for herself. From now on, at least for as long as Lord Raby kept the girls under his care, they would continue to grow worlds apart. They would rise to the height that they belonged, or at least move in the same circles, until they were old enough to go on their own, and she would sink further down the social ladder. Unless she could get a position as a companion too. If only one of her letters would bring a positive answer. She didn't have much hope at this date, but a little hope was better than none. Never had she thought that being the companion would be a step up the social ladder, but the longer she remained in the factory, the more she learned it was so. It had only been weeks. How would she survive years? Glancing at the position of the sun, she hurried her pace. She did not want to be late.

* * *

When the girls returned to the playroom, they were delighted to see Brayden there visiting. They immediately offered him chestnuts. He took one, then looked at them thoughtfully. They were holding cones from the vendor. For a fleeting moment he wondered if they had gone out, then recalled that it had been a week that the girls were here.

"Was your sister here?" he asked them.

They nodded in unison. "If you look out the window, you can probably see her," Emily told him.

He didn't have time for that. He had wanted to see her. All week he told himself it was because he wanted to know how she could leave the girls, but the truth was he wanted to see her, watch her mouth as she talked, watch the way her eyes widened when they focused on him.

He took the stairs, two at a time and ran out to the stables, calling for Harry to get his horse—now. The groom barely had Nelson out of the stables before he launched himself on the beast's back and headed out of the mews. Thanks to his conversations with the girls he had learned quite a lot about Lady Jane Worsley. He still didn't believe that she was innocent of selling her sisters, but he was fair minded enough to know he had not let her tell her side of story. He would have remembered.

Due to the speed he was traveling, he collected a few strange looks until he cleared the area. By the time he drew close to the lodging house the girls had told him about, he had calmed down enough to walk his horse.

"Miss Jane's not here," the landlady told him, not disguising her interest in seeing a member of quality on her doorstep. "Went to visit some grand house to see her sisters."

Brayden nodded his head. "She left there. Where is she now?"

"I reckon she went on to the factory," the woman told him. "This is her late-in day."

Receiving directions, he gave her a brisk nod and started on his way. A factory! What had Collin been thinking of? The man had to be more corked brain than he thought. The closer he drew to the soot billowing factories, the tighter his lips became. He knew what went on in the factories. He had requested reports and read every single one of them. He could be just as progressive as the next man, but one had to remember these were people in the factories, not just machines.

Reining his horse, he dismounted and called one of the younger boys to come and hold him. He gave him one coin, with the promise of another when he returned, then strode into the building.

It must have taken a full two minutes before the supervisor realized he had a member of quality on the floor. News traveled fast. Brayden quickly glanced around the ill-lit building, but from where he was standing, there was little to see. The overseer came bustling down the stairs.

"My lord," he said, bowing. "It is a privilege to have you here. What can I do for you?"

With his most aristocratic face, Brayden turned to the man. "I have come to see your operations, of course."

"Come with me," the overseer told him. "Everything is most efficient and modern."

Brayden said nothing, just followed the man across the floor. He stopped, frozen, when he heard a scream, and looked at the overseer. The man got red in the face, but said nothing.

"No, please!" He heard it again. There were genuine sobs of terror in the voice. It sounded like a child, but he knew that a man's voice could be pitched that high too if he were terrified enough.

"What in blazes is going on there?" Brayden asked, striding toward the sound.

The overseer scurried to catch up, and tried to make his way in front of him. "I'm sure it's fine, m'lord."

Brayden stopped where he was. From the top walk he could see the floor and the small knot of people. The sobs seemed to be coming from the middle. He turned toward the overseer for answers.

The man shrugged. "One of the children must have caught his hand in the loom. I can take you to another room if you would like to see one working."

"I would like to wait for this one." He had read enough to know what to expect. What he did not anticipate was the flash of brown and *her* voice commanding the man to halt. He was on his way down the stairs when he heard the foreman growl at her. What did the woman think she was about?

"Ain't stoppin' any longer. Already lost too much time."

Brayden snorted in disgust. It would be easier to cut off the child's hand than halt work.

"That is a child!" Her voice carried well through the building. Brayden hurried his steps. The little fool didn't realize that she would be the man's next target.

He wasn't fast enough.

He saw the man's fist strike out before he could form the words. She staggered backwards while the man raised his ham fist again.

"Touch her again and you will never be using that hand." Demme, he was still too far away to do anything but he had the satisfaction that his voice carried.

"Who sez?"

Brayden could hear the overseer puffing behind him. "I am Lord Raby." He was close enough now to see Jane still on the floor, but struggling to her feet. He came to a stop in front of the man. He held out his hand to Jane, but never looked at her. When he felt her hand in his, he pulled her so that she was partially behind him.

The foreman was large and strong from years of hard labor. "What is the problem?" Brayden asked. He ignored the intermittent sobbing that he could now tell came from behind the man.

The overseer stepped between them and looked nervously at Brayden. "It's an accident, m'lord. It won't slow the factory work none." He motioned to the foreman to continue what he was doing, until he caught Brayden staring at him.

Jane was shivering to such an extent that she kept bumping Brayden. He tried to ignore her trembling body and turned his attention to the foreman, demanding to know the extent of the problem and the solution.

"They'll cut off the child's hand," Jane said from behind

him.

He turned to the overseer. "Is this true?" he demanded. "Explain," he said when the man nodded nervously. He tried to ignore the fact that Jane had gripped his arm in her nervousness.

The man's nearly bald head bobbed nervously. "The boy's hand is caught in the machine, m'lord. There's naught we can do." He started to wring his hands.

"Let me see," Brayden demanded. Walking toward the foreman, he pushed the man aside to see a boy of about seven or eight. His hand was indeed caught, and his body was stretched tight over the edge of the frame from where he had been reaching.

The boy sobbed harder when he saw him.

"Take it easy, lad," Brayden told him. "We need to see the problem."

"Know what the problem is," the foreman grumbled. "See, 'is hand is twisted in the threads."

"How does this thing work?" Brayden demanded. He had heard descriptions of such devices, but never the opportunity to see one. Not that he cared to do so at this point.

As if sensing he was in charge, the foreman took it upon himself to explain how the loom worked.

Brayden took off his coat and handed it to Jane who had come up when she saw what he was about. "Is this information correct?" he asked her.

"Mostly." Stepping closer to the loom, she pointed to the boy's fingers. "See, his hand is mostly twisted in the threads. If the loom were to run, it would crush his hand and tear at his fingers. But with it stilled, it might be possible to remove his hand."

"Not without destroying a day's work, it won't," the foreman said.

"The day's work will be lost anyway," Jane snapped. "Blood does not go well with thread!"

Seeing where the problem lay, Brayden reached down and slipped a knife from inside of his boot. Jane tried not to blink at that. Did all men carry knives? Collin hadn't.

Leaning close to the boy, Brayden said something in a low voice and stretched over the loom, his knife ready to cut the threads.

"See here, you can't be doin' that!" the foreman said. As he reached out to grab Brayden's hand, he stopped.

"Very good," Brayden said in a dry voice, recognizing the man's sense in halting before he touched him. "I will pay for the damages, of course." He turned back to the boy who was sobbing louder now, at least until Brayden cut through the warp threads, releasing pressure on the boy's hand. If the loom had even moved once it would have snapped his arm, and then most likely pulled his body into the machine as it finished its move. Brayden had heard of that. And now that he had seen it—or nearly so—seen the results first hand, he vowed to become more insistent on the bill passage to protect the workers.

When the child was released and stood in front of him, Brayden patted him on the shoulder and gave him some direction quietly enough so that the others did not hear. "You may go now," he finally told the lad.

"M'lord," the overseer protested. "He must stay to finish the day. He has only just begun."

Brayden straightened his shirt and reached for his jacket, allowing Jane to assist him in donning it. She would have stepped away, but he grasped her arm tightly. "You will stay with me," he practically hissed.

He felt her immediately stiffen at his words, but she did not move.

"The boy is finished here," Brayden said. "My man will be by later with the funds for your damage."

"If he is not? Beggin' your pardon, m'lord?"

"I am Raby. He will be here." He drew himself up to his full height, and without slackening his grip on Jane's arm, headed toward the door, practically dragging her along. When she tugged at her arm, he let it free and strode toward the door.

He was seething. He couldn't even turn to see if Jane was indeed following him. If she was not, he would go back and shake her until her teeth rattled in her head. How dare she subject herself to such a situation? Which was exactly the question he asked her some time later when they arrived at his Town house and she was immediately led into his study.

He closed the door with a definite click, but paused before he turned around to face her. She hadn't moved from the spot where he released her.

"What was the meaning of that?" He bit out each word in a clipped voice. He had the vague suspicion that he sounded just like his father when he had been angered by his mother!

She flinched at the sound of his voice, but didn't move. "Of what, my lord?"

"And stop calling me my lord." He ran his hand down his face, trying to regain his temper. "Call me Brayden." When she didn't respond, just wore that stony look, he sighed. "Try Dere, if it sits better."

"Dere?" Her hands dropped to her sides from where she had them crossed against her midriff. "Dere!" There was disbelief in her voice.

"Yes." He said the word cautiously. "Did Collin mention me?" Why did she look like that? Surely she had known his family name was Derrington, or maybe she hadn't. Either way it should not have made her look as she did now. If he had physically slapped her she would not have looked any more shocked.

She released a brittle laugh. "Oh, he mentioned you all right! All he ever talked about was Dere did this, and Dere did that." She waved her arms, emphasizing her points. "He wanted to be like you, you know."

Brayden shook his head. "Not like me. Like my brother."

And that was the crux of the problem. Everyone expected him to be like his half-brother. He was trying to fit in where Nigel left off, but it was deuced hard. Especially since Nigel had few redeeming qualities—at least in Brayden's eyes.

"He was called Dere too? That is difficult to believe!" He heard the skepticism in her voice.

"No, it's not. It is our family name." He shrugged. "We've all been Dere: me, my brother, even my father." He waved his hand, waving away the issue. "That is not the problem. The problem is that you—a lady by birth –you were in a *factory!*" He took a few steps away from her, then abruptly turned on his heel and gave a mocking laugh and ran his hand through his hair. "What am I saying? You were working there. *Working!*"

Jane took a step closer. They were practically nose-to-nose. "What kind of work could I get, my lord? Women have very limited choices."

"They do, but you did not." Only his anger kept him from reaching out and grasping her shoulders. He was afraid if he laid his hands on her he would shake her. "You were born a lady, the same as your sisters, and you were very careful to point that out."

"Ladies have even less to look forward to. Did you think I wanted to be someone's paramour? I assure you, even if I were attractive enough to catch someone's attention, it was not—is not—what I want to do."

Brayden' mouth nearly dropped. Not attractive enough? What was not attractive? Her gorgeous green eyes that were brighter than the highest grade emeralds? Or her lustrous hair that she kept tied back so firmly that only tendrils escaped?

He examined her more closely. Her mouth was a shade too wide, but her teeth were white and even. Even as he looked, he wondered when he began to notice those things about her, certainly not on their first meeting. Well, true, he had noticed her eyes, that would have been impossible to miss. With a sounding clarity, he realized that he may not have noticed them, but he always *knew* of them. How could that be?

"There are other things," he said weakly. Even as he said the words, he knew that was only partially true.

"I had hoped to be a governess, or a companion. I wrote to all of my mother's relatives asking if they or their friends had a need. There was no response."

Brayden shook his head, trying to clear it. "Tell me why we are discussing this now? You live with your brother."

"My home was lost," she reminded him. She had not moved from when she first entered the room, while he had felt the need to pace about.

He winced at that. A direct hit. If he had won the house, chances were that she would still be in it. Collin would have told him what he needed to know about the artifact that had the Regent in an uproar, and he could go on to be the Earl of Raby. Now, none of that was happening and he stood a good chance of losing his property, and the earldom that had been in his family for generations.

"Something had to be done so I went to find employment. Little girls like to eat and be warm."

"What about big girls?"

Jane nodded. "We like that too, but know it can't always be."

"I had thought that you would stay with relatives. Actually, I thought Collin would have been home and had this whole mess cleared up."

"What are you talking about?"

Brayden motioned for her to sit as he pulled his chair closer to hers. She sat gingerly on the edge of the seat, her back ramrod straight. "I was looking for your brother—"

"You said that. That was why you were at the house."

"No, I was looking for your brother before that. I had been searching for him, hoping he could give me some answers. Now he's missing."

"And I'm out my home." Her voice was quiet, but it

carried.

"Things will work out, Jane."

Her head snapped in his direction as he said her name. He knew she hadn't given him permission, but if he did not use it, she would never get past his title. "I feel like I know you from the twins." He watched her expression soften and he wondered if she would ever look at him that way. Just once without hostility. Although he had to admit, he had given her little to think kindly of.

"May I see them before I leave? For a proper visit?"

"You may see them, Jane, but I don't expect you to leave."

She stood up at that, her eyes wide.

"We have a lot to discuss, you and I."

She wasn't sure she liked the tone he had taken, but recognized that he had the upper hand.

He ignored her look. "Don't you realize how dangerous those factories are?" he started.

"Of course I realize it!" she hissed back at him. "Why do you think I didn't want my sisters there?"

She was surprised at the look that crossed his face, and then realized what it meant.

"You thought I wanted them to work! That I would benefit from it?"

She saw the truth in his gaze, though he quickly dropped it, not meeting her eyes. He had thought it. She gave a half-sob, then a bitter smile.

"The last thing I wanted my sisters to do was work. Ever. They are ladies. I told you that."

He nodded. "You did."

"But I thought if they had to work, at least if they were in familiar surroundings they would not mind so much."

"You do not know me. You had no idea what kind of house you were putting them into? What if I had other designs on them?"

She felt the blood drain from her face, even as she raised

her hands to her cheeks. "I had never even thought of that," she admitted, raising her stricken gaze to him. "I...I trusted you because you know my brother."

"Yet, he told you of Dere's reputation."

"I did not know that was you!" She lowered her hands and crossed her arms over her midsection. "The girls trusted you."

"Think, Jane. They are nine years old; they trust everybody."

"Of course." She gave him a quivering smile, hoping that it appeared more brave than she was at the moment. "I will remove them immediately." She stood, and headed toward the door, intending to do just that, but Brayden grasped her arm, stopping her.

"There is no need to do that." He gave her arm a little shake, forcing her to look at him. "I *am* trustworthy, Jane. The girls are under my protection and are treated the same as my nieces."

"They said that. I thought they were companions."

He shrugged in response. "They are in a way. As long as they are here, they keep my nieces entertained and I am less involved."

"Why would you do that? I can never repay you, and it's less likely that Collin will ever be able to do so."

"I am hoping that you can help me, in turn."

"Of course, my lord." Hope stirred in her. To think that the girls might have the life they were entitled to, at least for a period of time. She wasn't naïve enough to think he meant forever, but long enough for her to get a position where they would be welcomed, tolerated at least, would be wonderful.

He pulled on her arm, dragging her closer to him, and nearly off balance. "I thought we were past that."

She nodded quickly.

He sighed and released her. Obviously, he did not believe her. Later she would ask him for recommendations. Perhaps he had relatives that knew of someone. She could hope.

"My sister is here—"

"With your nieces," she interrupted him.

"No, that is my older sister. My younger sister, Arabella, is in residence also. I know that she would enjoy your company."

Wonderful! She could be a companion in the same house as the girls. "Do you mean it? It is more than I hoped for, my lord." She would be safer here than at Mrs. Beetly's. That was more than she hoped for, and she told him so.

He had started to release her arm, but now he tightened his grip again. From the sudden tensing of his muscles, she had the feeling he would like to shake her.

"You could stay as our guest," he said.

"No, I couldn't," she said. "Surely you see that."

"As you wish." His voice was clipped.

Why would he offer her a position of sorts, then be angry that she accepted? She turned to face him. She didn't care that he could read the pleasure in her gaze. "I wish, my lord."

Standing, he turned from her and walked to the bell pull, giving it a vicious tug.

One of the footmen answered his summons almost immediately. Giving his message in a quiet voice, he sat back in his chair.

A moment later, the girls came rushing in and threw themselves at her. "Bella said you were here, and that we could see you. Are you going to stay?"

Jane dropped to her knees and gave them a hug. "Only for—"

"A few days," Brayden interrupted her.

"Oh, Jane! That will be wonderful!" Evangeline gave her a hug tight enough to threaten her air.

"If you release her, imp, she can stand," said a woman who stopped in front of Jane.

About Jane's own age, she was lovely and dressed in what Jane guessed were the latest fashions. Jane stood. Was this Lord Raby's wife? He had said that he wasn't married, hadn't he? She didn't understand the wave of disappointment that went through her.

"This is Arabella," Brayden said from behind the woman, "my youngest sister."

Chapter Six

Jane curtsied when she was introduced.

Brayden practically hauled her to her feet.

"Arabella will show you to your room."

"I want to show her," Emily insisted.

Jane sank down on her knees to shush the little girl. "Perhaps you can come with us, but you must ask Lady Arabella."

At the other woman's nod, the twin eagerly set off.

Brayden reached down to assist Jane in rising. She looked up in surprise. It had been a long time since someone had extended such a courtesy to her. She did not mistake his good manners for anything more.

"We dine at eight," he told her, giving her rough-worked fingers a squeeze before releasing them.

The room Arabella showed to her was welcoming. It matched the rest of the house in its blend of comfort and elegance. The counterpane was a soft yellow and matched the pillows on the window seat. The curtains were a heavy yellow brocade. The yellow rose-flowered wallpaper made it all seem like perpetual spring. Jane could not help contrasting it with the room that had been hers at Collin's house. That now seemed cold and Spartan. She did not think of the lodging house.

Arabella looked Jane up and down. "You are similar in size to my sister, Anne. A trifle shorter, perhaps. I will send one of the maids in with a dress that you can wear for dinner. And if it needs tucked up, one of the maids will be happy to do it."

"Please, it is too much trouble," she said. "Perhaps if someone could show me where to press my gown, it will do."

"Impossible."

She sounded like her brother.

"Brayd will not hear of it." She looked at the twins and encouraged them to stay and visit with their sister until it was time for bed.

Visiting not enough, the girls insisted on telling her everything that had transpired since they arrived, and she put them to bed, too.

Dressed better than ever in her life that she could remember, Jane was half-afraid to even touch the food on her plate. What if she should spill or drop something. But the rumbling in her stomach told her that she would just have to be careful. She had not seen so much food at one time in years.

Brayden seemed to have recovered his good humor and was more relaxed, amusing the girls with general talk about town. While his stories were entertaining, Jane was almost relieved that she would not have to face the situations he described. Companions blended into the background.

"Caroline's ball is sure to be a crush."

"And you plan to add to it, I suppose," Brayden said.

"But of course! It will the perfect place for Jane. She can meet everyone at one time without really having to meet them."

Brayden's eyes crinkled at the corner and Jane had a difficult time pulling her gaze away. At least until he looked in her direction. "Do you think you will be ready to face Manchester society in the next two days?"

It would be such a pleasure to go out. She could hardly wait to see the ballrooms her brother often talked about. "It would be lovely," she said. "Collin spoke so often of all of the people and places. I never hoped to see them." She fingered the fabric of the gown she wore. "If I might again borrow this dress...?"

Brother and sister exchanged glances before Arabella reassured her. "Jane, the dress is yours. I may have not made that clear. Anne has no use for it; it is just something she left here."

Brayden had to look away. The wonder in her eyes hurt him to look at her. Didn't Collin ever give his sisters anything? From what he learned from the twins, they had been well cared for and always had warm clothes. Even he knew that what they had been wearing was not strictly in fashion, but they were neat, clean and very well made. He could not say the same for the dress he had seen on Jane earlier. In fact, if he did not see it again, he would be well pleased. He would have to tell Arabella.

After dinner, Brayden excused himself, insisting that he had to go out, but that he would meet with them at breakfast.

* * *

He was rather surprised at the reluctance he felt in leaving. Dressed in one of his sister's old dresses, Jane looked at least as well, if not better, than many of the other women of his acquaintance. It was a wonder that he had not run into her on any of his previous trips, but then, from the reactions he got when they discussed society, perhaps not.

Inside the club, he looked around until he spotted Kit near the Baccarat tables. When the other man saw him, he used his chin to point to a quiet corner. Kit joined him moments later.

"They plan to ride tonight," he said.

"Thought that might be the case, it's certainly dark enough."

"Do you really want to go through with this, Brayd?"

"I don't see that I have a choice, do you? I'm Dere—remember?" He slipped his hands behind his back, and rocked on the balls of his feet. He glanced at his friend from the corner of his eye. "Do you know that Collin's sister thought I was my brother?" That rankled more than it should.

"Well what do you expect, Dere? How many people manage to have the same nickname—all in the same family?" He gave his friend a lopsided grin. "Besides, I can think of a few instances where it was not unwarranted."

"True. But never for malice." The escapades that he had got himself into—and out of—when at Oxford were nowhere near the troubles that Nigel had caused. Instead of his brother leaving him a legacy to follow, he left a mystery to unravel and the threat to the earldom in his hands. Brayden's one meeting with the Prince Regent convinced him that if he didn't unravel Nigel's problems, and find and return the missing artifact, the family name would wear mud for many years. That was the best scenario. The Prime Minister took care to explain anything the Reagent may have forgotten to mention.

"No," Kit agreed. "So, what do you want from me?"

"The same as always." Half way between his estates and town. He wanted to be at his home, not here. He was only in town because Liverpool made it imperative that he be here. He had to admit either place was equally good for his operations, but he would rather not have his home sullied with Nigel's nonsense. But the first chance he had, he was for Raby Hall.

Kit clapped him on the shoulder. "I'll always have your back, Brayden. Do you know where they ride?"

Nodding, Brayden quickly gave his friend the directions. At least he knew that Kit would watch his back. If anything would go wrong, Kit could extradite him, or witness, whichever the case may be.

* * *

The night was dark enough that it was difficult to see his hand in front of him. Brayden detested these rides, but there was nothing for it now. He was merely following orders. Liverpool had suggested that he ingratiate himself with the group to flush out the person responsible. It sounded a reasonable enough plan. Only Brayden had thought it would be well finished by now. Instead the rides seemed to be increasing in frequency.

While waiting for the other riders to appear, Brayden again wondered if this was the only path to finding the damn statue and clearing his family name. He had his own doubts, but the Prince had made it known that if he couldn't retrieve the statue, but at least was able to name those responsible, he would be doing a favor to the Crown. Brayden didn't think he could afford to pass up favors at this point.

The others traveled as silently as he had, and they were quite close before he realized their presence. Amazing how covering the horse's hooves had such an effect. He had a better understanding as to why the smugglers were so successful in their endeavors.

Ascertaining that the small band was ready, they moved to the crest of the hill. As if on cue, the crested carriage drew into sight. The men charged and surrounded it within a moment, demanding that Lord Darlington and his party exit.

Looking the man over, the leader held out his hand, palm up, demanding his lordship's watch fob. With shaking hands, the man handed it over, looking relieved that was all they asked of him.

One of the men chuckled. "Don't need to be so relieved, m'lord. We need to check your bags. Understand you're carrying something we may want."

"There's nothing, I tell you."

"Let's hope for your sake, you're wrong. Get in the carriage," the threatening voice continued. He turned his attention to the driver, "You will not move." He motioned to one of the other men to stand in front of the horse. Fortunately, it looked as if both men would obey.

Brayden' gritted his teeth. He hated this. It would be over in a moment. He couldn't decide if he would be glad or not to find anything. For the past several months, everything pointed to this group of men as being the ones responsible for missing artifacts throughout London. He just hadn't planned on being one of them.

At first, the Demons, with Nigel at the head, had performed small robberies for a lark. They only took from the men of their class, men they knew. And it was never anything of value: a watch fob, a tie pin, something small. It was an open secret. Then the tone changed shortly before Nigel's death. It was the same time that Collin wanted to join and Nigel refused. There had to be a connection, but he hadn't found it yet.

"Nothing here," one of the men said after a few moments of searching through Darlington's goods. Brayden felt the relief course through him, even knowing that he should be hoping for evidence. He was simply not up to it tonight.

Once the carriage left, the men turned their mounts and headed to the nearby copse of trees. They didn't bother dismounting.

"I know the old goat has something," Miles Wright said. "Saw that statue at his house, then overheard him say he would be shipping it off. Tonight should have been the perfect opportunity to snatch it."

"I realize I'm new to this," Brayden said, "but isn't it difficult to...sell the artifacts?"

Donald Turner, Lord Smythe, shook his head. "You disappoint me, Dere! You should know that anything can be sold to the highest bidder. If someone asks, it's our job to get it—any way possible."

That was exactly what Dere feared.

And what he relayed to Kit later.

"I still fail to see how this will help your case," Kit said.

Not even to his best friend would Brayden reveal the Prince Regent's threats. "If I can see *how* they do it, I might still be able to track the Indian statue and return it to its rightful owner."

Kit reined his horse in, allowing Brayden to take to the narrow path first. His voice carried quite well. "Bet a pony that they've already sold it."

"Let's hope that is indeed not the case."

"Not going to say more, are you?"

Brayden smiled, even if Kit couldn't see it. That was just like the man. His voice held no rancor, he just spoke the facts as he knew them. They both knew he was right.

* * *

The two days sped by. Initially, Jane worried that without having a household to manage or working the long factory hours she would be bored. That couldn't have been further from the truth. After half a day in Arabella's company, she longed for some quiet time. None of the sisters could dispute the fact that it was nice to be together for the day in such pleasant surroundings. She managed to get in a few drawing lessons for the girls and delighted the kitchen staff with the sketches she did of Cook and Stevenson and the housekeeper while the girls were busy practicing on the sleeping cat.

She further endeared herself to the staff when she insisted that they keep their likenesses when they seemed so enthralled with them.

"They seemed so pleased with them," she told Arabella later.

"I'm certain they were," she said, "especially if they were good."

"Tolerable, I suppose," Jane said. While they were sitting in the parlor, she brought along her sketchpad and started to do Arabella while the woman bent over her embroidery.

The twins were with the governess employed for the Tilston children, and for the moment, Jane found life quite pleasant. Enough so that she commented on it to Arabella.

"I like more lively amusement," Arabella said. "The ball

tonight will be great fun. I just wish you would have let me choose another gown for you. Anne has so many of them."

"The one I'm using will be fine, but I am nervous. What if I do the wrong thing?" She already vowed to keep her mouth closed so that she would not say anything amiss. She planned to keep her ears open, and if someone needed household assistance or a companion, she would find out from Arabella who was asking. It promised to be a worthwhile evening.

It was more than she imagined. The only disagreeable point had been when she insisted that she would go in unannounced, but she was able to convince Arabella it was for the best. Once they were in the room, they only spent a few moments together before Arabella was claimed for the first dance. Jane excused herself; the only reason Arabella permitted it was because Jane had stated that she did not know how. After that, it was easy to make her way to where the other companions and matrons sat. Not feeling comfortable with people she did not know, she did her best to blend in with the potted plants.

The whole experience was more than she expected—the light, the heat, the noise and the music. Collin had said very little about the balls or soirées, other than that they occurred. Sometimes he would mention who was there, but mostly he named the men, most of whom she did not know. A few names she would recognize from the occasional newspaper that came her way, but that was a luxury Collin had not believed in. For living in one of the busiest cities of the world, she was sure she led the most sheltered life. She had not realized how much so until she met Lord Raby and Lady Arabella.

"Haven't seen you here before, gel," said one older woman. Jane smiled at her in reply. Dressed in deep purple, and wearing a turban, it was difficult to tell the woman's hair color. "Nothing to say?" she continued.

"I have not been here before." Of course she hadn't.

What a stupid comment! The woman would think she were a real imbecile for sure. Balls such as these were held only once in lifetime, surely.

"Just look at those poppy cocks," the woman said, using her chin to point to a group of young men gathered around the most exquisite woman. She was petite and fit the English beauty mold of blonde hair, blue eyes and dewy complexion. It was small wonder all of the men were there.

"As if any of them have a chance!"

"I don't understand," Jane said. "Why wouldn't they. Almost all of them are as handsome as she is beautiful."

The woman gave her a sharp glance. "Very well spoken. Know you're a plain thing, don't you?"

Jane didn't answer. What could she say, but it was true, she had no illusions. It was not as if she had been a pretty child and grew to a plain woman, or the other way about, which she had often longed for.

"Doesn't matter how handsome they are," the women continued. "Her parents are determined that she shall marry Lord Raby. Not that he ain't handsome. But you don't see him there, do you?"

No, she didn't see him there, but since she wasn't sure if he would be coming this evening that hardly surprised her. "Surely that would make her happy."

The woman gave another cackle of laughter. "Happy has nothing to do with it. That's what her parents want. At least she has the bloodlines. The Raby family has enough scandal going on without that."

Jane desperately wanted to know what scandal, but refrained from asking. She wouldn't have minded listening to the woman speak more about Dere or his family, but she could hardly continue to ask. She was saved from that temptation when the woman spotted someone she knew across the floor and excused herself from Jane.

For her part, Jane couldn't help but follow the progress of Arabella or Dere's fiancée, though she realized she might be too premature about that. She would have to ask Arabella later.

Just as quickly, she stopped that line of thought. First, it wouldn't matter to her, and secondly, she only agreed to a few days at Raby House in hopes that he would receive word of Collin. It wouldn't do to get too attached to them, although she had to admit to herself at least that becoming a companion was not an option she had foreseen since she had not received any responses to her letters. She knew she would not be treated the same as she was by the Derrington household, but the fact that she had spent time there would make her more appealing to other families. She recognized that. Enough so that she smiled for the first time that day.

Brayden immediately spotted Arabella. That was easy enough. His sister hardly need the chandeliers to help her glitter. His eyes narrowed when he realized that Jane was not with her. He scanned the room without appearing to do so. Finally, he spotted her standing with the matrons and chaperones. Now what was the chit up to?

Brayden greeted her before she could make her escape. She curtsied; he raised one eyebrow, which she promptly ignored.

"Arabella is dancing," she told him, indicating the floor with a tilt of her chin.

Brayden still stood facing her, with his hands behind his back, but swiveled on the balls of his feet to locate his sister, then back to Jane. "So I see. That is not in the least surprising. Why are you not dancing?"

Because you haven't asked me, she wanted to say. Fortunately, she knew how inappropriate that would be as a response. "I don't dance," she told him coolly.

This time both eyebrows went up. "Why ever not?" He held out his hand. "Come, give me your dance card so that I may take my pick of dances."

"Companions should sit quietly."

"Perhaps they should," he agreed affably.

He seemed totally unaware that he had cut her to the quick. It surprised her that no blood appeared anywhere on her body. He only spoke the truth; what had she expected?

"Excuse me, my lord," Jane said to him, turning to—she didn't know where. She was already behind the plant. If she could slip under it, that might be the best solution. Dropping a quick curtsy, she turned and would have headed for the row of chairs farthest back.

He grasped her arm, but her momentum was such that he barely caught her fingertips. He held them fast, forcing her to stop or cause a scene. If she hadn't already done so, she thought.

"What just happened here?"

She gave him a tight smile. "I was reminding you of my station."

He tugged on her hand so that she felt a little off balance and would have fallen into him if she had not caught herself. "You are not a companion, so I do not see what that has to do with you."

She raised troubled eyes to his. "Then what am I? I agreed to stay with Arabella, to serve as a companion, so that I might learn how to move in Society a bit, making it easier for me to get a paid position. That is all."

"I neither agreed, nor asked, such of you." He grasped her hand tighter, pulling her closer to him.

Even she knew it was wrong and tried to stop from falling into him.

The music had stopped, but now started again.

"Perfect. A waltz. We shall dance." He practically dragged her to the dancing area.

"I do not know how to waltz," she practically hissed under her breath, trying not to let everyone know her reluctance to dance. There were certainly enough stares coming their way.

"Relax," he said as he positioned her for the dance.

He talked to her, coaching her around the floor. After

the first few minutes she was able to follow easily.

He was right, the dance was an easy one, and once she relaxed enough, she had no problem following his lead. She allowed herself to enjoy the sensation of being close to him. She inhaled his scent of sandalwood; spicy and clean. She would always remember this. No matter which position she took next, this is what she would remember each night before she fell asleep.

"I saw your fiancée tonight," she said to him.

"That's interesting since I don't have one."

She bit her lip. Drat! She hadn't actually meant to call her his fiancée. Evidently he had not asked yet. "I apologize for being premature. One of the matrons, the one on in the purple turban, pointed her out to me. She's absolutely lovely."

"Who are we talking about?"

"The woman in the purple turban?" She looked at the woman standing near the terrace doors.

"That's Lady Drummond, but I was referring to my supposed fiancée."

"Oh. Lady Drummond didn't give her name." She tried to peer over his shoulder to point her out.

"Stop that!" he said, laughing down into her face. "I feel like I'm dancing with a monkey. It doesn't matter since I don't have a fiancée. You can show me later."

Jane bit her lip. She hadn't meant to annoy him.

He grasped her hand a bit tighter, indicating that they would be making a turn, and she looked up at him, giving him a shy smile. This truly was delightful, but the things that it made her think being this close to him also made her understand why there had been a furor when the dance first came out. Even Collin had told her that much.

When the dance was completed, Brayden led her to where Arabella stood with a small group of admirers. Jane graciously thanked him; she hoped her reluctance at leaving him did not show. He could not have made it any more plain that he no longer desired her company. He was a true gentleman, she reasoned. He could have set her back among the plants.

Excusing herself from her admirers, Arabella made her way to Brayden.

"I see you found Jane."

"I was hardly missing," Jane told her. Immediately she closed her mouth. Wrong! She *knew* that wasn't the way a companion behaved. She put her lapse down to Brayden's presence at her side. She did wish the man would leave. He unnerved her.

Arabella smiled at her in response and patted her on the arm. "I phrased that poorly. I wanted to leave and I was looking about for you to see if you were ready."

So that was why Lord Raby had come to find her, not to dance as he claimed. She kept the disappointment out of her voice. At least he had been a gentleman and had danced with her. It was something to remember.

She sensed Brayden stepping closer to her and hemmed in by brother and sister, she had little choice but to do as they wished. Not that it was against what she desired. She should never have come the ball, but then if she had not, she would not have experienced being close to Brayden.

"I will see you to the carriage," he told them.

"Which means that he is not leaving," Arabella told her in a side whisper as the small party made its way to the foyer. After leaving instructions for his carriage to be brought around, he left them to retrieve their cloaks.

Once they were situated in the carriage, Arabella started to talk about the ball with a great deal of enthusiasm. Enough so that Jane questioned if the woman had really been ready to leave.

"Lud, yes! While I enjoyed myself, I have had enough. This was by far the most boring ball I have attended in some time."

Boring? It had been the most excitement she had ever

experienced. She could not even imagine what it would be like to be courted like Arabella. And the woman had thought it boring. "Then why go at all?"

"That was easy enough! Brayden insisted," she said. "Really, Jane, he thought this might be a good way to introduce you to society. I cannot begin to tell you how peeved he is with me over your gown." She slapped her hand across her mouth as if just realizing how tactless she had been. "I am so sorry, Jane," she said, reaching across the seat to grasp the other girl's hand. "I cannot seem to say one thing correctly tonight."

Jane gave her a weak smile. "It is of no consequence, Lady Arabella. I fear that your brother and I were at cross-purposes for a while, but I believe we have straightened them out this evening. In that respect, the ball was a success."

Arabella gave a delighted laugh. "Jane, I swear you are as big a tease as Brayden."

When Jane did not respond, but merely turned her head to look out the window, Arabella heaved a loud sigh. "I've done it again. I vow to keep my mouth shut for the rest of the way home."

Since they would arrive in a matter of moments, Jane did not look on her vow as a particular hardship.

* * *

Breakfast was a solitary affair, or it could have been. Instead of sitting in the breakfast room alone, she asked Stevenson if she could breakfast in the nursery with her sisters and the other little girls. They were delighted to see her.

"You must check my sketches, Jane," Evangeline said. "I have been practicing."

"Have you, sweetling? Then as soon as we are done clearing the table, then we may look at them."

"We don't have to clear the table," Emily whispered to her rather loudly. "The maids will do that."

Jane watched Miranda and Hannah looking at her with wide eyes, but ignored them as she addressed her sisters. "No, we will assist them, then we will talk." This was not going to work well, she could see that. Already her sisters felt they were above the chores that would be necessary for them to do.

"Does that mean I can't show you my sketches?" Evangeline asked.

"I would like nothing better, but first we will clear the table."

"My mama does not make me clear the table," Hannah, the younger of Lord Raby's two nieces, piped up.

"Ladies don't need to do that," Brayden' deep voice said as he entered the room. "And as you are all ladies in my home, no one needs to do so." He pointed to the table, and the maid immediately removed the settings.

"I would like to talk to Miss Jane, he told the girls. Perhaps you will excuse us?" He gave them a bow, which made his nieces giggle even as they curtseyed. Jane was pleased to see her sisters did the same.

"But I want to show Jane my sketches," Evangeline said while the others turned to other amusements in the nursery. "Please, Uncle Brayden."

Jane drew her breath in sharply, but before she could say anything, Brayden shot her a warning look.

"If you're quick about it," he told her.

She had her sketchbook nearby and was busy flipping through the pages before she got to the one she wanted and handed the book back to Jane.

"Evangeline, this is wonderful," Jane told her, completely truthful.

"The other ones are not as good," the little girl said.

"Good God!" Brayden had come to look over Jane's shoulder. His scent tickled her nose and she wanted to breathe in deeply. His voice rumbling in her ear called her back to the task at hand. "Did you really do this?" he asked the girl. At her nod, he looked at it again.

It was a remarkable sketch of Nelson, his horse, as he stood in the stables. Only his head was visible.

"It is a wonderful likeness," Brayden said.

Thanking him, Evangeline took her book, gave Jane a hug and joined the other children.

"Where did she learn to draw like that?" Brayden asked her later as they walked in the garden.

"She has always had some talent—more than Emily."

Brayden stopped where he was and turned to look at her. *"Some* talent? That is marvelous for a nine-year-old. Did you teach her?"

"Of course. I taught them both, but Emily..." she shook her head. "Emily gets the merest outline and says that she is done."

"What do you sketch, Jane?"

She shrugged, then resumed walking. "Anything that strikes my fancy." She snapped her mouth shut after that. She didn't want him to ask to see the pictures. Heavens, since she had arrived, she must have a dozen sketches of him to every one other one she had done. She knew she would have to hide them until she left.

She tried to ignore the way his hand rested against her back as he guided her in the direction he wanted to go. It meant nothing, but she could feel the heat from his fingers seep through her clothing. "Somehow, my lord, I don't think you called for my attention to discuss sketches."

"I didn't. But now that I know you do sketch, it might help tremendously."

She waited for him to speak.

"Do you have any recent sketches of Collin? So far, I have very little to go on and none of my inquiries have yielded concrete answers."

"I do." She gave him a considering look. "I suppose I never thought of using them to find him."

"Which makes me wonder why?"

"I saw Collin when he left, I told you that. It is no

mystery that he is gone." She didn't point out the fact that she certainly did not have the resources to have a description of him printed and posted. Aside from that, since he did leave in the middle of the night, as it were, she supposed he had his reasons.

"Don't you want to know where he is?"

She gave him a wry smile. "Dearly. But Collin is a man grown. If he wants me aware of his whereabouts he will tell me."

"I wonder, Jane, if you are always this truly complacent? Just think, a man would not have to worry if he married you that you would be upset if he were late. It would not bother you at all!"

"I did not say that!" she snapped at him. That was far from the truth. If she were married to someone like Brayden she would always wonder where he was. Good thing she could be spared that anxiety. Handsome, kind and powerful did not often come together, and when they did, they would not be for the likes of plain women. "I just know Collin."

"He has done this before?"

"Not to this extent." At his questioning look, she continued. "This time when he left, it was in the middle of the night. Well, early morning," she corrected herself. "He did tell me not to worry."

"That's it?"

She could hear the suppressed anger in his voice. "No. He did tell me that he was sorry, and that he would be in touch, but chances are it would not be soon."

She stopped and looked up at him. "Do you think that was wrong? That I should be concerned?"

"Given the circumstances, probably not." He looked to the horizon, seeming to contemplate an issue. As if making his decision, he turned back to her.

"Why is it so important that you find him?" she asked before he had a chance to say anything. She had been studying him, but now she turned away. She busied herself with the leaves of one of the plants. From what Dere had already told her, everything seemed rather straightforward.

Seeming to reach a conclusion, he told her.

"Morris—Lord Hawke—" At her quickly indrawn breath, he stopped. "Have you met him?"

She nodded. "He made himself known the night before I came to visit the girls."

He did not like the way she stiffened when she said that, or her choice of words. They implied something sinister; easy enough to believe with Morris. It was a moment before he realized that she said nothing more, just increased playing with the branch.

He touched her arm, and when she flinched, he knew there was more than she was telling him. What had the cad done? This time he grasped her arm, turning her to face him. She made to pull it out of his grasp, but he held firm, only easing the pressure of his hand when she calmed. "You can tell me, Jane."

She gave him a weak smile. "I am making more of it than there was, I assure you."

"Where did you see him?" His voice was clipped. When she raised her wide eyes to him he could see the shadows in them. At his voice, or at Morris's behavior he had yet to learn.

"He was waiting for me outside of Mrs. Beetly's—the boarding house where we stayed. It was night." She shrugged. "I didn't know who he was at first, but he introduced himself."

Brayden swallowed the growl that was building in his throat. Morris must be convinced that Collin knew something. Her next words confirmed it.

"He wanted me to tell him where Collin was. I...I couldn't do that." She looked away from him. "I told him I didn't know where he was."

Was she ashamed of that? It wasn't her fault.

"Perhaps he merely wanted to settle things with him." He ran a hand through his hair, ruffling it and showing his agitation. "You understand that it was a debt of honor—"

"Living with my father and Collin, I have certainly learned of those and understand," she interrupted him. Seeing the pained look on his face, she reached out her hand and touched his. She wasn't sure who was more surprised. She quickly withdrew it. She merely intended to offer comfort, but she could see that such a forward motion on her part was not what he wanted. Obviously the pained look was for her interruption! How often had she seen that same expression on her brother's face when she said something that he found extremely inappropriate or what he considered stupid.

"So sorry," she said. "I just wanted you to understand that I realize the blame for our current situation rests on Collin's shoulders."

"You do not appear overly angered by his shabby behavior."

She studied him for a moment, as if trying to choose her words. "I suppose that I always knew there could be no good that came from this." She couldn't stop the cynical chuckle that erupted. "My failing was not in better preparing for it."

Brayden grasped both of her arms, forcing her to look at him. "No, that was your brother's responsibility. He had a duty to care for you and for his holdings."

"I agree, but he has not."

Brayden released her arms and ran a hand down his face. "I fear I'm a great one to talk. Regardless, that is not why I brought up the matter."

Jane felt dread gather in her stomach. What if Collin actually owed more? That would explain why he took off as he had, as well as Dere's reluctance to have them stay in the house any longer than necessary.

"The truth is, I think Collin has been used by his supposed friends."

"You are not one of them?"

"I told you, my brother was the 'Dere' they refer to. Now they believe that I can take his place."

"You don't sound very sure."

"I'm not."

"I see." What else was there to say? She cocked her head as she looked at him. "Lord Hawke did want me to go back to the house with him. He seemed certain that I knew where Collin had something hidden."

Brayden focused all of his attention on what she was saying. "Think, Jane. What exactly did he say, word for word."

Jane felt ill. Because Dere had been so kind to them, she tended to forget exactly what her brother had told her about the man—well, his brother. It wasn't much, but it was enough. She knew how to fill in the missing pieces. His quickened interest in Lord Hawke proved Collin did have the man summed up correctly.

She told him what she remembered. She didn't tell him about how she managed to get away from him. "I'm sorry I couldn't be more help in finding Collin, but now I should see to my sisters." She dropped him a brief curtsy and all but fled to the house.

Brayden watched her go. That went as completely opposite of well as it could, he thought irritably. There was something about her that always distracted him.

He rather meant what he had said. Collin appeared a bounder, but in truth it wasn't entirely his fault. The men had used him—were using himself too, but at least he was aware of it. He encouraged it. It was the only way he was going to find out anything about Nigel and more importantly, who really stole the statue.

He watched Jane walk away. There was little he could do about it. Until he had the family name cleared he was hardly in a better position than Collin.

Chapter Seven

Kit invited himself to breakfast the next morning, and Brayden was glad of the company. No one was in the breakfast room when he had come in, and he did not want a repeat of yesterday's visit to the nursery. No surprise to him that Arabella had a tray sent up—the little heathen darlings, as she called the young ones, were too much to bear constantly.

No surprise to Kit either evidently since he didn't ask for her. They made general talk through breakfast and coffee, then migrated to Brayden's study.

There, Kit wasted no time in coming to the point.

"There was another raid last night."

"Raid?"

Kit shrugged. "I can't think of what else to call it. These men knew what they were after, and they went for it."

Brayden perched on the arm of one of the stuffed chairs and watched his friend pace.

"This has to stop, Brayd."

"Are you saying that you believe I was involved last night?"

"Weren't you?" Kit asked. "You have been following Dere's Demons for the past several months."

"Wait a moment. Think about what you are saying!"

"I know what I'm saying." Kit took a step closer so that they were nearly toe-to-toe. "You have to end this now, Brayd."

"Kit, I didn't ride last night. You should know that since I didn't ask for you to watch my back." He jammed his hand through his hair. "Hell, I didn't even know that they were planning to ride. Obviously, I'm not as much a part of their group as I thought."

Kit gave him a thoughtful look. "Do you suppose that Nigel was any different? What if he didn't know everything that went on in the group?"

"I've considered that, believe me. But he had to have known. The group bears his name and some of his exploits are a little too well known."

"Brayd, the group bears your name too now, and you don't know everything."

He gave a bark of laughter. "I don't know *anything*. But it would be much too brazen just to take the name. Nigel *had* to have approved it."

Kit shrugged. "You are most likely right, but consider, just for a moment, that he did not."

"The truth is even if Nigel *did* know, there was no guarantee that he understood the full ramifications." His half brother was known to be beef-headed.

"There is that," Kit agreed. "But the question remains, why haven't they confided in you? And what is their purpose?"

Brayden stood, then paced a few steps in one direction, then the other. "It's to the point that I almost no longer care what their game is. All I want is the damn statue."

"You and how many others?"

"For a start, Prinny and the Indian Prince. After that, I'm not sure. Liverpool ranks up there."

Kit let out a whistle and stared at his friend. "No wonder you didn't want to name anyone earlier. Rather high-ranking list there."

"Don't I know it? Makes life uncomfortable, let me tell you."

"Why do I think there is more to the story?"

"Because there is." He finally threw himself into one of the chairs. "You'd better ring for more coffee. This is going to take time."

Kit did as Brayden requested, then sat in the matching

chair.

Brayden told him the entire tale, pausing only long enough to wait for the servant to set down the coffee tray and leave. "Are you sure you don't want something stronger?" Kit asked.

"I would love something, but I know that I need my wits about me, especially now that time is running short."

"Never thought Prinny would continue to hold you responsible."

"Compliments of Dere's Demons. That's all the Indian Prince knows and he's insisting that the Regent do something about it since he knows that 'Dere' is still active."

Kit gave a bark of laughter and shot his friend a sideways look. "You are joking."

"Look at me. Does it look like I'm joking?" He jammed his hands in his hair. "I don't have much time to find that artifact and get it into Prinny's hands. After that, I may not have to worry about anything, since the man has threatened to do everything but kill me."

"He knows you're not at fault!"

Brayden nodded once. "But he also knows someone has to be responsible, so if the statue doesn't appear—preferably by my delivering it—then he can lock up this estate, if he doesn't choose to claim it."

"That would be insane! He would have to be as mad as his father to do such a thing. Your family has been more than loyal to the Crown."

Brayden nodded in agreement. "Did I mention that he is really angry?"

"Did he come out and say all of that?"

"Of course not," he said with some disgust. "He left that part to Liverpool."

"Only Nigel could cause such a mess."

Since Kit was such an old friend, Brayden took no offense at the comment. It was the truth, after all. Hell, even Liverpool had said as much, though not so bluntly.

Rising, Kit moved to sit behind his friend's desk and looked about for paper. "We need a list."

Brayden shook his head, more in exasperation than disagreement. "What we need are answers. We need to find what was taken last night, and how it ties in with the statue I'm searching for. And most importantly...where are these artifacts going."

"What are you thinking, Brayden?"

"That I need to get it back. What else could I be thinking?"

Kit stared at his friend. "Naturally."

"I need to have everyone together and see what happens. Surely someone would let something slip and give me a lead to go on."

"Ah, one of the reasons for your attendance at so many assemblies lately."

Brayden gave him a wry smile. "That would be the reason."

"I was beginning to worry that you didn't trust me with Arabella."

Brayden focused his full attention on Kit. "Something you want to tell me?" He hid his grin; he swore the man actually blushed. He had long suspected that Kit held a tendre for his youngest sister, but she had not said anything to him. He would hate to see either of them hurt.

In an unaccustomed manner, Kit dropped his gaze. "You know I care for her, Brayd, but I don't know what her feelings are." Finally he looked his friend in the eye. "You don't mind?"

"Quit being an ass, Kit, and work on the problem at hand."

"As to that, I like your idea."

"Enlighten me. I seem to be out of ideas." Brayden turned back to stare at the fire burning in the grate.

Kit stood and came around to the front of the desk, leaning against it. "You said have everyone together. Why not do it? You could have a house party at Raby Hall and invite the lot of them."

* * *

After sharing breakfast with the girls, Jane was shooed from the room—in the nicest possible way, of course—by nanny. Stopping in her room on her way down from the nursery, she saw that Arabella's door was firmly closed. No surprise there. It didn't take Jane long to realize that her friend preferred to sleep late.

Stopping in her room, she picked up her sketch tablet and charcoal intending to head out doors to sketch new subjects. She hurried down the backstairs, where she was stopped by the downstairs maid, telling her how much everyone enjoyed the picture of Cook that she had done.

"I never see you, Miss, or I would have told you before," she said, grasping her duster tighter.

"Thank you. Would you like me to do you sometime?"

"Really, Miss? I could send it to my mum."

"Then I will surely do it as soon as you are free."

Thanking her again, the maid gave her a quick curtsey and went on her way.

Jane felt a warmth deep inside that she hadn't felt in years. Her sisters were the only ones who ever seemed pleased to be with her, look forward to it. And she with them.

Continuing on her way, she stopped in the kitchen and borrowed one of the cloaks there for slipping outdoors. A few minutes in the kitchen garden and she would find something that appealed to her; making her want to draw. Instead, as she sat there, she held her charcoal poised over her paper. The cat lying under the plant captured her attention, but when she began to draw, the only face she could see was Brayden's. She blinked, working to clear her mind's eye of the image that would not leave. Within moments her hands were sketching the face that she thought of. Repeatedly. Finally, as the chilled morning air warmed, she realized the passage of time.

Closing her book, she made her way back to the kitchen to return the cloak.

"The maid said you would do her likeness. That's right nice of you, Miss," Cook said. "Her mum hasn't seen her nigh on five years."

Jane finished hanging the cloak on the peg before turning back to Cook. "That must be hard on her mum."

"That's the way it goes, Miss. Gots to make a living."

True enough, she mentally agreed as she headed to the parlor. Wasn't she one to know that more than even some of the servants, she thought wryly. And really, it was time that she made some move. If only she knew in what direction. It was obvious to her that she would get no further direction from Brayden. In truth, he had done a lot of good for her; she couldn't expect that he would actually find her a position. It was up to her. Not that she wanted to leave, but if she didn't make the move soon she was afraid she would become too comfortable. She looked around the hall as she made her way to the parlor. Everything was the way it should be here, not the way Collin's house had been run with just herself and two old retainers helping. This was a gentleman's house.

She found a chair in the corner of the parlor and made herself comfortable while waiting for Arabella or someone else from the family to make an appearance. She fingered the dress she was wearing, caressing the material as she smoothed it over her legs. She never owned anything as fine as the clothes she was given when she arrived here. Arabella and her brother had been very generous with her and her sisters.

Learning not to overstay her welcome was one lesson she had remembered from her mother, although need won out over courtesy when it came to the girls. If Lord Raby was willing to let them remain for a time, she would do nothing to gainsay it. She realized she would be severing ties with them, if not now, then at some time in the future, but there seemed to be no way around it.

"Why the long look?"

Jane sat up with a jerk. She hadn't heard anyone enter. Immediately behind Arabella came her brother. She didn't know if she was ready to face him, but even so, she couldn't resist studying his face even more. She quickly shifted her gaze back to Arabella when she realized what she was about.

"Not long, surely!" She smiled warmly at them.

Arabella seated herself near her embroidery frame while Brayden looked at her a moment longer, then headed to the window. Jane was glad he found something else to stare at. His gaze was unnerving.

"Perhaps not," Arabella said, as she sorted through her threads. "But definitely thoughtful. It's much too nice of a day to tax your brain."

Jane rose from her chair to stand closer to Arabella, the better to converse without having to shout her responses across the room. "You are such a tease—making people think you are a widgeon."

Sitting up straighter, Arabella graciously accepted the compliment.

"Not many people would think it was a compliment," Jane admonished her.

"I know, but can I help it if they make it so easy for me?"

"See why I fear I will always have her on my hands?" Brayden said with a mock sigh. "Who would ask for her hand? And if they were simple enough to do so, she would have none of them."

When Arabella started to protest, he quickly interrupted. "Not that I would let them."

His sister wrinkled her nose in his direction. "Beast," she said without heat.

In a way, Jane was jealous of them. She had never shared such a relationship with her own brother. She hadn't even known it was such a thing to miss. Again, she was glad that the girls would be staying with Lord Raby and his household, and she told him so.

"It will be nice for you all to be together again," Arabella said, her voice rather cautious. She shot a look at her brother, but before Jane could wonder about it, Brayden interrupted.

"That almost sounds as if you plan to leave."

Jane took a deep breath before turning to face him and raising her eyes to his. That was a mistake. His jaw was hard set but his eyes were positively ice-like. She stared at him anyway and raised her chin. "I do plan to leave. There is nothing I can do here. Your home is so well run that I am more in the way than I am a help. The children don't need me—you have a governess and a nanny."

"Yes. That is what children need."

"I appreciate what you are offering my sisters, but as I said there is nothing for me here."

"You don't need anything? Is that what you are telling me?"

"I would not be so foolish. I would dearly love to have your recommendation for a post."

She heard Arabella's indrawn breath.

"As what?" Brayden drew her attention again. "A factory worker again?" There was total disgust in his voice as he bit out the words.

"A companion would be wonderful, but it seems relatives needing such are in short supply." She tried to make light of it, but Lord Raby still wore a stony look. If anything, she would have sworn his jaw was clenched tighter, though she would not have believed that were possible.

He moved closer to her before she had finished speaking. "I would prefer not to do that," he told her.

How could she think of leaving him? It angered him that she obviously did not care for him in the way that he thought of her. He would prefer that she never left his side, but at the least not leave his home. And where had that thought come from? he chided himself. There was no way she could know of his thoughts when he had been totally unaware of them himself. What she proposed would not only take her away from his home, but from the very social sphere of his existence. He did not like to think of not seeing her again. Lord knew when he would find Collin—if he ever found him. By then he might have lost all trace of Jane. It was not to be considered.

Arabella must have had some inkling of what he was thinking because she came to join them, pushing aside her embroidery hoop. She laid her hand on Jane's arm.

"Jane, please sit down. Let's discuss this."

"There is nothing to discuss," she told the siblings in a flat voice.

"Consider that if you leave now, there is really nowhere for you to go, but if you stay we can send out letters and inquiries. Perhaps you will find somewhere you would like to be. In the meantime, you will be with the girls—your sisters will enjoy having you."

He could see that she was weakening to that argument, and felt his jaw relax somewhat. She was considering it at least.

"It's wonderful weather," he said abruptly. "Perhaps we should go for a drive. The grays could use some exercise anyway."

"That's a wonderful idea, Brayden!" his sister said. And if he were not so tense he would have laughed at her antics. She hated going out. "But I really must wait for Madame Celeste. I simply must have this fitting. Why don't you and Jane go?"

"Jane?" He was afraid to breathe lest she refuse him.

She looked at him for a moment, her gaze unwavering as if trying to determine what he was really about. He let his eyelids fall half closed. If she knew how much her agreement meant she would refuse him for sure!

Finally, she nodded her head.

* **

They didn't really speak until they were headed to the park. Brayden had the phaeton in excellent control, and his tiger stood behind them.

"I'm glad Arabella decided not to come," he finally said.

"You are?" There was no mistaking the surprise in her voice.

"I needed to ask you a favor and I'm afraid if Bella would be here you would agree just to please her and not yourself." He could see that she took affront to that. Good.

"You may have noticed that Bella can tend to be a bit spoiled and try to get her own way whenever possible –"

"She has been nothing but kindness to me," Jane insisted.

He liked that she stood up for her friend.

"Oh, no argument there," he told her." Bella is one of the kindest people I know. But, I assure you, she can be spoiled." He shrugged. "She's the youngest and I fear we all had a hand in spoiling her." He grinned at her. "You have made me forget what I started to say!"

She gave him a tight smile. That was better than a closed look, he told himself.

"I think you were under some misapprehension at the Durand's Ball," he finally said. "I blame myself."

"In what way? I apologize if I overstepped my role."

He gave her credit for not glaring at him. In her eyes, he was the one that made her 'overstep.'

"Jane, that is precisely what I am talking about." He pulled the team over to the side of the lane and instructed the tiger to watch them as he helped Jane down. "I need to have my wits about me," he said teasingly. Although he did briefly wonder if he should have had his hands occupied so that he wouldn't be tempted to wrap them around her pretty neck.

"You insist that your sisters are ladies."

"They are," she said.

"Yet, you are the elder, and you almost never refer to yourself in that manner. Is there something I don't know about your family?"

She gasped and stared at him. He wondered if she would pick up the insult, not that he had intended it that way, and he told her so.

"Of course I am a lady by birth."

"Then why will you not let yourself be treated as one?"

They had stopped strolling, and she turned to look at him fully. "There are several reasons." She looked down, seeming to hesitate in looking at him. "I have known since I was tiny that I was not a pretty child. My mother told me that I would always have to be careful of how I spoke, how I behaved... She told me that it would be my job to take care of everyone. The twins were merely infants," she said then shrugged. "I understood that. My father would tell me the same thing. After all, he was a busy man, and he made sure that Collin would follow in his footsteps and behave a true gentleman."

Brayden bit back the retort he would like to make. He reached out and brushed a loose tendril of her hair from her face, tucking it behind her ear. He let his gloved fingers rest on her cheek a moment longer than necessary. "That is not all quite true, Jane. You know that, don't you?"

She shook her head. "It is true. Don't you see, it was exactly true. I do have to take care of everyone. Well, Collin is old enough to care for himself and he has done so. But there is no one else to care for the girls."

He reached out and clasped her shoulders. "I see where you feel responsible for them, but Jane, it is Collin's failing. He is the head of the household. It is his responsibility to care for you, not the other way around."

"But I am older than Collin," she explained, raising troubled eyes to his.

"What of it? Anne is older than I and until she married, I cared for her."

"Perhaps that is the difference," she said quietly. "My mother realized that I would not marry. So did my father. Perhaps him even more than my mother. After all, he knew there would be no dowry, and for someone with my looks a dowry would be essential. A big one would be essential," she pointed out.

Brayden let his hands slide down her arms until he clasped her hands. "Jane, I have no idea where you got these ideas, but please desist in airing them when you are with me."

She nodded in agreement, but he didn't see agreement in her eyes, it was more like fear. What did she think he was going to do to her? "Jane you are beautiful. Your eyes...your hair...your mouth is generous and looks positively enchanting when you choose to smile." He reached out a finger and tapped her on the nose. "Your nose is perfectly proportioned, if a bit impertinent, just like the chit whose face it is on."

Jane gave him a shy smile. "Thank you for saying so, my lord. No one has said such things before."

For that he was grateful. He couldn't help that others had been blind, but he didn't feel compelled to share his good fortune.

"I wanted to talk to you." If she wasn't going to stay with him because it would benefit herself, perhaps she would stay if it were for her brother. He daren't think it would be for him.

He started to stroll along again, close to her, but certainly not touching. He could hear the horses, not quite impatient, but getting restless. "I hoped you would agree to a series of assemblies—"

"That is out of the question," she interrupted him.

"Do let me finish, Jane." He gave her a slight smile. He already noticed that impatience was a big part of her personality. "At my home, I am going to have a house party. Before you refuse, know that it would not only help me, but help Collin too."

She gave him a thoughtful look, but he would not elaborate further until she asked.

She did. "How so?"

"I believe that many of the things your brother was involved in were not of his own doing."

"Such as? No one told him that he had to bet his home."

"Not directly, no. But I believe that there were sources that orchestrated it. Maneuvered him into behaving as they wanted."

"But what could they want?"

Brayden turned, heading her back to the phaeton. "There is more that I would like to discuss with you about it, but the horses are ready to go. I'm not sure Jem can hold them much longer. For now, I would like your agreement that you will stay, as my *guest.*" He stressed the word and held her gaze with his as he said the word. "You will do as Arabella does. That means that you will wear appropriate clothes, do the appropriate visits, and so on. That is Arabella's forté."

"How will that help you and Collin?"

"I will tell you as we go along. That can be discussed at the house, but for now I need your agreement before I can even proceed."

"I would give it, but I do not understand how this will help."

He helped her into the phaeton, then hopped in himself, taking the reins from his tiger. "So, you agree? With no more nonsense about leaving, or finding a position?" he asked while holding the horses steady for the tiger to jump on.

"But I will have to face that at some point."

"Let us put a time on it, then. You can bring the matter up however much you desire after everyone leaves the house party. Is that fair enough?"

She gazed at him for a moment, then slowly nodded her head.

He took a deep breath. One hurdle down. That would at least give him time to convince her that she would always want to stay and never leave.

* * *

Back at the Town house, Jane immediately went to her room. She had to think about what she had agreed to. It was well beyond any dream she ever had—to spend time at assemblies; talk to people. Living in one house and seeing no one save Collin's friends or some areas of Manchester that she knew real ladies never ventured to unattended was dramatically different from seeing the glittering ball rooms. Now that she had been to one ball, she knew they were magical. Even though Lord Raby had danced with her, she had known it was not the right thing to do. That was not her place. Now he was telling her that she would have the right to do that. Other men might even ask her to dance. She took a few tentative dance steps around her bedroom. She would have to practice, if she could remember the steps. She wasn't exactly sure what was involved in a house party, but Arabella would know.

Rather than go downstairs, she made herself comfortable in the window seat and took out her sketchbook again. What luxury.

From her window, she could see the gardener potting about the shrubbery so she sketched him. Now that Cook had mentioned that her sketches were prized by the people who received them, she felt she must sketch everyone. Even if they were poorly done, if they brought some happiness to the recipient, she would be equally happy to share. From that moment, her goal was to sketch every person who worked at Raby House. She riffled through the pages left in her sketchbook, briefly wondering if she would have to perhaps draw smaller sketches in order to accommodate her goal. She already had the gardener sketched out for the full sheet, so he would stay, and she did promise the maid. After that, she would have to conserve her paper.

When she completed her sketch, she laid her book aside, stretched and decided to take inventory of exactly how much money she did have. She agreed to be Brayden's—Lord Raby's—guest, so she would not add further insult and insist on offering anything in payment. She gave a wry smile. As if she could afford anything. Besides, his lordship did say that he had a request in payment. She would wait and see what it was.

In the meantime, she had enough money that she felt she could take a few coins for a new sketchbook and charcoal. Pleased, she closed the drawer and headed to the nursery to see what the girls were up to.

She certainly need not have worried. With his lordship's nieces present, the girls were enjoying themselves immensely and were making plans for an outing.

"We're done with our lessons for today," Miranda, one of the nieces told her.

"Miss March is taking us to the park," Evangeline told her. "Will you come with us, Jane?" Emily asked.

Jane thought about it, was tempted, but had to decline. Lord Raby had not said at what time he would meet with her and she felt responsible enough that she needed to be present when he called—even if it were not until after dinner.

"How about if you tell me all about it after tea?" Even if his lordship had tea, it would not be the exact same time as the girls.

In the end, Brayden did not have a chance to meet with Jane until well after dinner the next day. In the meantime, he had to talk to Arabella, and explain that Jane had agreed to stay, to participate, and his sister was to do everything in her power to make sure it was successful for her.

"As if I would do anything but make her welcome," she protested.

Brayden gave her a thoughtful look. "I know that, Bella, but I sense that she's very nervous about this. She has never had a season, never any exposure to real society. So I'm not sure she has any idea how to really go on."

"This house party that you suddenly want to have will certainly be easier than facing a different group everyday."

"I do intend to socialize, Bella, so there will be different people."

She waved her hand, dismissing the problem. "True, but

there will be a core group that she will be comfortable with. Now, give me the list today and we can get this started."

"Just like that?"

"Just like that. You know Nigel never wanted to do any entertaining. I know the mourning period was not as long as you like, Brayd, but it will be acceptable and a house party will be ideal. Everyone will accept, Brayd."

Of that he was sure.

"My only concern in all of these arrangements is Jane's wardrobe."

"What of it?"

"She doesn't have one," Arabella said flatly. "She won't wear anything else of Anne's and I'm not entirely sure it's seemly for you to pay for her gowns."

He raised an eyebrow at that comment.

"Oh, don't give me that look. You know what I mean."

"True." He thought for a moment, then told her to pay for it from her allowance.

She gaped at him. "Brayden!"

"Settle down, Bella," he laughed. "I'll make it good. In fact, as soon as I do the accounts I'll settle it. You do have enough, don't you?"

She sniffed at him. "You know I'm only doing this because you're my favorite brother, Brayden."

"I'm your *only* brother," he said dryly as he left the room. At least one matter was taken care of. Now to meet with Kit.

That did not go nearly as well as his meeting with his sister.

"I wasn't sure you would go through with the gathering. Can't understand it," Kit told him as they settled into chairs in Kit's Town house parlor.

"You have to be more specific," Brayden told him. "The artifacts have to come from somewhere, and we know they're surely going somewhere. And someone is keeping it very close. Now, that's a lot of loose ends."

"Maybe."

"If you know something, now might be a good time to share it with me. I'm not getting any younger, and Prinny is getting more impatient."

"Still threatening you, is he?"

"Nearly every day there is some message from St. James. Then there are messages from Liverpool."

"You may not like this, but I'm wondering how involved Collin really is in the whole affair."

"Why do you ask? I figured him for a dupe, maybe even an unwitting courier. If they used a courier."

"Do you think that's why he's disappeared now?"

Brayden stared at his friend. "You mean you think that he took off with some of the items? It could well be." He wiped his hand down his face, and with it, the suggestion Kit had put forth. "But I don't think so. I really think Collin is running scared. As for leaving, what would you do if you lost everything—including the respect of your sisters, and left them poverty bound, but you didn't want to put a gun to your head?"

"Not a lot of options, I agree." Kit stared straight ahead for a moment, gathering thoughts. "Did you mean what you said about his sisters?"

"Losing respect?" he asked.

Kit shook his head. "That's easy enough to understand. I meant about the poverty. Don't they have some money of their own—dowries, and so on?"

Brayden shook his head. "It seems that Collin's father was as much of a bounder as the son. Maybe more so. He made no provision for the women in his family."

"Behavior of a cad. Did the man have no sense of responsibility?"

"Apparently not. But Kit, if that information is not already making the rounds, I would appreciate that it not be spread."

"I have no problems with that. But what are you thinking? She already appeared at one ball dressed—well, not exactly at the height of fashion. Even I could tell that."

Brayden grinned at his friend and settled back in his chair. "Hush. Don't let Anne hear you say that."

Kit gave a mock groan. "So, what are you planning?"

"Several things, but in regards to Lady Jane, it will be known that she has a small dowry from her uncle, and that she and her sisters are guests at my house. After all, my nieces and the young girls are close enough in age, and Bella and Jane are close in age and appear to get on well, though I daresay their experiences are vastly different." He shrugged. "The point is, this may be as close as she gets to a season."

"Are you playing matchmaker?"

Was he? Good Lord, he hadn't really thought this through. What if in giving Jane this little taste of society she found someone that appealed to her, someone she loved, someone who wanted to marry her? Maybe he *wouldn't* give her that dowry!

"Not at all. Merely giving her a chance to see the society that her brother and father knew about."

"Is that wise?"

Brayden shrugged. "I have no idea. The point is that it is her birthright. Do you realize how old that family is?"

Kit nodded. "Daresay older than many of the other titles around."

It was Brayden's turn to nod. "I could wring Collin's neck. If I could find him."

"When do the Demons ride again?"

"Tomorrow night. At least that's the message I got. It appears that I do not get invited to all of them," he said bitterly.

"What if there is a second group, Brayden?"

He shrugged. "What if there is? The point is that I need to find that dratted statue and at the moment I can't even determine who has it!"

"Or if anyone does."

"I hardly think it likely that Prinny would be threatening

me if he didn't have some very damming evidence."

"Think, Brayden. What evidence could he possibly have? The artifact is missing and the person he is accusing is dead." Kit spread his hands. "What does that leave?"

"Not much. But I will jump through hoops, and Prinny knows it. I have no idea why he suddenly has it in his head that he prefers my Lancashire property, but I'm not willing to give it up. If I have to find the artifact to do it, whether Nigel is involved or not, that's what I'll do."

* * *

Finding it was much easier said that done. And that was never more evident than when Brayden met with the Demons the next night.

"I think it's time that we decide what this group is doing," Lord Parke said.

Brayden couldn't agree more, but held his silence.

"Thought it was all for a lark," Sir Mitchell said.

"It started that way, then it changed. The question is: do we want to continue in this manner?"

Changed? In what way? Brayden was all ears. All he needed was for someone to really talk. And they did seem to be in a talkative mood tonight.

"Nothin's changed," Lord Parke insisted.

"It has. It's one thing to steal some small token from some of the older lord's. They give it up in good fun. But when we start stealing because someone is asking for a particular item, then that is another matter."

A hanging offense, Brayden thought, but still said nothing.

"What do you think, Dere? After all, it was Nigel who changed the group the most. Do we go with his plans or do we follow as we intended?"

Brayden shifted his weight in his saddle. Definitely as they intended, was his thought, but going in the manner

Nigel intended would perhaps give him the clues he needed. "I think this needs more discussion, but certainly not in the rain while the horses grow restless." Not that he really could come up with a time or place.

"Does have a point, there," one of the men said. Brayden could not place the voice and with the man's hat pulled low over his face, it was difficult to determine who it was.

"Shall we meet here tomorrow—when it should be dry?" Lord Parke asked.

"Not up to making a run tonight," Sir Mitchell agreed.

"With the way this rain is coming down, it would be foolish."

In agreement, they each headed their own way.

Brayden met up with Kit some way toward home. "That was the last thing I expected."

"That they would have enough sense to get out of the rain?"

Brayden chuckled at that. "Partly. They have ridden in the rain before, you know."

"True. But I think different things are at stake from what you say. So, do you think that Nigel really was behind the robberies?"

Brayden tightened his lips. He didn't want to think that at all. Even if Kit was his best friend and had known him and Nigel forever, he wasn't ready to condemn his half-brother. He and Nigel had not seen eye-to-eye on many things, but perhaps blood was thicker than water.

"Nigel seems to have had quite a bit in common with Collin," was all that Brayden could get himself to admit. That was certainly appearing to be true enough. And who knows, perhaps he would have been in the same situation as Jane. Although at the rate he was going in discovering the artifact, he still might end up with nothing.

"Tell me again why Prinny is so intent on finding this particular artifact," Kit asked him later as they shared a glass of port at his Town house.

"Why this Indian prince suddenly needs to have the item accounted for is beyond my knowledge. You would think if you gave something to someone, that was it; it would no longer be your responsibility. Suddenly, Prinny needs it."

"Typical."

"Actually, I think Prinny learned that Nigel was somehow involved and sees it as an easy way to get his hands on some property. From things Liverpool has said, I got the impression that some prime Lancashire property was promised to someone. Liverpool only hinted there, but it wouldn't surprise me if it were this Indian prince."

Kit shook his head in denial. "He'd have every lord in the realm up in arms."

Brayden laughed at that. "True. But it has happened before."

"English history and all that rot."

"Hardly rot if you were affected, Kit."

"So, should you just drop a word or two in the ears of certain people and see what happens? Prinny can't afford to alienate anyone else."

"No, he can't. But the fact remains that he can ruin me. Besides, I don't even know if Nigel really is guilty or not."

"You say that as if you think something else is involved."

"I do. I think he's also using me to shut down the Demons. But after tonight, I'm not sure that my role will be necessary. They seem to want to shut down on their own."

"Tomorrow will tell."

Chapter Eight

Jane didn't know what to expect when she met with Brayden. Was a little nervous in fact. What more could he have to say that he hadn't already said the other afternoon? And how in heaven's name did he think she could help him? A question she asked as soon as he closed the door to the library.

"Women like to talk," he told her after inviting her to be seated while he took the chair next to his desk.

She didn't know if she should be affronted by that or not, but apparently that showed in her face because he chuckled.

"No need to be offended, Jane. I'm relying on that."

"You want me to talk to people about something for you?"

"It may come to that, but for now, I want you to listen to what some of the other women tell you. To show how fair I am, I will also tell you that many men like to talk, especially to pretty women."

She felt the heat creep along the back of her neck. Was he saying that she was pretty? He had said so before, but she didn't believe him then and didn't now.

"What am I to listen for?"

After swearing her to silence and keeping her own counsel, sharing only with him or Kit, not even Arabella, he told her.

"There are certain men who are stealing small artifacts from different great houses through the ton."

"You've had something stolen?" Was he blaming her? It didn't sound like it, but you couldn't be too careful when you were in the position she was.

"Not exactly. I'm helping someone recover what was stolen from them."

"How can I possibly help? I don't know anyone or what items were stolen."

"I'm counting on the fact that you don't know anyone to help. Someone may tell you they have it, and you will know to tell me, and I can see if it really is the item I'm looking for."

Briefly, he described what he knew of the statue for her, giving her rough dimensions as he understood them, since he had the disadvantage of not seeing the statue either.

Finally, she nodded. "I think I can do this."

"It won't be difficult, Jane. I just want you to keep your ears open, be alert. You never know when someone will say something."

"First I would have to have someone interested enough to speak," she told him, her tone wry.

Brayden shook his head. "You do not see your potential, Jane. I am sure that once you are dressed the way you should be, every buck in town will be aware of it. I'll find it hard pressed to get anywhere near you."

She giggled at that, but realizing the conversation was over, she stood, dropped a quick curtsy and left. Suddenly, life seemed to be an adventure. One that continued the next day as Arabella insisted on fittings and fingering every length of material in the shop; holding different ones up in different lights as she waited for Jane to be measured.

When Jane joined her, they sat down to look at the variety of sketches Madame Celeste had available, as well as some of the journals in from France that had more current sketches.

"Jane, this would look lovely made up in the green velvet," Arabella said, holding a sketch of a riding habit Jane would love to have. Except she didn't ride. Which is what she told her friend who quickly dropped that sketch and picked up two others with day dresses and walking ensembles.

Jane studied them critically. They were beautiful, no doubt there, but they also looked frightfully expensive. In spite of what Lord Raby had said, she did have an eye to what would be suitable when she left. Sighing, she placed both of them on the table and reached for a much plainer gown. "Perhaps this is a dark blue," she said to Madame.

Arabella snatched it out of her hand before Madame could take hold of it. "Absolutely not! Try this one," she said and pushed another sketch into her hands. This was more elaborate than the first, and Jane said so.

"Then stick with the first one, " Arabella said, "But on no account are you getting this one," she said about the plainest one.

Madame removed the offending sketch. It was clear who was in charge.

Jane looked over Arabella's dress "The other one would serve me well," she said quietly.

"And this one," she shoved the sketch in her hand, "will serve you better."

Finally acquiescing, Jane accepted Arabella's orders. There was no other way to consider them.

When they exited the shop, it was some time later and Jane was tired, thirsty and cross. Not a good combination, even if she had been all of those before.

"I think it's time for tea," Arabella said. She looked about for their driver.

"I would love to, but I truly must ask you make another stop."

"That's no problem, Jane. Tell me what you need."

"I would like to get a new sketch book and perhaps a sweet for the girls."

Arabella looked at her and nodded.

"I had not even thought such a thing," Arabella told her brother later as she gave him an estimate of the bill.

He shrugged in response. "Why didn't you let her buy her sisters something more?"

Arabella laughed. *"Let,* Brayden? She counted out her own small bits of coins. She refused to take anything more." She tilted her head to one side as she stood there watching her brother leaning back in his desk chair. "She seems to think that the only reason she has for doing this is because she owes you something."

"No, she doesn't owe me anything, but she has agreed to help me with a problem."

"Something I can help with?"

At her brother's surprised look, she straightened. "Brayden, I know you think I'm a widgeon, but really, I would do anything to help you any way I can. I didn't even know you needed help."

How could she, he reflected. He hadn't told anyone. "Perhaps, but I think Jane is in a better position to do so." He caught the surprised look on his sister's face. He hadn't meant to call her by her Christian name, but that was the way he thought of her. That's what he called her.

"But I'm your sister."

Brayden stood, leaning on the back of the chair. "That's precisely the problem, Bella. Everyone knows you're my sister. Because of that most men are very careful about what they say to you, because they know they will ultimately have to deal with me."

"Jane has no one to protect herself."

"Her brother," Brayden said. "I'm sure anyone would be answerable to him whenever he makes his appearance. But in the meantime, the point is that no one will have any of their facts checked—to their knowledge."

"Brayden, you know as well as I that most men will not be paying much attention to her. She has no dowry and she is not so beautiful that men will be drawn to her."

"You think not?" he said softly. He waved his hand, as if waving away the issue. "No matter. She does have a dowry. Not a great one, but enough to attract some men."

Arabella clasped her hands together in delight. "She did

not tell me! Then why did she refuse to stay?"

"She only recently became aware of it as I went through her brother's papers." He couldn't quite meet her eyes as he said it. No need for her to know differently. "When will the gowns be ready?" he asked her. The sooner he got his plan in motion, the better it would be.

"Madame Celeste promised that she would have one day dress and one evening gown ready by tomorrow evening. Where are we planning to go? I had planned on attending supper at Lady Tull's and then staying since she always has dancing afterwards. It will be a small party though." She cocked her head to one side. "Didn't you already accept?"

"I did, but that was before I planned the house party. You did send the invitations?"

"Of course I did. In fact, we have already received responses. Everyone is quite looking forward to it." She clasped her hands, then released them with a loud sigh. "I didn't think of it until after, but would you mind terribly if we added a few more to the list?"

"Bella, you can invite whomever you want. But remember they do not all have to stay. There will be other activities. I thought you already had those planned."

"Oh I do, Brayd. Everything is in order. But I just had the most marvelous idea." She walked closer to the desk and leaned her hands on it so that she was quite close to her brother. "Kit—Viscount Hulton—has some friends who would be wonderful partners for Jane. I think we should invite them."

He felt himself nodding agreement and watched numbly as his sister spun away from the desk and set about her task. Prospective husbands for Jane? That's what his sister meant. He wasn't sure he liked that idea at all.

* * *

Jane had made an early night of it. Brayden had gone to

his club and stayed there for dinner, leaving the two women alone. After visiting with her sisters, she headed to bed herself. She never would have thought the past several days of shopping and fittings could be so tiring, but she found them so. Before falling asleep, she had a better understanding of why Collin often complained of being tired. She did wonder where he was. In spite of his negligence, he was her brother. It didn't matter what Brayden—Lord Raby—thought. She knew that as the eldest it was her job to care for him as well as the little ones. Yet, she couldn't see searching about for a grown man, especially one who might not appreciate being found.

Early to bed meant she was early to rise, even earlier than her usual time, before the sun even thought of making an appearance. Deciding that fresh air would be welcome, she slipped into the old clothes she had kept. They had been Collin's when he had been much younger. They were loose on her and suited her just fine. She often wore them when she would go down to the docks and to the markets early in the morning when she lived at home. In spite of the vastly improved lifestyle she shared at Bray...Lord Raby's, she realized she missed some of the constant activity and exchanges.

Once her transformation from girl to young lad was complete, she took her sketchbook and made her way outdoors. She had to be quiet and make sure she used the main entrance, for the servant's entrance would soon be busy as they went about their work and coming to the house and leaving on errands. She nearly stopped in fright thinking someone might see her once she was on the docks, too. Calling herself foolish, she continued on her path.

Long before the docks were in sight she could hear the men calling to each other in their loud voices, or at least voices that sounded loud in the quiet air. She made her way down to the line of trunks piled high and hid behind them, deciding exactly where she wanted to go next.

From her vantage point she could see the different ships. Some of the wares from each were quite evident. In the past, she had seen ships back from America, India and even from the orient. Those were fascinating. Today didn't appear to be anything out of the ordinary. Choosing one of the smaller ships, she opened her sketchbook and made her way closer to the ship. She sat on the ground close to several of the piled up barrels, where she would go unnoticed, and started to sketch. The damp from the river seeped into her clothes, but that was not unusual or bothersome. She did notice when the sun rose and it began to get hotter. With a snap, she closed her book, tucked her charcoals in her pockets and sprinted for Raby House where she was able to slip inside the house through the servant's entrance this time, and made it to her room without mishap.

After breakfast, Jane and Arabella joined the girls in the garden for a game of lawn bowling. Brayden finished his accounts and looked about the house, wondering why it was so silent. After being directed to the girls, he joined them in the garden.

"May I join you?" he asked Arabella.

"We're still waiting for Miranda," his sister said. "Why don't you take her place until she gets here?"

He didn't wait for a second invite, but set the pins and joined his sister and Jane at the other end of the court.

"I'll start," Arabella stated to absolutely no one's surprise.

"You have to watch her," Brayden leaned over and said to Jane in a sotto voice, "She'll cheat through the game, just to make sure she's won."

"I heard that," Arabella said as she eyed up the pins before sending her ball down the court. "And I don't cheat." She watched her ball and gave a grunt of disappointment when she only managed to knock over two of the pins. "See what you made me do," she rounded on him, though she was smiling as she said it. She joined him and Jane as they waited for the younger girls to take their turns. None of them managed to knock over more than five pins each.

"Tell me what to do," Evangeline insisted when it was her turn. "Please, Uncle Brayden. I want to beat you," she said candidly.

Brayden let out a bellow of laughter. "I believe you can, too. But I think the best person to talk to would be your sister."

Evangeline looked at him in surprise. "Jane doesn't know how to play either."

"I stand corrected. Then you had best ask Arabella since she manages to beat everyone nearly all of the time."

He turned to Jane as the other girls took their turn. "Do you really not know how to play?"

"I do not make up stories."

"I didn't think that you did. But I know that Collin's house has gardens along the back, so naturally I thought you would have done so."

"The back garden is mostly flowers," she told him. "A vegetable patch and a small place for some fruit."

"I hadn't realized..."

"Aside from that, I would imagine that you need to have some room to play the game. This space is larger than Collin's...was."

"Would you like to learn to play? The game is simple."

"So your sister assured me or I would not be here." She smiled up at him. She could tell that he was trying to be kind. He had no way of knowing how very different their circumstances truly were. He had probably learned to play on his estate and merely transported the game here.

"While the game is simple, I have to warn you that the strategy can be formidable."

"I thought it was a simple game."

"No game is simple. How do you think Arabella always wins?"

"I thought you were joking."

"Not by much," he said wryly.

"First, the object is to knock over all of the pins, or failing that, as many as you can." He stood in front of her and demonstrated. She had no complaints. He really was a very good looking man, and in his shirt sleeves he seemed especially approachable.

She demonstrated for him, and he told her to stop. "You have to stand with your feet apart a bit," he told her. "You need to balance before you throw the ball."

"Like this?" she moved her feet slightly apart, but even she could tell that she seemed too tense. She knew her arm would not have that graceful swing that she had witnessed in nearly everyone else's save the youngest there.

Brayden came to stand behind her. He reached out to put his hand on hers and stopped at the sound of her indrawn breath. "Excuse me," he said formally, and stepped back.

From a few feet away, he gave her verbal instructions again, and this time she did slightly better. They played for only a short time before Miranda came tearing out of the house to take her uncle's place.

* * *

What had gotten into him? Brayden poured himself a scotch when he got back to his study. He had nearly wrapped his arms around her! Outside! He did not miss the look his sister shot his way, but even that had not been enough to stop him. It barely registered. What did register was the way Jane had quickly drawn her breath, In fear that he would touch her? He tossed back a good portion of his drink. At least he would not be seated next to her at dinner tonight, and unless he had a reason to stay, he planned on leaving before the dancing.

It was a nice thought, but not one that came to fruition. Dinner was bearable. He was right, he was not seated next to her, but from where he sat, he could see Kit sitting to her left and Nathan to her right. He ground his teeth in frustration as he did his best to pretend that he was listening to Lady Jenkins. Once in a while the woman paused long enough that he could speak to Miss Bailey on his other side. He could feel Arabella watching him. He never saw if Jane ever looked his way.

After dinner was slightly better. As the women withdrew, the men poured their port and lit their cigars. Brayden was tempted to do neither. He didn't care for the smoke and he probably had more port than he should have had today, but he had to do something. Port seemed the lesser of two evils.

He was conversing with Kit, but heard Jane's name mentioned. It would have been amusing to hear how her dowry had grown, if he were not so aggravated by it all. Kit seemed to sense it, and encouraged him to talk about almost anything else except the women in his household, even though he knew that was not entirely fair. Kit did like to hear about Arabella, not that she would stop to talk to him at all, but that never stopped the other man from wishing she would, and Brayden knew it.

Ready to make his excuses, his host decided that they had left the women alone long enough. Brayden silently agreed. Why in heaven's name did he want to sit here with the men he liked, and disliked, when the woman he wanted to be with was in the other room?

By the time he made it to the salon, he found Nathan sitting on the sofa next to Jane. He looked much too interested for his peace of mind.

Jane stifled another yawn and fingered the material of her dress. She owed this to Brayden—Lord Raby. All he had asked in payment was that she listen to what the men had to say. Suddenly, Nathan had her complete attention.

"I didn't realize that you owned ships, my lord."

"Not many people are in favor of it, you understand. Smacks too much of trade."

"There is nothing wrong with trade, from my point of view, so rest easy."

He gave her a grateful smile. She had to wonder what the people of the ton thought was so horrible about trade. She was beginning to understand Brayden's horror when he found her at the factory. If they thought that of trade what would they think of factory workers? No wonder he had tried to protect her. From her own folly, she didn't doubt.

"Have you ever gone to any of the ports of call?"

"No, that would be too much for my family to bear. It is enough that I get reports from my captains and get to see first hand the wonders that they bring back with them."

"You mean spices and such?" She couldn't imagine anything else. Until she entered Brayden's life she really didn't even know there was anything else other than what was found in the market stalls in Manchester. And she really seldom looked there since she never had the coin to spend should something appeal to her.

"It sounds adventurous," she said after he described some of the ships.

"The most interesting has to be when they come from India or the Orient. The things that one finds is astounding!"

Perhaps he was one of the people Brayden would be interested in. She would have to encourage him to talk even more, but that was not to be. One of the other men came to join their small circle. Before they were interrupted though, Nathan quickly asked permission to stop by the next morning. Of course it was granted.

After that, there was little time to speak to anyone quietly. Arabella joined the group too and informed her that the musicians were set up and they would all be making their way into the ballroom.

Kit appeared next to Arabella and offered to escort Jane into the room. Arabella stared at him in surprise. "Your brother will do the honors," he told her, whisking Jane off.

"That was most unkind, sir" she told him.

"Do you think so? I assure you that in a few minutes Miss Arabella will be hard put to recall that I was even in the room with her."

Jane picked up a bitter note in his voice and instinctively laid her hand on his arm for a quick squeeze. "I think you underestimate the lady."

"Thank you." Kit squeezed her fingers in turn.

Jane found that being in the ball as a properly escorted young woman and knowing that she was a guest was vastly different from her last attendance, and she had thought that one was beyond grand. Now she knew it was the merest hint of what really could have been hers if Collin had shared his interests with her, if he had acted differently from their father. She knew she should be sorry that he was not there, but all she could think of was that she hoped he stayed away for some time. She immediately realized that was foolish, because she would not be staying in her current place just because he was gone, but it was a nice dream all the same. As soon as Brayden found what he needed, she would not be necessary, if she even was so now. She was aware of that, but she also knew she would do whatever she could to ensure he got the answers he needed. She could not be fair any other way. Heaven knew she would not be able to pay him back in coin for all that he had done for her, and proposed to do for her sisters. That he would keep them for several years defied anything she could have imagined. No, she would do her best to help.

* * *

The next morning, she was greeted by several bouquets of flowers in the front hall as she went to breakfast.

"These are beautiful," she said to Arabella as the other woman read the cards.

"Any you like in particular?" she casually asked.

"Any! They're all so lovely. I especially like this one," she said, pointing to one of the smaller nosegays with spice scented white carnations in the mixture.

"That's good," Arabella told her, "because it's for you, as is this one, and this one, and this one," she said pointing to three of the other bouquets. Some were quite large.

Jane's eyes widened in surprise. "Whatever for? It's not my birthday even."

It was Arabella's turn to stare. "I imagine they are from the men that you met last night. That's one of the ways they send tokens of affection."

"Truly?" Jane was totally unaware of such a thing. "But they are so costly."

"True. But it means you are worth it to them, Jane. Honest." She plucked the cards from the bouquets and sorted them out, the four she gave to Jane and the rest she kept for herself.

"Do you always receive so many?" Jane asked as they walked to the breakfast room where they were greeted by Brayden.

He had overheard the remark evidently. "The flowers? Bella manages to capture quite a few every night. I'm surprised you haven't seen them before today."

She didn't bother to tell them that she would breakfast alone, and then scurry out of the way until much later in the day when she knew the girls would be about or Arabella had something in particular for her to do.

"Jane spends a lot of time in the nursery," Arabella told him, while pouring her tea.

Brayden raised his eyebrows at that. "Why ever would you? You are welcome to bring the girls down any time you want. It's not as if they have to stay in the nursery." He put his paper down. "Good heavens. Is that what you thought?"

At her slight nod he really did look perplexed. "No wonder it has been so quiet around here. We'd better bring them down immediately, else Anne will hear of it and roast me alive."

Arabella put up a warning hand. "Please, Brayden, let me finish my breakfast in peace."

He leaned back in his chair. "So that's the reason they're really still up in the nursery? Minx," he said without heat and returned to his paper. After another moment, he sighed and put it down again.

"Do bring them down as soon as you're finished, Bella. Remember that we leave for Raby Hall this afternoon. I have already informed the staff."

"It will be good to be home, won't it Brayd?"

He answered her, but was looking at Jane. What would it be like to have her in his home?

Jane wore a puzzled expression. "I thought this was your home?"

"When Brayd, well when any of us have to come to town, it is, but our real home is Raby Hall. We all grew up there, Jane. You'll love it."

This house was already grand enough,; she couldn't imagine owning another.

"Once everyone arrives—" she stopped herself and turned to her brother—"You did remember to invite Mr. Burke and the others, didn't you?" She allowed him a moment for a brief nod before she continued. "Jane and I will spend the rest of the morning packing. We'll be ready." She took a sip of her coffee. "You know, Brayd, this is the best idea you've had in ages."

"Really? I'll have to tell Kit. He's the one who suggested it."

"Tell me what?" Kit said as he strolled into the breakfast room. "I just love being a friend of the family; never know what you'll hear when you wander about."

Brayden gave a bark of laughter, but noted the way his sister's gaze followed Kit about the room. That was good as far as his friend was concerned.

* * *

The morning was one of constant motion, but they made

it to the carriage in the time that Brayden planned to leave. The young girls, their governess and nanny all traveled in the large coach and started out as soon as everything was packed since it was a slower moving vehicle. Brayden, Jane and Arabella followed in the lighter carriage, and all of the luggage was piled into another and would make its way along to the Hall. After seeing them into their conveyances, Kit assured them that he would meet up with them later than evening.

Arabella had told her that the trip was not a long one, no more than two hours, just enough time for her to get a nap in.

* * *

Jane could not imagine how Arabella could sleep instead of watching the passing countryside. It was a different world from what she had known. It was vastly different from the park. She would have liked to talk to someone about it, but Lord Raby would think her foolish, and Arabella was asleep. She gave a sigh.

"Are you tired, Jane?"

She looked at him, startled. Why would he think that? "No, my lord. I merely wondered if you had any word on Collin yet."

"Not much, I'm afraid, or I certainly would have shared it with you, Jane."

Jane tried not to start at the familiar use of her name when his sister was about. It was one thing when they were in the house, but when they were out was another. Evidently Arabella felt the same since she managed to awake in time to hear him. Jane had no trouble interpreting the look that she sent Brayden's way. Evidently that had little effect on him since he merely smiled in her direction. Jane was very much afraid that being in Brayden's close company for so much of the day played havoc with her senses, even when he was not trying to charm her. That was not a good thing. The more she learned about the man, the more she liked about him, and the more she realized they moved in totally different spheres. She couldn't tell him, but she was beginning to think that she was attracted enough that it could cause her some uncomfortable moments if she stayed. She should think of leaving. She hadn't given any serious consideration to the matter since he asked for her assistance. So far, that has been scarce indeed. Then she fingered the fabric of her dress and knew that the truly feminine side of her would not allow her to do that. She enjoyed where she was too much.

"We have been looking," he assured her, and she had to blink to recall what question of hers he was answering. "With the help of your sketches, we have been able to post some at the ports down by the dock, and I do have a man there who takes care to show the likeness to any of the new captains who come in."

At the mention of ships, she turned to Brayden and leaning a little closer told him that she did have to talk to him soon.

Arabella watched with narrowed eyes and Jane had the feeling that the girl suspected that there was more going on between her and her brother than she liked. She would have to take care to explain to Arabella that there was nothing, merely that this was how she was assisting Brayden.

After that exchange, Jane went back to staring out of the carriage window. Brayden broke the silence nearly half an hour later stating that they were now on Raby grounds. There was no mistaking the pride in his voice. It was another fifteen minutes before the drive came into view, then the house itself. It took Jane's breath away.

The house was the solid stone of the area and rose four levels that she could tell. The windows reflected the afternoon sun.

"Welcome to Raby Hall," Brayden said quietly.

"It's magnificent, Brayden," she said.

She didn't seem to notice that his name had slipped out,

and Brayden hid his smile. It sounded delightful. He certainly wasn't going to remind her. He reached out a hand and shook his sister's arm. "We're home, Bella."

* * *

While the outside was magnificent, Jane had no words to describe the interior. Her gaze moved from one costly item to the next. Everything was in good taste, or at least to her taste, and nothing was out of place. She did her best not to gawk, but it was difficult. After being introduced to the maid who would assist her and Arabella, she didn't know what to think. The woman's dress was more luxurious than what she had worn as she lived with Collin. No wonder Brayden—Lord Raby—insisted on her getting a new wardrobe.

The evening passed quickly, between getting the younger girls settled, the arrival of Kit, and dinner. Tomorrow, brother and sister assured her, there would be much more activity as their guests arrived.

The next morning was a dry one and Jane again found herself up earlier than most in the household. She repeated her exercise of sneaking out as she had done the other morning, but now she had a whole new area to explore. They had passed the village on the way in, so she was confident that he could find it. This early in the morning not many people paid her much attention, and she found that she could sketch all she desired. The village people cast a glance or two in her direction, but no one bothered her.

As she made her way home, even though she knew she was going to have to stop thinking of Brayden' house as 'home', she spotted him out for a morning ride. He must have been near the end of it because he was walking his horse, heading for the stables. If she continued on her path, she would surely run into him. Thinking of what to do, she scurried around the side garden to not be seen—at least by him. The gardener was out and asking what she was doing.

Masking her voice and making up tales, she managed to get out of his sight and into the kitchen, From there, she made her way up the servants' stairs and into her room. Only then was she able to take a deep breath.

Chapter Nine

Brayden threw his cards on the table. Another win. That wasn't a problem as far as he was concerned and in this case it might be better than he actually won. What he wanted was information and that seemed to be in very short supply.

He did not particularly want to come to join the card party, but that would truly be bad form since he was the host. A few hands and then he could join the women in the ballroom. On some level, he knew that Jane appearing increasingly attractive to him should be a problem, but he couldn't think of why that should be. Tonight she looked lovely. Her excitement at being at Raby House had not diminished, and tonight's assembly had her glowing with anticipation.

Kit tapped him on the shoulder, asking if he was ready to leave the table. Brayden shook his head. "Another hand at least." He indicated the pot of chips in front of him. "As you can see, it would be impolite to leave without giving these gentlemen a chance to win back some of their money."

"Go 'way, Kit," one of the older men told him. "Dere is right; we need to win our money."

Brayden was half-afraid of what they would do if they had indeed lost it all. More than half of the men at the table were Demon riders. Of them, they were the group that were most likely to want to continue to raid the homes and look for items of value, not sport. He had purposely added to his house collection and left various artifacts on display. He could only hope someone found something worth stealing.

A little over an hour later, Brayden met Kit in the foyer. "Hope the wait was worth it," Kit greeted.

"It was." How could Kit think that he had wanted to be

there any longer than he had been? He started walking toward the library and indicated Kit should follow him.

Once inside the room, Brayden told him what he had learned. "Probably the most interesting is that Robinson also wants Worsley's house."

"Why do you say that? And what could he want with it?"

"That seems to be the question. I would love to find out. He was trying to get Morris to pony it up."

Kit gave a bark of laughter. "You're serious?"

"Entirely. I think it may be time to pay Morris another visit."

Kit leaned against the desk, watching Brayden pace the room. "It can't have escaped your notice that Morris is here."

"Not at all. I plan to use that to my advantage."

"Just so I have this straight, you plan to visit him while he's visiting you?"

"Something along that line," Brayden agreed, "But first, I need some answers from Jane. I want to know why someone would be interested."

"Do you think that Collin really was behind it? That would be nigh impossible. I wasn't friends with the man, but I knew him. Ran into him at all of the clubs, events and so on. He's totally hare-brained. If he hadn't lost that house to Morris it would have undoubtedly been someone else. Soon."

Brayden stood in front of his friend and nodded in agreement. "Jane has said very much the same thing. I just wondered if someone set Collin up to lose."

"I can't see it. The man didn't appear to need any help in foolishness."

"True, but there must be some reason everyone is interested. Consider that the house is not in a wonderful section. It's not bad. Genteel, but definitely not the most desirable neighborhood."

"You wanted the house, too," Kit pointed out, "and you already have several. So what does that say?"

Brayden gave him a tight smile. "But I didn't want

Collin's house. We just decided that it would be best if Morris didn't have it, didn't we?"

Kit had to admit to his part in it. That much was true.

"So why would he want it?"

"I simply don't know. And nothing I've discovered from Jane at this point suggests that she knows. Collin has lived a very quiet life. It would be best if I could find him and shake the answers from that dunderhead brain of his."

Kit laughed. "I can see you're taking this to heart."

Brayden turned a cold glare on him. "Wouldn't you?" When his friend didn't answer, he continued. "We also know that for whatever reason Nigel did not encourage Collin to join the group and the man seems to have wanted to. I have no clue why."

"Since we're not coming up with the answers here, I suggest we join the party in the ballroom."

Brayden shot a grin his way and headed for the doors. He wouldn't mind a match between his sister and his best friend, but they did have to spend time together before that happened.

Once the men entered, they took a moment to look around and get their bearings as they looked for the women. Brayden greeted many of them while searching for Jane. He spotted Arabella on the dance floor, but of Jane there was no sighting. If she were hiding behind a plant again he was going to have to drag her out, forcefully this time. The woman was going to drive him mad.

Kit poked him in the shoulder. "Isn't that Lady Jane talking to Burke?"

Brayden's glance slid over the couple, then abruptly came back to rest on the woman. Demme if it wasn't his Jane. "She looks different," he said.

"Of course she does. One does clean up for a ball, you know. I daresay *you* even look better than normal."

That wasn't what Brayden meant, but he was too taken with Jane and making his way to her side to care about correcting Kit.

Jane did look different. She looked exactly the way he constantly pictured her. He had been able to see the real her without all of the trappings, but for the men around her, it was as if they spotted the caterpillar turned into a butterfly.

He came up behind her, just standing there, waiting for the other men to acknowledge him, or better yet, go away.

She didn't turn to greet him. So he leaned close to say hello.

She turned her head, not realizing how close he was. He could have captured her lips with no trouble at all. As if she realized his thought, she quickly turned her head to face the other men in front of her.

"I'm here to claim my dance," he told her, still talking to the back of her head.

"You're mistaken there, Dere. She's promised to me for the next set."

Brayden looked at him, letting his gaze slowly travel from the man's eyes down to the toes of his dance slippers. "Really?"

"Really?" This time one of his friends spoke up. "And after that, she is promised to me."

Brayden raised his eyebrow in a question. So his Jane was popular. He wasn't very happy about that, though he could see that she had few, if any, qualms. Tugging at her dance card hanging from her wrist, he studied it for a moment, then scribbled his name down in two spots. He took care to scratch out the first gentleman as he put himself down for the supper dance and the last dance. Two of the men were staring at him with open hostility. He touched her arm lightly and said that he would see her later, before heading off to the card room.

Two of the riders were still present. They acknowledged him with slight nods and encouraged him to play.

"I'm promised for a few dances," he told them, "but I would be delighted to stay until it's time for me to claim my partner."

They nodded in turn and invited him to pull up a chair. Since he had already done so, it was a moot point.

In quiet tones, they continued their discussion from the other evening. "What do you say, Dere? It's your group."

How convenient for it to be his group when something came up. "I know what I believe. I want to know where you fit in. Are you wanting to continue?"

"Don't know that I want to risk Newgate or having my neck stretched."

"A valid point," Brayden said. One he agreed with whole heartedly, but he couldn't say that at this time. These men did not appear to be out for gain from their exploits. That made him feel somewhat better.

"Heard you were trying to win Collin's house," the other man said.

"That's not quite correct," Brayden said. "I was in the original game before Worsley decided to throw the house in. Now I find that several people seem quite interested in getting the house from Morris." He didn't mention that most of them were from this small group.

When he heard the strain of music he knew would be the supper dance, he excused himself from the small group. He hoped that Jane knew he would be there, even if it were not as early as he had planned.

"Did you think I wouldn't appear?" he asked as the set formed.

"I do have other partners, you know."

He gave her a mock growl, and she giggled in response.

He really didn't need a reminder. He was well aware that he was the one who scratched out the man's name and took his place. He would do it again if he needed to.

As they moved through the set, their talking was kept at a minimum, but he could look at her all he wanted, and how he wanted. The candlelight gave her already translucent skin a pearly glow. And the pearls she had woven through her hair as it was piled on her head shimmered in the light.

He knew other men were watching, and he wasn't sure what he thought of that. He was glad that she was with him. He just wished that she would have done so more willingly. Like purposely saved a dance for him, he mocked himself.

"I see you have been practicing your dancing," he told her.

"Is it so obvious? I still do not know if I have it correct," she told him as she passed by him again.

He gave her a smile filled with warmth. "You do it wonderfully. I was watching you earlier. I could see how effortlessly you moved."

She blushed at his words, then moved from his side. He wondered if he had embarrassed her. Because he had been watching?

"I see no reason to tell you something that is not so," he told her. That much was true. From the first moment he met her he had been more forthright with her than anyone else, ever. Perhaps Kit was the only one who could come close.

"Your sister looks lovely tonight," she told him as they joined for the next steps, their gloved fingers touching. "Not that she doesn't always. She enjoyed being with Lord Kit and it shows."

Brayden found himself distracted by her words. He would have rather kept looking at her, but now he did give his attention to his sister and his friend. He knew how Kit felt, but he wondered about his sister. He would question Arabella. He didn't like the thought that she would tease the man.

Something of that must have shown in his face because Jane commented on it. "You must not quiz your sister. She will know I have said something to you and will be embarrassed."

"Arabella?" He couldn't keep the surprise out of his voice.

"Yes, Arabella. Sisters do get embarrassed by their brother's behavior."

That gave him something to think about as they continued on their way about the floor. He was sure she was mistaken. Arabella was never embarrassed by anything. She often was the cause of it though. As for Jane, he suspected that she had more than her fair share of embarrassments. This was probably the latest of many that Collin had perpetuated. Hopefully, it was the worst. He was not upset at all about the outcome, but he knew the way he wanted it to play out. Neither Jane nor her brother did. Nor did anyone else for that matter.

As the dance ended, Brayden lead her to the supper room. He quickly found seats for them, and waited to see who else would be joining them. He didn't have long to wait for Arabella and Kit. Now that he could see them without the dancing, he could see that Jane might be absolutely correct. They did seem to have a tendre for each other.

"Aren't you eating?" Arabella asked.

"Of course. We were merely waiting for you," Brayden told her as they made their way to the table lavishly set up with shrimp pasties, Croquettes and sweets.

Jane looked at all of the food with wide eyes. He wasn't certain she would have taken anything, so every so often he made sure to put a tidbit on her plate so that when they had finished going through the line, she had a nice plateful. It didn't quite match his, but fair enough.

Seated again, the foursome talked over the party at length. At least the three of them. Jane sat rather quietly. Brayden sometimes wondered if she were even listening, she had such a pensive look on her face.

It was too much to hope that no one else would join them, just as Brayden felt himself relaxing. He had forgotten how entertaining Arabella could be when on her best behavior.

"Lord Raby, I have been trying to catch you for several days," one young man said as he made his way over to the table.

Brayden greeted him, but felt no need to rise. The young man looked to be a clerk of some kind, and he couldn't imagine what he was doing here at his house. He raised a querying brow to his sister, who just shrugged.

No clerk. He introduced himself and then learned he was a friend of Collin's.

"If I might speak with you, my lord," he addressed Brayden.

Quickly, Brayden excused himself, and the two men wandered toward the terrace doors, but remained inside. "I cannot leave my party for more than a few minutes, Mr. Greenberg," Brayden told him. "You could make an appointment."

"No, that won't be necessary," the man said. "I had heard that you were interested in selling Lord Worsley's town house and I might be interested."

Brayden raised his eyebrows at that. "You heard wrong. I do not have the house. Now, if you'll excuse me." He stepped around the other man, but didn't get too far since the man stopped him, putting his hand on his arm.

"I would like to speak to you on another matter, if I may?"

Brayden studied him from head to toe. It didn't seem the man had any sense. He was sandy-haired with light blue eyes. Otherwise very nondescript, but to have stopped him the way he had showed that he had some backbone. What he said next made Brayden wonder.

"I would like to know when you ride?"

"Most days," Brayden answered him, though he knew that was not the question the man was truly asking; at least he did not think it was.

The man leaned closer to him. "I mean Dere's Demons," he practically whispered.

Brayden wanted to pretend ignorance. Which would be best? "There is no such thing," he told the man. And if he had his way, it would be true sooner rather than later.

"I beg to differ, my lord."

"I must see to my companions," Brayden said and walked away.

The rest of the supper was spent in lighthearted conversation and when the dancing began again, Brayden had to let Jane go, reluctant though he was to do so.

He knew his instincts had been right when he saw Greenberg come up to her for the next dance. Since she did not refuse him, he must have been on her card.

"It is so nice to meet a friend of Collin's," she told him as they followed through the dance. "I seldom had a chance to talk to them. Did you come to the house?"

"Not often, Miss Jane," he said. "In fact, if you would not mind, perhaps we could sit out the rest of this dance."

"Of course." Privately, she thought it rather odd that he would need to sit out the dance right after suppertime, but perhaps he was too polite to say that she was stepping on his feet, though she didn't recall doing so. The man did not have a particularly healthy look about him. Perhaps he was ill and did not want to admit it.

He led her to the terrace doors, and stepped through, leading her. "We won't go far," he assured her. "I just thought a bit of fresh air would be welcome."

She gave him a tepid smile of agreement.

"I really needed to ask you something and am hoping that you can assist me."

"I will do the best I can, sir. Are you not feeling well?"

"No, nothing like that. I'm fine." He indicated that she should sit on one of the benches against the wall of the house, which she did. "I have a favor to ask."

He loomed above her, though when they were standing he did not seem so very much taller. Nor did she like that he was requesting a favor. What did he imagine she could help with? With a growing sense of unease, she listened to him.

"As a great friend of Collin's I would really like to purchase his house. I believe that would alleviate some of your difficulties."

What gentleman would say such a thing? A strange person at that! Even Brayden, when he had told about Morris's winnings had not been so high handed and he had done far more for her than she imagined this man could ever do or more important, desire to do.

"It is not mine to sell," she told him coolly. "That is a matter for you to discuss with Collin." If he did not know that Collin had lost the house in a wager, she was not about to tell him.

He shook his head. "I, and the rest of the ton, already know that the house was lost and that Lord Hawke has won it."

What could she possibly say?

"What I want is for you tell Lord Hawke that he wants to sell it to me. If he does so, then I can give you part of the selling price."

"First, I do not know Lord Hawke." The little she did know from their encounter, she did not want to consider. "Why would you do that? You don't know me."

"But I do know Collin. This would be a favor to him. We might even make arrangements so that you can perhaps earn the house back from me."

She looked at him and made to rise, but found that she could not; he stood too close. She perceived an insult, but wasn't sure. In the next moment, she was positive.

"I would advise you not to say one more word." Brayden's voice floated across the darkness. In the next moment, he had joined them. He held his hand out to Jane. "I believe you owe me this dance."

She nodded, glad to escape the other man. She was equally sure she did not have Brayden down as a dance partner, but she didn't care, regardless of the leashed tension she felt in him.

"Do you want to stay for the remainder of the dance?" he asked once they were inside the room.

"Of course. Why would I not? I am having a lovely time," she insisted. And she would have been if it weren't for the bounder she just finished visiting with.

"Naturally everyone thinks being insulted is part of a lovely time," he said, a sneer evident in his voice.

"Do you believe that is the first insult that I have heard, my lord? I assure you I have heard much worse."

"Directed to yourself?"

"At times." It was difficult, but she managed to look him in the eye. It was the truth, after all. In fact, it was after such incidents that she decided wearing Colllin's old clothes and disguising herself as a male as she made her way around the docks and vegetable sellers. But that was even before she dressed as a maid. In the first early days after her mother's death, she still looked fashionable, and was still young enough that her youth alone brought her many of the crude comments. As the years went by, they became less so, but more sinister in their offerings. That's when the disguise became more of a necessity. She lifted her chin. "It's not as if I am innocent of the way the world works."

He nodded, acquiescing to her words. He held his hand out to her. "So shall we dance the next set?"

"I'm afraid I am promised for the next two," she told him.

"You are having a delightful time, I can tell," he finally said, slowly.

She appreciated the sincerity she heard in his voice. "I am, my lord. I thank you so much for the opportunity."

"You are mistaken. Bella has vouched for you in no uncertain terms. I believe half of the ton is dying to meet this paragon." He smiled down at her.

She could have stayed there forever. He looked pleased with her and she was pleased with him all over again. It seemed each time she saw him she found something new to like about him. Now he had been ready to defend her virtue, as such. Something that Collin would never have bothered with. He would most likely not have even seen it as an insult, but rather as an opportunity for her to further herself.

Her partner came to claim his dance, and she went with him, but her thoughts lingered with Brayden for far longer than they should have. It didn't help matters when she saw him dancing the next set with a tall red-haired woman, lovely to look at, and she also seemed younger than Jane. She also seemed to be on extremely good terms with Brayden. That should serve as a reminder, she told herself, that she was definitely moving in the wrong sphere. People such as Brayden and the red-haired women, Kit and Arabella—they all inhabited a more rarefied section of the ton than she could ever attain, even had hoped to attain when her family was intact. She would have this for her sisters though, and Brayden had promised it. She had no reason to believe he would not follow through with it.

Of course, with the opportunities of a house party, she might have the chance to meet someone who would want to marry her. She knew she would not be in the market of someone wealthy, but even someone who could afford a household would be good. Someone would not only have to care for her sisters, but be willing to set aside some portion so that they would have a dowry. That would help tremendously when they came of age.

With new resolve, she set her mind to trying to find a husband. Perhaps a vicar would be good. She was familiar with hands-on workings and would not be afraid to work with him through the village. Even for him there would be benefits for that would give him more time to study books should that be his desire.

She shared her plan with Arabella later as they stood around between sets, asking her to point out likely candidates.

"There are several good men," she told Jane. "I can think of three that would be wonderful for you. In fact, I made sure that Brayden added them to the guest list."

"They're here?"

"No, Brayd didn't see any reason to invite them to be part of the party staying since they do live close-by. They were invited to all of the events, though."

Brayden had agreed; had invited them. That certainly put her firmly in her place. Strangely enough, while it upset her, it also proved to her that he was a kind man to put himself out to make sure she was cared for.

Arabella's voice brought her back to the present. "They're friends of Kit's and they are amusing men."

"Then what is the problem with them?"

Arabella laughed at her. "Nothing that I can tell. The chief problem is that they seem to be in trade of one kind or another."

"That is nothing to me."

"Exactly. That is why they may work very well. Your title is an old one, after all, so they would be marrying up."

Jane wondered why she did not feel happier about the situation. She refused to let the image of Brayden get in her way. She looked around the room, trying to see where Kit might be standing, but everywhere she looked she seemed to see Brayden and the redhead.

"Are any of them here?" she asked again, as if Bella hadn't just answered her.

"Not tonight. Brayden has no problem inviting them, but some others would never do so."

Jane nodded her head in understanding.

Arabella gasped and covered her mouth with her hand. "I was not thinking, Jane! You will have to find some other men."

"What are you talking about? I haven't found anyone yet."

"No, I mean rather than Kit's friends." She waved her hand up and down, seeming to get more agitated by the moment. "It will never do. There are too many hostesses who will never invite you to one of their balls."

Jane had been growing alarmed, but relaxed when she realized what was worrying her friend.

"Calm down, Arabella. I have not even met the gentlemen, so it may all come to naught. Besides, it doesn't matter if I don't attend these balls. I have never done so before now. I don't imagine it will be much of a hardship to not attend from now on."

"But that is one reason the men will want to marry."

Jane tried to hide her wince at that hit. She knew she was no beauty, no matter how many nice compliments Brayden sent her way, but she had not thought she was a complete antidote either. Besides, before she thought she had nothing of value to barter; now she knew she had her title. It would be good for something.

Arabella patter her on the arm. "That did not come out quite right."

"Never fear, Arabella. It will be fine. When do you think I might meet these men?" She didn't want to say that her time with the Derrington's was growing short, but that would be the case. She wanted to give an inward smile at her own plan. Now she could even hold to Brayden's decrees that she not talk about working when she left. If things worked out, thanks to his generosity and that of his sister, she would not have to work in such a menial capacity again. She would if she had to, but any of the men might be quite pleasing. She had to thank Arabella—and Brayden, for opening her eyes to that fact.

"Do remember to point them out," she managed to say before Arabella was claimed for her dance.

She hadn't realized it was the final dance of the evening until Brayden came to claim her for their dance.

"You look quite pleased with yourself," he said. "What has my sister been proposing now?"

"A suggestion that I gave to her, and she agreed with, that is all."

They danced mostly in silence, and she was glad to do so.

To be held this way, well she had never realized how suggestive a waltz could be. Not that she had been familiar with many of the dances before she arrived at their house. Let him think she was concentrating on the steps. She was, to an extent.

What she really wanted to do was memorize everything about him, the way he smelled, the way his eyes crinkled in the corners when he smiled. Even the way he managed to look down his straight nose when someone said something he was not particularly pleased with—as long as it was not her. She liked the way his hair managed to fall over his forehead when he was engrossed in something about the house, but tonight, it stayed put. She wondered how he did that, and it saddened her to realize that she most likely would never know.

"You look thoughtful," he murmured. "I hope it is something good."

"It is," she agreed, and gave him a smile that she hoped held some delight in it and did not show how unhappy she was with her decision: Satisfied, but unhappy. Some things could not be helped she thought as he whirled her into the turns of the dance.

At the end of the dance, Arabella and Brayden made their farewells to those who had come for the evening, and their good nights to the guests who were staying. She had agreed to Kit's suggestion of a nightcap, so followed him to the library.

"Several of my friends will be joining us tomorrow evening," Kit said to her as he handed her a glass of sherry.

She looked at him, curious as to why he should mention that.

"Arabella said you might want to know."

She hadn't heard brother and sister enter the room, but suddenly Arabella was beside her, giving her hand a squeeze, but addressing her remarks to Kit.

"That will be marvelous. I have told Jane a bit about

them. I am sure that one of them will suit."

Jane wanted to fall through the floor. Did she have to talk about her as if she weren't there? Or worse yet if she were going to market? It was humiliating. She hoped she wasn't blushing, but from the warmth she felt on her cheeks, that was unlikely. Brayden proved it.

"What have you said to make Jane blush now?" he said from somewhere near her left side.

Arabella turned to face him with a bright smile. "Nothing. She is being sensitive! We have decided the perfect answer is marry Jane off."

She didn't know which was more uncomfortable: the increased heat in her cheeks or Brayden's gaze boring into her. He should not be angry, she thought as she tossed back the rest of her drink defiantly and put the glass on a table.

"If you'll excuse me, I'll say goodnight." She walked past them, head high, not looking at any of them. As soon as she cleared the doorway she felt a hard male hand grab her arm, jerking her to a stop.

"What do you think you are doing?"

Brayden had spun her to face him. Even in the near dark of the hall she could see the sparks of anger shooting from his green eyes.

"My lord?"

He pulled her closer with his one hand, and she used her free hand to push him away. She would be bruised in the morning.

"I thought we were past that?" He practically growled the words into her face. "Who are you thinking of marrying?"

She pushed at him again. "You're hurting me." It wasn't until a whimper escaped her throat that he seemed to realize the crushing hold he had on her arm. Immediately his grasp gentled, but he did not release her. His other hand came up to brush her hair from her face.

"Ah, Jane," he whispered. "I did not mean to frighten you."

"It is all right," she said, but when she moved to pull away from him, he did not release her.

"I have no right to say what you must and must not do, but promise me that you will tell me who you are interested in. I would not like you to make a mistake."

She nodded. So, he would treat her the same as Arabella, that was what he meant by his comment. For that reason, it was all the more surprising when he bent his head and gave her a quick kiss on the lips, then instantly disappeared. That did not feel brotherly to her.

Chapter Ten

"So, what have we found out?" Brayden asked Kit the next day, when they met in his study as planned.

"Not a whole lot. I think we are simply going to have to go over that house nail by nail to see why everyone is interested in it."

Brayden moved to pour them some coffee from the service left on the table and handed a cup to Kit before going back for his own. Both men settled into the winged back chairs facing the fireplace.

"I just cannot picture Collin being intelligent enough to be the mastermind behind this. If a mastermind is involved, and if there is anything at all going on!" Brayden shook his head over the complexity of the sentence he just stated.

Kit chuckled. "Then why else would they want the house? And why all of a sudden?"

"It's not that sudden." Brayden took a sip of his coffee. "It's not all that long since Morris won the house. It's only been a few days since some of the riders have insisted that they need to be split."

"What do you propose to do about that?"

"What do you think I plan to do? I hope the whole bloody mess dissolves itself. Preferably after I find the statue."

"You know, Brayden, I've been thinking about that, and Prinny's involvement."

"Well, that makes two of us, then."

"What if there was no statue?" Kit took a sip of his coffee and watched his friend over the rim of the cup.

"That would make no sense. Why would he send me on a wild goose chase?"

"That's exactly what I'm wondering. And I think perhaps now would be a good time to seek audience with him."

"Audience?" Brayden snorted. "I'd have more luck running into him at an orgy."

Kit put his cup on the saucer and sat up straight in his chair. "Do you really attend those?"

Brayden gave a bark of laughter. "No, I don't."

"Couldn't picture it myself," he said as he settled back in his chair. "So you'll talk to Prinny."

"If I must. Liverpool seems to think that he'll be at Lancaster in the next few days."

"Is he following you?"

"Hell, no. He's undoubtedly checking out the lands around Raby Hall."

Kit started at that. "He must already know the land, his duchy is here."

"He probably knows it quite well. It's the person he plans to give it to who will want to see it." He didn't bother to hide the bitterness in his voice. "All I can do is plead for more time. To answer your earlier question, I do believe there is an artifact, I just can't believe there are no clues."

"But you believe that Nigel is involved."

"Not entirely. I can understand that he would be, but I don't know that he was." He ran his hand down his face. "I guess that's one thing I will never know."

Finishing his coffee, he put the cup on the table between the chairs and stood. "I may as well write and beg for that audience. In the meantime, I think I need to come up with some kind of plan. At the least, one that involves getting into Worsley's house."

"Do count me in," Kit reminded him.

"Naturally."

Brayden went to his desk, wrote the brief note, signed and sanded it. He added the wax and his seal before calling Thomas to ensure that the missive was delivered immediately.

"We shall see what happens now," he told his friend.

Kit had finished his coffee and was slouched in the chair, his feet extended toward the flames, and crossed at the ankles.

"What I am thinking is that perhaps it would be best if Lady Jane joined us in the search at the house. She will surely know where everything is better than we could hope to find it."

Brayden moved from behind the desk to perch on the end of it. He crossed his arms over his chest. He had no doubt Jane knew every nook and cranny, but he wasn't sure he wanted her there on this trip, and he mentioned that to Kit. "Let's see what we discover on our own. The servants are still there so I'm sure they will assist us if we need it."

"When do we go?" Kit was already on his feet as he asked—a motion that caused Brayden to smile. "It looks to me that you're ready now. No reason not to." Brayden called for the carriage to be ready.

"Thought you would prefer to ride."

"I would, but I would also prefer that not everyone know was heading there. After all, I am leaving my own house party, and Morris should be on his way here now."

* * *

The house was much as Brayden had left it those weeks ago. He met with Williams, who confirmed that Morris was indeed on his way to Raby Hall. He encouraged him to talk about when Miss Jane and the little ones lived there.

He was sure Kit wondered why, but he could hardly tell him it was because he hungered to know more about Jane than just to learn anything they might have to say. That talk naturally enough led to Collin and his wicked ways. By then, the men had made their way to the kitchen and joined Williams and the housekeeper in a hot drink. They might have felt uncomfortable entertaining such men in the kitchen, but Brayden assured them that was their preference.

"I understand that he used to have friends by fairly frequently," Brayden finally said to the housekeeper.

"Not frequent-like, m'lord, but some of the ones he did have..." She shook her head in dismay. "Miss Jane and he would get into frightful rows about some of them. And she always made sure those little ones always stayed in the nursery."

Thanking the woman, he said that he and Kit would be in the library discussing matters. "I'm sure Lord Hawke won't mind," he told the servants, "since he is by now availing himself of *my* hospitality." Agreeing, they led them to the room and left.

The matters were not what Kit anticipated, he was sure. "The man was a bounder."

"True," kit said. "But what has you so worked up?"

"How he treated his sisters for a start. Those little girls are the sweetest things—"

"And the older one too?"

Brayden's temper flared as he stared at his friend.

Kit laughed at him and held his hands, palm outward as if to ward him off. "No offense, Brayd. She is sweet."

"Leave it at that."

"I can, but I thought you might be sweet on her too. I think you should be careful until you get this straightened out."

"You can't think she's involved?" His voice was incredulous.

Kit snorted. "Hardly. What I'm saying is that you don't want to be accusing her brother on the one hand, and courting her on the other."

"I'm doing neither!" He practically growled the words at him. He moved around to the working side of the desk and started opening drawers. Not that he knew what he was looking for, but doing something would be better than nothing. After a few minutes of riffling through pages of accounts from one book, he tossed it to Kit.

"Make yourself useful. See if there's anything in there that would make someone want this house."

Kit sank into one of the chairs, but didn't look through the book. "I can do that, but I suspect what you're looking for isn't here. Why would anyone want to buy this house just to look at account books? There are other ways they could obtain them."

"So what are you suggesting?"

"Maybe we should be checking for passages."

"Thumping walls?"

"That would be a start," Kit said, "But I was thinking more along the lines of asking the butler. He's probably been here for years. Or the housekeeper."

Brayden stared at his friend for a moment, then started laughing. "That would be the sensible thing to do."

Sensible, but not particularly productive. The housekeeper agreed to take them through each of the rooms, the attics and the cellars, as soon as she understood that they were helping Miss Jane more than offending Lord Hawke. There were small rooms that Kit thought had potential for investigation, but they did not interest Brayden nearly as much as the rooms the girls had. The twins' room was charming. A little bare, but it had nice counterpanes, with matching curtains. There were several dolls and stuffed animals about. He swallowed hard when he saw them. "Wonder why they didn't take them," he said aloud.

"They couldn't," Kit said. "They belong to Morris, remember?"

"Quit saying that," Brayden said. "Do you think the man would miss something like toys?"

"Then why don't you bring some of these things back for them. Better yet, why don't you bring them over and let them collect them?"

Brayden leaned against the doorframe, looking at his friend. "That's a really good idea. Why didn't you suggest it when we were already in town?"

Kit looked at him in exasperation. "I was being facetious."

"But it's a wonderful idea. Except that it would have to be done tomorrow at the latest while Morris is still at my house."

"Speaking of such, shouldn't you be there?"

"I'm good until this evening. Arabella has everything under control and activities planned to the minute." He watched the expression on Kit's face. "Oh, you want to be there." Brayden straightened. "Tell you what, let's pick something from the girls' room, search around a bit more and leave it at that." He wasn't entirely comfortable in looking about the house anyway.

Sending Kit to tell Williams of their plans, he took the stairs two at a time. He stopped in the girls' room and picked up a doll similar to the one he often saw Evangeline with, and two small stuffed rag babies, and a battered copy of Pilgrim's Progress. He looked in the armoire to see if there were any clothes he could bring them. Nothing. Could Morris have already cleaned them out? He didn't think so. He was more inclined to think they really had taken everything with them when they left. He was no longer sure how much he wanted to catch up with Collin. He needed him to settle his own affairs, but his shabby treatment of his sisters showed him to be a real cad.

Setting his finds on the floor in front of their room, he set off to finish exploring the upstairs and attics.

Kit passed him on the landing as he headed for the attic and Brayden went to the other bedrooms. Collin's room looked not much different from his own room. Perhaps not as opulent, but similar. He pushed aside the curtains to check the view. Opening the drawers of the dresser showed that there were still plenty of clothes within, as did the armoire. Which meant that either Collin hadn't gone far or didn't intend to be away for any length of time. Why else would he not need clothes? A question he put to Kit when the man came down from his search.

"Could be planning to buy colours."

"With what?" Brayden asked instinctively, Then stopped. "If he had the artifact, and sold it, it would certainly pay for a nice officer's commission and more besides."

"That would be one answer. Perhaps that is the avenue to search."

Brayden ran his hand through his hair. "Would he join without saying anything to the girls?"

Kit merely shrugged.

He instructed Kit to gather up the few items near the twins' room. "I want to finish looking about, just to see if there is any irregularity in the walls, anything like that. I'll meet you in the hall in a moment."

He wasn't much longer than that. He poked his head into the other rooms as he passed and quickly searched them, running his hands over the walls and mantles. One room held very little indeed, as if the house was not used to receiving guests, which Brayden could well believe. The other room was Jane's. He could still detect traces of her scent in the room. He walked in and stood, looking around.

He was loath to touch anything, but he did. He needed to know, he assured himself.

The dresser yielded few clues and even fewer clothes. The wardrobe held nothing but a cloak. He ran his hand down the length of it, tamping down his anger. How dare Collin have a full wardrobe and dresser of clothes with the finest lace and handwork on them, and his sister have nothing. There was literally nothing. He was sure that what she had when she left was all of her belongings.

There were no knick knacks about, as he often saw in his sister's room, even in the rooms of the women he occasionally visited. There was a candle in a holder near the bed. No rug underfoot. A glance at the bed itself showed him the thinnest of covers was on it. He wondered at that until after searching, he saw the window seat there bore a cushion, covered in the same material as the counterpane in the twins' room. It didn't take long to figure out what had happened here. The question in his mind was how and why had it happened?

With a snort of disgust, he joined Kit in the hall,

thanked the staff, such as they were, and headed home. Now he had more questions than answers; the only discovery, if it could be called that, was a safe under the floor in the library. At any rate, it was something that had been there for some time and not recently added. Besides, it was empty. He checked.

* * *

One of the events Arabella had planned before leaving town was to schedule a musicale at Raby Hall. It was more than Jane had hoped for. Arabella had assured her repeatedly that the gentlemen only attended such things to have a chance to talk to the women. "I'm sure there are one or two who are there for the music, but generally, if they are not married, they are pressed into service to escort a relative. Aside from Kit's friends there must be a half a dozen gentlemen who will be here for a relative."

Before heading down the stairs, Arabella again told her that she looked lovely and the men were the nicest there were.

She discovered the truth of that herself not long after she was there and introduced.

"This was a marvelous idea," she shared with Arabella later that evening as they sat in the library after most of the people had gone. The men she had met tonight showed her that there were other nice men out there. They could not all be Brayden, none of them made her feel the same way he did, but they were nice. She could lead a very contented life with nearly any of them, at least as soon as she could get Brayden out of her mind; she didn't tell Arabella that part. "I cannot believe that it was not something that occurred to me before." She gave a little laugh. "No, I can believe I never before thought of it. I had no means to think or dream of anything."

"That is not true, Jane."

"Very true, I'm afraid," she said. "I cannot count Collin among the most conscientious of brothers. He is nothing like your brother," she pointed out. "He cares for your well being and he looks out for you. That is a wonderful gift."

Arabella sighed. "It is, but sometimes it is quite tiring. After all, he asked you to help him. He didn't ask me."

"He explained his reasons for that, and I agree. The only difficulty is that no one has really said anything to me."

"You've hardly gone out," Arabella said.

"That's not true. There has been entertainment nearly every night this week."

"And you have the flowers to prove it," her friend teased.

"Perhaps it is time that you took one of them up on the offer for a drive or to come calling. I bet you would learn a lot then."

"That is true," Jane agreed. What did it matter that she didn't care for any of them? She would have to learn to do so. After all, this was a two-fold game as far as she could tell. She would help Brayden, she hoped, and in turn, she would meet more young men. Eligible men. But somehow, the idea didn't sound as appealing as it should.

Still, she did as Arabella suggested. It could only work to her benefit in several ways, not least was if she would hear of anything from the gentlemen.

To her surprise, she found that she enjoyed herself more than she thought possible. Perhaps because she knew none of it was real. The men, for whatever reason, seemed to insist they must spend time with her, and she was delighted to let them do so.

She didn't ride, so that left mostly walks about the estate and carriage rides into the countryside. In the evening, Arabella always had something planned.

Lord Parke, Mr. Burke and Mr. Robinson were steady in their attentions. Lord Parke and Mr. Burke seemed to be well acquainted with Collin, and often asked his whereabouts. Even Lord Hawke made it his business to be close by whenever he was not with the men in their shooting, or billiards or other activities. She silently thanked Brayden for keeping him away from her, though she knew that was not his sole intent.

It wasn't until a carriage ride with Lord Parke, perhaps the third time they were out that she heard anything that might be of interest to Brayden.

"Surely Collin would have told you of our adventures," he said to her as the carriage rolled along at a sedate pace through the park.

"I'm afraid not," she insisted. "Collin and I lead very different lives." That was one way to put it rather delicately, she thought. She could hardly tell him the truth that they had been more like master and servant.

"Collin and I were at school together. After that last outrageous bet, it was no wonder he left town."

Didn't he know? "He did, for a time," she told him. She couldn't help but notice how his attention perked after that.

"Do you expect him back any time soon? I do need to catch up with him."

"I'm afraid not."

"Would Dere—Lord Raby—know of his whereabouts? Or Lord Hawke. They were in the last game with him before he left."

She shook her head again. "I'm truly sorry, my lord. You might find more information from the other gentlemen, but if you merely wanted information on Collin, then you are wasting your time talking to me about it." It was interesting to see the way the red crept up his neck to his ears.

"Forgive me if that's what it seemed," he told her. "That was not my intention at all." After driving for a few moments and exchanging trivialities, he turned the horses back to the park entrance.

Before they drew up to the stables at Raby Hall, he spoke of Collin again. "I did not mean to be so heavy-handed," he told her. "It's just that Collin was to hold something for me and I would like to retrieve it."

"I'm afraid I can't help you with that. Perhaps Lord

Hawke..."

He nodded, then stopped the carriage, coming around the side to help her alight after the groom came to hold the horses.

* * *

She dressed with care for dinner. Apparently, Lord Parke was only interested in what information she could give him, and that was none. Perhaps Arabella's plan was not a good one. It all came back to the fact that she had no looks to speak of, although she had seen other men interested in women nearly as plain as herself. She would see what the evening brought. The highlight would be that she would need to speak to Brayden alone for a few moments. Unfortunately, it wouldn't take longer than that to convey the information. She had to admit, after their last meeting, she was a bit apprehensive about meeting with him. Since then they had only shared the slightest pleasantries in rooms full of people.

There was nothing planned for the evening, so after dinner the men joined the women in the drawing room. Card tables had been set up should anyone desire to play, and several of them did. Brayden appeared in a subdued mood, but spent the evening close to his sister or with the other men. There was no opportunity to talk to him. With some encouragement, Arabella sat at the pianoforte and gently played a few songs until Brayden suggested she play something more soothing. Since she was already playing a rather refined tune, Jane couldn't imagine what would be quieter.

"A dirge, perhaps?" she asked him since he was standing close by.

Brayden looked at her sharply and then gave a bark of laughter. "I deserved that," he said as he came to stand near her chair, just as she stood.

"If you'll excuse me," she said. "I have a bit of the

headache and find that I need to be somewhere quiet."

Brayden gave her a curt nod and watched her disappear. It wasn't until Arabella mentioned that Jane had gone for a drive earlier in the day that he wondered if her headache was real or if it was a means to escape his presence. He would find out.

He found her sitting in the library in front of the fire, staring at the flames, although she held a book in her hand, her finger marking her page. He perched on the arm of the chair next to her so that he was quite close.

"Where have you been these past few days?" he asked idly, though his eyes were sharp.

"Here and there," she told him. She turned in her chair to look directly at him. "I realized that I was not being of much help to you, so I thought if I accepted some invitations with some of the gentlemen, I might learn more."

"And did you?"

Again, his voice seemed unconcerned, but she had a feeling the answers meant something to him.

"A bit." If he was going to be reticent, she could be too. It would be a lot easier if he were not sitting so close that she could inhale his scent with every breath. But when he continued to stare at her, she continued. "It turns out that Lord Parke is a friend of Collin's. An old friend." She tilted her head to one side as she looked up at him. "I did not know that, yet he thought I should have."

He shrugged at that. "I'm sure there are other men that Collin knows who are still unknown to you."

Brayden stood. His standing made him seem closer than he had been before. And more intimidating. Quickly, she relayed what Lord Parke had told her, that Collin was holding something of his. She tilted her head to one side, looking up at him. "It doesn't sound right to me. Why would anyone who knew Collin trust him with anything of value?"

Brayden wondered the same thing, but doubted that he and Jane were considering the same item of value. Just looking at her made his heart stop. How could Collin have possibly not cared for her?

"I thought it strange too that he thought Collin *should* have left. That did not surprise him at all." She traced the edges of the book before looking at him again, asking if he had any word of her brother.

"Very little." He walked toward the fireplace, not looking at her as he spoke.

"Has he ever said anything about buying colours?"

Jane gave a little laugh at that, which brought his attention to her. "He always talked about it. First it was for the cavalry, then it was for the dragoons. I'm hard pressed to remember what it was for this time."

"Did he say where he would get the funds?"

Jane shrugged at that. "As you know, he said precious little to me about funds or anything else. I have no idea. I guess I always supposed that he was just talking, not entirely serious about the venture."

"Could he have been serious this time? Is it possible that he has gone to join some regiment or another?"

"I...I suppose it is, my lord, if he had the funds, which as we both know he does not." She thought for a moment, then shook her head. "You know, it is possible. Collin had a small collection of jewelry that he had never wagered and never touched. It's entirely possible that he has cashed them in."

"Jewels?"

Brayden walked back toward her. "A gambling man does not normally hold on to jewels, Jane. Are you certain they were the real thing and not paste?" Why would he hold on to jewels? The last bit was more of a question to himself, but Jane answered him anyway.

"They were to go to his wife."

"That is not enough of a reason for a gambler. And Collin was most definitely a gambler."

It saddened her to hear him say it, but she suspected that it was true. Knew it was true.

She gave a self-depreciating smile at his comment. "You are correct. But my father was a gambler, and I suspect my grandfather before him. One of my great-great-mothers put a 'curse' on the jewels." She shrugged. "The women in my family always referred to them as the Curse. If they were used for a debt of honor, the original owner would be cursed." She smiled up at him. "Pretty effective so far. I can't picture Collin going against it."

Brayden let out a loud laugh. How perfect! If there was one thing a gambler was, it was superstitious.

"The problem is that I would guess the jewels now belong to Lord Hawke, if he finds them."

The laughter quickly died.

"Jane, it pains me to admit this, but I have been to your house. I have gone over every inch of it. There is no place to hide anything."

"I knew you were there," she said softly.

"You did?"

She nearly giggled. He sounded dumbfounded. "Did you think that I wouldn't notice that the girls now had some of their favorite toys with them?" She dared to reach out and give his hand a slight squeeze. She didn't care if it was forward or not. "I am most grateful and have wanted to tell you so."

He heaved a sigh of relief. "I was afraid you would be angry."

"How could I be? That was a great kindness. But there is a place where the jewels are hidden. Any small item really. No one outside of the family is aware of it."

Did he dare to hope that Parke was in the right of it? That Collin had held something for him. "Can you tell me?"

She shook her head. "I wish I could say yes after all of your kindness, but I cannot."

He felt his heart drop. "Jane, it would—"

"It is not that I would no tell you. Merely that telling is not enough. I must show you or you may miss it. But I cannot imagine Lord Hawke letting us in."

He looked at her sharply. "There is something about the way you say his name. What is it? Has he said something to you?"

Chapter Eleven

It wasn't so much as what Lord Hawke had said as the manner he chose to say it, she thought the next morning as she prepared to go to breakfast. There was nothing for her to tell Brayden, so she let the matter go. It helped that Kit had chosen that time to look for his friend. That had been rather humorous, although she could see the potential for disaster.

"I came to make sure you hadn't been caught by one of your houseguests," Kit said when he saw Brayden.

When Brayden moved away to respond, it was quite evident that Jane was also present.

Kit's eyes widened at that. It was the first time she had seen him without a comment ready at his lips. Even Brayden's lips twitched.

Deciding the joke had gone on long enough, Jane stood and faced him, still holding her book. "I was reading when Lord Raby came in," she said, showing him the book. "I merely asked for information on my brother, but we are finished." After bidding them both a goodnight, she left the room.

Fleetingly, she wondered if it had crossed his mind that they had been alone together. She had never thought anything of it until Lord Hulton had come in. Thank goodness it had been him and not someone bent on mischief. Never would she pay back Lord Raby's kindness with such shabby behavior.

Checking that she had enough time to visit the nursery before breakfast, she did so. The girls were delighted to see her. Emily assured her that they had been so busy they hadn't missed her. With the house party, that meant there were several extra children in varying ages. The twins were delighted to have so many playmates.

"I've sketched everyone, Jane," Evangeline told her as she brought her book over to share with her sister.

Jane looked through the pages admiringly. "These are so wonderful, Evangeline," she told her quite honestly. "Perhaps you would like to give them to the families. Or would you like to keep them?"

"Do you think they will laugh, Jane? I shouldn't like that."

Jane gave her sister a hug. "They will love them, I am certain of it."

After Emily came over for her fair share of conversation, Jane told them that she would be back later in the day.

"It's really nice here, Jane," Emily told her. "Are we going to stay here?"

Jane stooped down, skirts billowing about her, so that she was eye-level with her sister. It was important that the girls understand this was not permanent. "No, Emily. The house party is nearly over, so everything will soon go back to normal. That means that I will have to leave. I am not sure, but I think that Lord Raby intends that you will stay here for a while yet. That is one of the things I must discuss with him."

Evangeline wound her arms around Jane's neck. "We want to stay with you!"

Jane hugged both of them. "Sweetheart, we've talked about this before. Now, there is nothing to be sad about. It will not be like the last time." She broke their contact, rising, but keeping an arm around each of their shoulders. "Now, let me have those sketches Evangeline, and we will make a lot of parents very happy."

Nodding agreement, Evangeline gave her the book, along with the reminder that she would need more paper and charcoal soon. Dropping a kiss on each of their cheeks, she left the sketchbook in her room and then continued to breakfast. To her misfortune, she found that she was not the only one headed in that direction. Before she could duck into one of the other rooms, Lord Hawke noticed her and came to join her.

"What did you have to tell Dere last night?" he asked, his voice low so they would not be overheard should anyone be passing.

At her blank look, he cursed. "Dere—Raby—What did you have to tell him last night that meant the two of you had to be alone?"

"I have nothing to say to you," she told him. When she started to walk away, she found her arm caught. "Let's not try that again. Now, there can be no other reason for you to talk to Dere unless it was about your brother. What did you tell him?" He gave her arm a shake.

How many people had actually seen them alone? "There is nothing of any concern of yours. I merely asked if he knew Collin's whereabouts."

At his questioning look, she said, "No, he does not." It galled her to have to answer him.

"If I find you have been lying, I will be delighted to tell everyone just how I found the two of you alone."

"There is nothing to tell," she told him, yanking on her arm. This time he let her go her and she staggered at the release. Turning her back on him, she rubbed the circulation back in her arm and headed for breakfast, though by now she had really lost any appetite she had.

The only people at the table were Brayden, and two of the women she recognized as having children in the nursery. She sat next to Mrs. Stevenson and joined her in coffee. She refused to look at Brayden.

"I have been to the nursery," she said to the other woman, "to visit with my sisters."

Mrs. Stevenson nodded her head. "Caroline and I were there earlier too. We must have missed you. One of the girls has drawn the most exquisite likeness of my little Samantha."

"Thank you. That was my sister Evangeline. In fact, if

you like, I could give you that sketch."

"Truly? Did you hear that, Caro?" She had turned to her friend, then back to Jane. "She is quite talented. I do hope that you see she continues on in her lessons."

Nodding, Jane concentrated on her coffee. She didn't look up until Lord Hulton entered the room. Only then did she know that Brayden no longer stared at her.

After breakfast, Kit offered to organize the afternoon's hunting party. "I suspect you have somewhere you would rather be this afternoon."

"I do. This feels like my last chance. My week is nearly up and I am no closer. The only thing keeping the men together has done was cut down on the rides. And my damn artifacts are still in place," he answered, seeing the question forming on Kit's lips. "I'm going to Worsley House again."

"Is that wise?"

"Probably not, but something Jane said last night makes it imperative that I go."

"You go alone?"

"That's the problem. I need Jane to go with me. I need you to be sure that Hawke stays with the party until I return, or damn close to it. I don't expect to be gone long."

"Even if you push the horses, it will take close to two hours."

"Then you cannot have him leave before three. But I plan to ride. That is only an hour each way."

He sent for Jane immediately and told her of his plans.

"I don't ride," she said.

"Can't or won't?"

"I haven't ridden in years," she admitted. "Horses terrify me."

"Jane, I don't know what you told Brayd last night, but I'm not sure you realize how important it is that he get to Worsley House."

He wished Kit would go away. "I do need your help, Jane. You can use one of the quieter mounts, and I'll be with you the entire time. I won't let anything happen to you."

She gave him a weak smile. "I suppose not. Then you would never find the answer!"

He wasn't sure if she were teasing or not, but it fell flat on his ears. Seeing Kit's slight wince, he supposed he thought the same. "Bella will let you borrow a habit."

She could not believe she was doing this. She was actually riding this beast. True to his word, Brayden found a gentle mount for her, yet they kept a brisk pace, but not one that terrified her. She didn't like what she was doing, but he had made it seem vital. How could she possibly deny him something in her power to give? Not after all he had done for them. An hour was not long, she told herself.

"Do you need to stop?"

She shook her head. "If I stop, you may not get me going again. It's best that we ride on."

"You may be sore tomorrow."

"I'll take my chances. We are half way there, are we not?"

He agreed, and fell into step beside her.

When they pulled up in front of the house, Jane had mixed feelings. After the grandeur of Raby House and Hall, her former home seemed shabbier than ever. If it had still been hers, she would have been delighted. But then, the house never was hers, it had belonged to Collin. If he married, his wife would have run the house, not her.

After Dere dismounted, he turned to help Jane. He gathered the reins and tied the animals to the ring and headed up the stairs. Jane walked extremely slowly.

"Miss Jane!" There was a commotion at the door as Williams opened it, then called for the housekeeper who came running. "Miss Jane is here."

She barely had time to greet them before they dragged her in and exchanged hugs. Mortified that Lord Raby had been left on the doorstep, she turned to find that he had followed them in and closed the door behind him. His smile was tender when he looked at her; she was relieved that he was not angry, though she would not have expected it.

"What brings you back here, Miss Jane. Lord Hawke is not here."

"He's never here," Williams sniffed.

Hiding her smile, Jane told them, "I really came to discuss some matters with Lord Raby, and I need to be in the study to do so, that's where Collin kept most of his papers. I don't suppose Lord Hawke has removed them?"

It didn't look as if the man had made any changes, which rather surprised her, but that was not her concern. The Curse was. In that regard, it didn't matter where the papers were. She just needed to get in the study.

The study! Brayden's brows snapped together as he followed her to the back of the house. He and Kit had gone over every inch. There was no false panel or false desk drawer. Nothing that they could detect.

When they reached the room, he let Jane lead.

She stopped by the desk, and laid her gloves and hat on the surface. "I suppose I should show you exactly where the hiding place is, but once we remove the Curse, there will be no need for it. I suppose the jewels truly belong to Lord Hawke."

He came close to stand directly behind her. He could feel the tension thrumming through her body. She might be doing this because he asked it of her, but it would be difficult.

"No, Jane," he said, his breath moving the tendrils of her hair. "If the jewels are still there, then they would belong to you and your sisters."

She shook her head and the slight movement sent a wave of her scent over him. He wanted to bury his face in her hair. "No, they would belong to Collin. They are his by right."

Brayden had his own thought on that score, but at the moment they needed to see if the jewels were even in place.

He watched carefully as she made her way to the ornate mantle. Her fingers skimmed along the underside, right where his had gone. She seemed to find what she was looking for, for she stopped and invited him to join her.

"It will do me no good to describe it to you," she told him. "You must feel it for yourself."

He could barely trust himself to step closer, but he did as she requested. She grasped his hand and placed it where hers had been a moment before. By concentrating, he could make out where there was a slight difference in the design. Was this the key, then? Evidently it was for she encouraged him to press at that point. He was disappointed when nothing happened, but she continued to instruct him and then again using her hands over his, spread his fingers in such a way that he felt two small bumps on the underside. "These must be pressed together," she told him, and pressed on his fingers. This time, he heard a slight click and faint dragging sound. He looked around the mantle and the side wall, but saw nothing.

He moved his hand, and she quickly released it as if burned by his touch. "I heard something, but I didn't see anything."

She directed his gaze to the bottom of the mantle. In the brick, perhaps one layer above the hearth, he could see that one brick looked slightly loose. She stooped down to pry it out of its place.

"Very clever," was all he said as he joined her. Together they pulled out the protruding brick. Instead of reaching in the hole, as he expected, she turned the brick and slipped out a key, which she handed to him.

"You didn't think anyone would make it obvious, did you?" she asked as she rose to her feet and brushed the skirt of her riding habit.

He tossed the key slightly, feeling the weight of it in his hand as he rose to join her. "So where does it lead?" He held the key in the light. It was rather dusty looking. Picking up one of his gloves where they had joined hers on the desk, he wiped it clean.

After that she lead him to the credenza, a piece of

furniture that he and Kit also had checked and found to be open; having no false panels.

"That is not so." She told him. She started to push the piece of furniture away from the wall. When he realized what she was about, he quickly joined her.

At the bottom of the credenza, on the backside, she slid a small panel aside to reveal a key hole.

He could hardly tell her that he had already checked it and would have sworn it was a solid piece of furniture.

"Very clever."

"Isn't it? My grandmother had it built when it was her husband's turn to guard the jewels. He never knew it was here."

"But he knew about the jewels?"

She smiled at him, causing the dimples on the side of her face to show. "Of course, but he had no desire to touch them. Any time my grandmother wanted to wear them she had to retrieve them herself since she was the only one who knew where they were kept."

It really was a fascinating piece of furniture. "It looks so solid."

She tapped against the side of it as he had done the previous trip. "It will sound that way too. But as you can see, there is a small compartment."

She held out her hand for the key, and he gave it to her, watching as she slid it in the lock. There was no protest. She reached in and brought out a velvet box.

Brayden found himself holding his breath.

She must have been doing the same. She looked up at him with beseeching eyes. He knew she was afraid to find the answer.

He took the box from her hand and slowly opened it, letting his breath out with a whoosh. The jewels were gone. At least some of them. It looked as if the necklace was still in place, but in the spot where the brooch should have been, there was nothing. The earbobs were also there.

She stood, but as she did so, something caught her attention near the opened spot. Reaching down, she picked something up, and turned it over in her hand before showing him.

Right now, all of her attention seemed to be on the box he held. He opened it completely and showed it to her. "Is everything there?"

She shook her head, and pointed to the empty spot. "Collin must have used it after all." She gave him a tremulous smile. "I guess if it's not for a gambling debt, it won't carry a curse."

"You're sure it was Collin, and not perhaps your father who took it?"

She nodded her head. "Papa never looked at it again after they were locked away, and Mama only told us once where they were to be found."

She opened her hand and showed him what else she had found. "I did find this with it. I have never seen it before."

Brayden put the velvet box on the credenza and picked up the object in her hand with reverence.

He held a small blue statue which could not have been more than eight inches in height. Could this be what the furor was about? He held it up to study it better. Then, thinking better of it, he placed it on the credenza too. It looked to be in perfect shape and he planned to keep it that way. His entire future rode on it.

"Do you know what it is?" Jane asked.

"Know what it is?" He grasped her hands and pulled her toward him, giving her a quick kiss. "This is what I have been searching for."

He could tell that his voice was getting higher as he grew more excited. "Finding this...finding this means that I may be able to clear my family name. This was supposedly stolen."

As he spoke, he gave no thought to his words. Now, seeing the expression on her face, he realized what he had said. "Do not look like that, Jane," he hissed.

"Like what, my lord? Like you have just accused my brother of thievery?" She had yanked her hands from his grasp and wrapped them around her midsection, protecting herself. "I'm glad Collin is not here," she told him. "Glad."

"What is going on?" Williams' voice came from the open doorway. They had heard his feet running down the hall. Now he peered in the room.

"Get out!" Brayden roared.

The man did not need to be told a second time as he backed out of the room. Jane moved around him, reaching for her gloves, but was not quick enough to escape his grasp at her arm.

"Release me," she demanded, her voice low.

She sounded totally lifeless, and Brayden could have kicked himself for his thoughtless remarks.

"We must discuss this, Jane," he told her.

"What can there be to discuss, my lord?"

She turned misery-filled eyes to him. "Do you intend that I should stand trial in place of my brother?"

He gave her arm a shake, which was nothing compared to what he really wanted to do. He wanted to shake her until her teeth rattled. "Don't be a goose, Jane. I want nothing but the truth." He gentled his grip and using his other hand, grasped her chin to make her face him. "We have much to talk about. This is not the time or place."

Nodding in agreement, as much as his grip would allow, she made to move, and this time he released her.

The ride home could have hardly been considered pleasant. Brayden wrapped the statue in everything he could find to best protect it. He let Jane carry the jewels. As far as he was concerned, they belonged to her.

They made it back to the Hall before the shooting party returned. Jane immediately returned to her room. She could not even talk to her sisters right now. Would Brayden use his discovery of the statue against them? She didn't believe that he would, but what if it came between her family's honor and his? When she thought about it rationally, she conceded that of the two, it would have to be his worth the saving. Collin had pretty much already dragged their name through the mud. She sat in the window seat, watching the wind move the tree branches. She had been living in a fool's dream. On some level she knew that, but it was so hard to come back to reality. With a sigh, she set her feet on the floor, literally and figuratively.

With resolve, she searched out Arabella. Tonight there was going to be a small assembly, but tomorrow there would be a ball. Arabella had sent out the invitations before they even left town.

"Will Mr. Burke and Mr. Robinson both be here this evening, you think?"

"Oh definitely. I'm certain that either one, if not both, will be delighted to dance with you."

Jane still wasn't confident on that score.

She had Arabella tell her what little she knew about either of the men, and what trade they were in, where they lived, anything that she could think of.

"Have you decided on either of them?" Arabella asked her.

"I have decided that they both seem equally nice and kind. I am hoping to learn more." She blushed even as she said it. It sounded so predatory.

She was still going over bits and pieces as they headed down the hall toward the dining room.

"Whatever are you going on about," Brayden said after listening to his sister for the past several minutes.

Jane gave her a sharp look, but from the expression on her friend's face, she could see that she was going to ignore her silent plea.

"Not much, actually. I was telling Arabella about a few of the men who will be here this evening."

"That much I gathered," he said dryly. "Is there some particular reason? I mean, should I know to take her out of the area at any particular time?"

Arabella gave a gurgle of laughter, but Jane turned her head so that he would not see her expression. "You are amusing, Brayden. Why should you encourage her to leave the room? We're trying to get her matched up with one of Kit's friends." She studied him. "Perhaps you can help. I can't decide who would be the better catch: Mr. Burke or Mr. Robinson."

"They're both nice enough," he shrugged. "I'm not sure it matters."

"I am present," she told them. "And it may surprise you to know that I am capable of thinking for myself."

Arabella snapped her mouth closed, then started again, apologizing. "I didn't mean to say that you couldn't make a decision, Jane. I know Brayden knows who the men are. It would be useful to know if someone is really mean, but it's not seen at social events."

"That is true enough," she agreed. "But surely any friend of Kit's would be known to him."

"See?" Brayden said. "She's right. Ask him."

Brayden was glad to arrive at the parlor where they habitually gathered before going in to dinner. What had those two been plotting? Jane chasing after one of the cits? He knew he was being unfair, but he didn't particularly care. He wasn't even sure if he was more angry or hurt. That they would—she would—think about chasing after someone else. Couldn't she see that he was the one interested? He ran his hand down his face and was determined to be a delightful companion, even if it killed him. And right now, with the rage welling inside, he wasn't sure that was far off.

"What has you acting such a squeeze-crab," Kit asked when he met up with his friend inside the room.

Brayden wanted to growl at him.

Kit grabbed two of the glasses of champagne from a passing waiter and handed one to Brayden. "This will make it better," he told him in a false soothing voice.

"Somehow I doubt it," Brayden said as he took a healthy swallow of the drink. "Do you know what those two are planning?" he asked, pointing with his glass to his sister and Jane on the other side of the dance floor.

"It can't be anything too dreadful, neither of them is the type." Kit calmly sipped his drink.

"That's what you think. Did my sister ask you about any of your friends lately? Single ones, around thirty years of age?"

Kit eyed him warily. "Yes. What of it?"

"You didn't think it odd?"

"Why should I?" he shrugged. "She's always asking something. This time it had something to do with Jane, but I can't recall what."

"You need to pay attention around women, Kit. How many times have I told you that?" He sighed with the experience of having to deal with two sisters and numerous female cousins over the years whereas Kit grew up in a house of boys. Three brothers, all of them close in age and temperament, often were the target of Brayden's envy, especially once it became apparent that Nigel had no use for a much younger brother who would not inherit anything.

"They are plotting to see who Jane should encourage."

Kit opened his eyes wide. "You are joking?"

"Ha! That's all I had to listen to on the way down. The merits of Mr. Burke versus Mr. Robinson." He watched as Kit carefully placed his glass on one of the nearby tables. "You look a little pale. Feeling all right?" he asked, then drained his glass and set it to his friend's.

"I did talk about both of them."

"Well, you did them no favors! Now those two will be in their way constantly."

"Is that really a bad thing, Brayd?" He started walking toward the outside of the room where the air was slightly cooler, and Brayden followed.

"Of course it is. What good can come of it?" He ran his hand through his hair and looked at his friend in exasperation. "I thought Bella had made her choice."

Kit stiffened until Brayden nudged him on the shoulder. "I meant you, you nodcock, though if this is a sample of your intelligence when you're around my sister, I might have to rethink it."

"Has she said anything?"

"'Course not, but it's pretty evident to me. Don't see what she's waiting for." He scowled at the thought that she was not the only one waiting for something.

"I think they're trying to match Jane up."

Kit relaxed. "That would be a good thing. I know you were concerned about her. And from what you've told me, it would be an improvement in her life. Both of the men are nice, good and solid. Just what you would want."

"Just not for my sister, eh?"

"Not for those reasons. Because I think she and I would deal well together."

"You will. But now you understand the problem."

"What problem? Kit's tone showed his exasperation. "You have at least two very eligible parti, and she may like one of them. What could be better? I should think you would encourage such a match if one were forthcoming."

"Do you?"

Kit stared at him. "What is wrong with you, Brayd? You're being particularly obtuse."

"I found a way that Collin could have bought colours," he said, abruptly changing the subject.

"How?"

Brayden waved away the question. I'm not at liberty to say, but it would be legitimate. I also discovered that some people might just have a very real reason for wanting to get inside of his house."

Kit looked around to see who might be listening. "I'll stop in your study after dinner."

"That would be good."

* * *

Jane looked at both men as they were pointed out to her. Mr. Burke was tall, and rather thin, but he had a kind enough face. And he was dancing with a young woman Jane thought just might be more plain than herself.

Mr. Robinson was almost as tall, built on the heavier side, and was very pleasant to look at. His blond hair was in a faultless windswept style, which suited him perfectly Everything about him was in order and to perfection. Jane watched him dance; so elegant. She sighed. Definitely, he would not be interested in her. He had many more social graces.

As if reading her mind, Arabella pointed him out. "He would be very interested, Jane. His family has been after him to marry into a title for ages. That's one of the reasons he is not married yet."

She knew a doubtful expression was on her face.

"Truly," Arabella insisted. "He has two younger sisters and his parents are pressuring him to marry a title. They have plenty of money, so the girls will be welcomed at any rate, but they would like the extra cachet."

Jane felt bemused and wondered if she looked the same. She had never really considered that it would come down to this. The few times she had thought of marrying, she had thought it would be for love. Now she knew differently. She also had learned that she really didn't want to be separated from her sisters and this seemed the most provident way of going about making sure they stayed together.

"What do you think he will say about the twins?"

Arabella laughed at her. "Jane, dear, he will se so delighted to have a title in the family, I can't imagine him saying aught. His sisters are older than yours, so he will be sure that people will welcome his sisters with open arms since they can hardly snub your sisters."

"Even if they do me?" Jane finished the thought for her.

Arabella gave a grimace. "True. But your sisters will not be held for blame."

"That is all that matters. I knew nothing of balls and such, so this will not be a great loss. It is fun, though."

"Finally, I have heard you say something is fun," Brayden said as he came up behind the women.

Jane couldn't help but wonder as to how much of the conversation he had overheard. But he looked innocent enough.

"I have come to claim my dance, Jane."

She looked at him, puzzled. "But I don't recall—"

"Of course you don't," he said, offering his arm to lead her onto the floor.

"What is this all about, my lord?"

"Brayden, Brayden," he told her, still smiling. He wasn't about to tell her it was all about ownership. She was his and she should be used to it by now.

"I wanted to get my dance in before the rush started," he told her soberly.

"What are you talking about?" Then she didn't really listen for his answer. It was marvelous to twirl around the floor in a waltz with him. He made her feel as if she were indeed one of the most graceful of dancers, yet she knew she wasn't. She was lucky she recalled the steps, not that she needed to with Brayden to lead the way.

How wonderful it would be if he were to always do so. When she sighed, he caught it above the music and his light grip on her waist tightened infinitesimally.

"What was that for? This is a beautiful night."

"It is," she agreed. "Really, Bray...my lord, I would like to make an appointment to talk to you."

He laughed down into her earnest face. "Jane, I am here now, surely you can talk here."

"Not freely. May we meet tomorrow after breakfast?"

Agreeing, they finished the dance and he lead her back to where Arabella was standing, now with Mr. Robinson waiting at her side, as was Kit.

Kit took the opportunity to introduce the man to her, and let them go on their way to the dance floor.

"What did you do that for?" Brayden growled in his friend's ear as he watched the couple go through the intricate dance steps. At least he had her for the waltz.

"Your sister asked me to," Kit told him quietly. "Besides, you mentioned it earlier, remember?"

"I also remember telling you that I am about to leave and invited you to come along."

"I don't recall accepting."

Brayden looked at his friend, then giving him a curt nod, headed out the door.

Kit showed up in his study less than half an hour later.

"What in heavens name is wrong with you?" he asked Brayden.

"Nothing that can't be cured." Waving his hand, as if waving away the problem, Brayden led his friend into the study and poured him a drink. But rather than sitting, he headed over to his desk.

Kit followed, carrying his drink.

"The reason every one seems to want Collin's house is because there really is a place to hide treasure." He watched Kit's eyes light up.

"What did you find?"

Placing his drink on the desk, Brayden went around to the working side and slid open the top drawer, taking out his key for the safe.

Kit stared at him. "This is the key?"

"No, this is the key to *my* safe. The one that is holding the treasure from Collin's house."

He walked over to his safe, kept below the credenza on the other side of the room. Kit followed. The safe and its contents were no secret to him, and Brayden never intended them to be.

Bending down, he unlocked the safe, and pushed aside

several packets of papers before pulling out a cloth-covered item. He heard Kit's quick intake of breath before he even unwrapped it.

He set it on top of the credenza and unwrapped it, letting the statue lie on the top.

Kit bent for a closer look at it. "This is it, then? You're sure?"

"As sure as I can be without talking to anyone about it." Brayden bent to peer at it closely too. "Do you think there's something wrong—that this really isn't the artifact? It's Indian in design, even I can tell that. The color alone proclaims it so. Then there are the markings." He used his forefinger to point out the intricate designs carved in the artifact.

Kit nodded, then stepped back. "Amazing." He started to wrap the artifact back in the piece of chamois that Brayden had it wrapped with and handed it back to him. "I'd feel a lot better if that was where it belonged."

Brayden returned it to the safe, locked it and then walked back to his desk to pick up his drink. "You and I both. I already sent a letter to Prinny."

"Waiting for a response tonight?"

"No, waiting to go. I already got the response." He drained his glass and left it on the desk.

"He must be desperate to get it indeed if he's willing to meet with you tonight."

"I got that impression. I'm not sure it's the right thing to do and I wish you would come with me."

"I hardly think you need a guard to go to Lancaster House."

"Nor do I. What I do need is a witness. I want someone else to hear it's all clear as far as my name is concerned."

"You don't sound overly happy if that is the case."

Brayden ran his hand through his hair. "I have the artifact, and my name is clear. I still don't know if Nigel was involved or not, but it looks as if Collin was—"

"Oh Lord," Kit said. This time, he imitated Brayden and ran his hand through his own hair. "Bella is introducing Jane with the thought that someone will want her title."

Brayden drew his own breath in, telling himself to calm, that Kit did not mean it the way it sounded. He would take Jane without a title.

"What if Prinny decides that Collin is the thief?"

"It sounds to me as if he is," Kit grumbled.

"Looks can be deceiving, Kit. What if Collin is not the thief? What if someone planted it there? After all, no one seemed particularly interested immediately after the house was lost. It took some time."

"True, but there were men quite eager to win it the first time."

"If he were the thief, why didn't he sell the artifact to pay for his colours? Instead he sold a family heirloom."

"Not Jane's?"

"No, nothing like that. It was his. But if he were not honorable, would he have not sold the artifact that meant nothing to him?"

"He could have been holding it for someone."

"Exactly. But who is the question. Who else would know that he truly had the artifact at his home and was willing to buy the house to get it?" He would not say they were willing to buy Jane too, though that was evident to him from at least one source.

Kit finally nodded, answering the question Brayden asked before. "I'll go with you."

"The carriage is being brought around now."

Chapter Twelve

The girls fully expected to see Brayden the next morning at breakfast. Jane had planned to meet with him afterward. He had left the assembly early, and left no word other than that he would return later that morning.

Arabella ground her teeth. "He took Kit with him."

Jane shrugged her shoulders. "They are great friends; why does that surprise you?"

"Kit was to drive me through the park this afternoon, but from the sound of the message they may not be back."

"They said later this morning," Jane reminded her.

Arabella gave a delicate snort.

Even though the host and his friend were away, Arabella managed to keep the party moving along. It helped that there would be a ball, so most people were delighted to spend a lazy day indoors reading, playing games or resting. Mr. Robinson had searched for Jane and finally found her in the middle of a game of spoons with her sisters. She had a feeling she had not come off in the best light.

"I did not realize you had such lovely young sisters," he said. Each of them dropped him a slight curtsy before Jane shooed them off to continue their game in the corner.

"I hope you can come for a drive with me this afternoon. If that would be permissible."

Whom was she going to ask! After setting arrangements for time, Jane exchanged a few pleasantries, then Arabella came into the room, to supposedly keep the twins occupied, as well as her own nieces and the other children.

As soon as Mr. Robinson left the room, Arabella demanded to know what he had wanted.

"To go for a drive," Emily said calmly, continuing to

study her cards.

"May we go, Jane?" Evangeline asked.

Jane smiled at the two girls and their friends, and told them definitely not.

"But Uncle Brayden lets us go with him," Evangeline insisted.

"That's not Uncle Brayden," Miranda informed her as if she didn't know who was who.

Arabella clapped her hands, for which Jane was grateful. Another few minutes and the potential for an all-out scene was very real. "I think that we should take a walk to the park now while the weather is lovely. What do you girls say?"

They scrambled to their feet and darted for the door, where Jane laughingly stopped them and told them to pick up their game before getting their cloaks to go outside.

Jane leaned against the doorframe after the girls exited the room, and stared at Arabella. "And what prompted this action?"

Arabella shrugged. "I didn't want them to come to blows If they did, Brayden would hear of it and blame me. He always does." She left to send a message to the groom that the carriage should be made ready for them.

Hearing the girls on the way back down the stairs, Jane and Arabella donned their own coats and waited in the hall for them to appear.

She couldn't help but think of her upcoming outing with Mr. Robinson. Perhaps it was to her best interest to marry a cit, as she and Arabella discussed. No matter how she thought about him, she kept comparing him to Brayden, which was not entirely fair to the man.

"You look miles away," Arabella told her after she failed to respond to the twins' comments.

"Are you thinking of Mr. Robinson," she asked.

Jane gave her a sheepish smile. "Is it so obvious? I must have it written on my face."

"Hardly that, but what else would capture your attention

so fully?"

There was no answer for that. She could hardly claim that Brayden captured it now and most of their waking moments.

They arrived home, in time for the girls to have their tea, which they were quite delighted to get. In honor of the outing, Arabella insisted that they all have tea in the parlor instead of the nursery—an idea that suited the girls just fine.

When they were nearly finished, they sought to prolong the adventure, and Arabella seemed to be in a mood to humor them. "Will you draw pictures of Miranda and Hannah?" Evangeline asked Jane.

"Mine aren't very good and I think they should like to have them."

"You do, do you?" She smiled at her sisters, looking and truly growing up so much here. "I'll get my things and be only a moment."

"You can use mine," Evangeline offered.

Jane ran her hand over her sister's head. "I appreciate the offer, but I have more paper in mine."

Getting her things took only a few moments, and the girls were pretty much where she had left them. Evangeline insisted that Miranda be sketched with her favorite book in her hands. Humoring her sisters was never a problem for Jane, but to be doing something she enjoyed at the same time was pure pleasure.

More pleasurable than her ride with Mr. Robinson. She feared that she was the dull party, merely responding yes and no to his comments about himself, his lifestyle, and the way his sisters were eager to be launched into society.

* * *

Brayden and Kit rode back to the house in relative silence. What was there to say, after all?

Kit changed his position in the carriage again. They

hadn't been traveling long; it wasn't that far from Lancaster House. "Everything worked out for the best."

"For who?"

"For you, and you know it. Prinny was absolutely delighted to receive that statue."

"I'm not so sure. Surprised would be more the word I was looking for. Even that wasn't enough, though. You saw that for yourself. He wants more. And mostly, he wants property. The title would be an added bonus."

"There were no papers."

"There better not be," Brayden growled. "I swear before you that if he gives me any, I will immediately go to the rest of the lords."

"That would hardly be necessary. Just send a message to one of the border lords. I'm sure even he has learned his history enough to heed it."

Brayden slapped his hand on his thigh. "The last thing I want or need is to have the Prince of Wales set against me. I swear if Nigel were not already gone I would do the deed with my bare hands."

"Calm down," Kit warned him. "Watch what you say."

"There is no one here but you, Kit, and nothing in my house is a secret to you."

He fell silent after that. The trip home was not long enough for Brayden to finish digesting all that had occurred in the past day and a half.

There was no reason to meet with Prinny that he could tell. It had wasted time that he could have better spent with Jane. All he had wanted was information on the Demons. Contrary to Kit's thought, Brayden believed that the Prince hadn't even cared whether he actually had the artifact with him or not. He did seem pleased enough the next day, but not overly so. All of his concern had been for who was involved with the Demons. He wanted names; names which Dere was glad that he could not give him, save his own, and that he already knew. Not that he had any fondness for the riders—he found most of them to be a bunch of worthless lordlings with nothing better to do than terrorize the countryside for a lark, but he did not believe that they were guilty of treason, either. The latest additions did have him wondering about their loyalties to the group, and if he probed long enough he might have to wonder about the loyalty to their country, but he hoped it wouldn't come to that. The group seemed to be on the verge of disbanding, and he would do anything he could to hasten that along.

When he entered his house, he realized deep contentment as he was greeted by the sounds of laughter and women talking in the parlor, and Jane's voice. He closed his eyes briefly, before snapping them open when he heard Harold clear his throat. Hastily, he threw off his coat and gave the man his hat and gloves.

He planned to just open the doors, but there was no need as the doors opened just at that moment. The little girls practically came tumbling out. Immediately, they called his name and flung themselves at him as if they hadn't seen him for years instead of the day before. He welcomed it, but his eyes sought Jane above their heads. He encountered his sister first, then slid past her to see Jane standing there. She did not come to greet him as he would have wished, but she stared at him in a thorough manner that made him forget anything else save that he was glad he was back.

He wondered what pretext he could use to speak to her alone, but when none was forthcoming, resigned himself to waiting until dinner. Then there was the ball. Greeting the older girls, he informed them he would be in his study until dinner.

Being there was one thing, but now that he had time to think, he didn't know if he could. He walked over to the window facing the garden, and pushed the curtain aside. It was a view he never tired of when he was at the Hall. It still amazed him that he was master there. He had always loved the land, and Nigel the city. It was the reason he had consented to manage the estates for his brother. They should have been born in opposite roles, but fate had other ideas. Or so he thought. Now, he was in Nigel's role, along with the role of working for the Prince Regent—at least for the moment.

What could Nigel have been thinking to get mixed up in—even start Dere's Demons? Even he should have known the Crown would not look kindly on terrorizing the lords. There was no one else for them to complain to.

Now he had to find a way to convince the rest of the riders that they truly needed to disband. He felt he would have the support of some, but would it be enough?

Dinner was not what he had anticipated. Arabella was animated and delighted in telling him about the day. Jane had little to say. That, he had not expected. With the prospect of the ball ahead of them for the evening, he thought she would be as buoyed as the rest of the company.

* * *

After standing in the receiving line with Arabella to greet all of his neighbors, he was more than ready to escape to the terrace for fresh air, but first he had to dance the first dance with his sister to open the ball. Then, he could escape.

"What is wrong with you?" Arabella hissed as they danced. "You have been like a sore bear ever since you returned from your mysterious errand."

"I have things on my mind."

"Does this have anything to do with what Jane told you the other night? You have been preoccupied since then."

"Partly. She has been a tremendous help."

"A tremendous help," he repeated to himself later as he leaned on the balustrade. Jane finding the statue quite possibly saved his earldom, in spite of what he had said to Kit. She had even braved riding a horse to help him. And what had he offered in return? That her brother was a thief?

Somehow, that did not sound right. If he had indeed been the one to steal the artifact, Nigel's group would have welcomed him. He could not presume to know Nigel's thoughts, but those of others in the group were quite clear.

He knew he should go back into the ballroom, but he could not face the bright lights. They were too exposing. Some host he was turning out to be. Thank goodness Bella took most of it on her shoulders.

"Hiding in the dark?" Lord Hawke joined him near the baluster.

Brayden turned to lean against the railing. He stopped himself from crossing his arms across his chest. Hawke would see it as a defensive sign, not one that meant Brayden was trying to control his impulse to flatten the man. "Hardly. Rather, enjoying the fresh air. What brings you out?"

Morris waited until he was quite close so his voice didn't carry. "I thought the reason to meet here was because it was close to the highway, yet the riders haven't gone out once."

That was good to hear. "I can hardly leave my guests."

Morris snorted at that. "Dere, you have been absent more than present. It leads one to wonder why you even invited everyone here."

"That part is easy. My sister requested a house party."

"You expect me to believe that?"

Brayden shrugged. "Believe what you will. You asked me a question and I gave you the answer."

"Then if you're in the mood to answer questions, tell me, when do you plan to ride again?"

"Tell me why you're so anxious to know?"

Morris shot him a glare, then turned on his heel and reentered the ballroom. The man would bear watching. He was the only one who seemed the most anxious to ride. He was also a few years older than most of the others.

Pushing away from the railing, he headed for the ballroom, standing just outside of the doors, letting his eyes become accustomed to the light before entering.

Arabella was talking with one of the matrons, Kit at her side. He was going to have to do something about that. Kit could get away with his constant companionship because of his close association with Brayden and the family, where another might not. Everyone in the area was well aware of the connection. Finally, he gave in to temptation and looked about for Jane. His Jane was dancing with one of the men he had seen following her about lately. Burke was his name, Bella said. His eyes narrowed. He would have to dance with her, as he would with all of his other guests. He saved her dance for a waltz, but he made sure she was aware of it long before the dance. He didn't want her promising it to another.

She held herself stiff in his arms, so he pulled her infinitesimally closer. When she tried to put more distance between them, he held her fast. "Relax, Jane. I thought you liked balls."

"That was before—" She bit her lip.

She didn't have to finish. He knew that she referred to before he discovered the artifact in Collin's possession. He appreciated that she said no more about it in public.

There was much that he wanted to say, but the middle of the dance floor was hardly the place for it. Instead, he concentrated on the way she felt in his arms as they swept about the floor, and the way the light from hundreds of candles added a glow to her skin.

As the dance ended, she sighed. It sounded suspiciously like relief to him. Others were leaving the floor to go in to supper, a place he did not want to be.

"Something seems to be troubling you," he said at last. "Is it something I can help with?"

Jane shook her head, but didn't look at him.

He offered his arm. She would have appeared churlish to refuse, so she accepted and followed him to the terrace.

Trying to take a neutral tone, he said, "The girls look well. I think Anne will be delighted that her daughters have such good friends. Practically family."

"They're not family," she snapped at him.

Brayden held both hands up, palm outward. "I didn't mean anything, Jane. I just thought they got along well."

He invited her to sit on one of the benches against the railing. He knew he surprised her when he sat near her.

"Is there something you wished to speak about in particular," she asked him.

"No." He looked up at the stars, then glanced at her. She was still sitting quietly.

"I've heard rumors that Mr. Robinson has been paying some attention."

Jane relaxed and smiled at him. "More than rumors, my lord."

He winced at her use of the title as much as what she had said. The anger he felt surprised him in that he thought he had better control over that emotion.

"What could he want, Jane? Why has he come?" He softened his voice so as not to frighten her with what he was thinking. It didn't seem to matter. She shrank away from him anyway. She probably would have moved farther but was stopped by the end of the bench.

"Actually, I think he is interested."

"In you?"

"You don't have to be quite so nasty," she told him smartly. He was relieved to see that she no longer seemed afraid of him. "I believe he is interested in me." She lifted her chin. "You're the one who told me that I should think of doing something besides working in a factory, and I have."

"What? Become Robinson's mistress?"

"That was a vile thing to say." She practically hissed the words at him.

Even so, he was able to pick up the hurt in her voice. "What more could he want, Jane? He knows that you are living here..."

"That can't mean anything. Arabella is here, too!"

Brayden gave a nonchalant shrug. "I'm merely repeating

what I've heard."

She turned away from him, trying not to cry in front of him. That would never do. This was not what she had planned at all. And she told him so.

"I'm sorry, Jane. I would not have wished for your plans to fail. It was perhaps unkind of Arabella to set it up in such a way."

She practically jumped to her feet. "You don't sound at all sorry."

Brayden stood, much more slowly, and stepped toward her until they were only a few inches from each other. He reached out, but she backed away from him.

"What are you doing?" she demanded. She stepped even closer, she was so angry. "You told me not to discuss what I planned to do after I left here. Not to discuss the issue with you, or with Arabella or even my sisters, so I haven't. Arabella is the one who thought perhaps gentlemen would be interested in me."

"There are many who are, Jane. So why would you settle for Robinson? The man is a bounder."

"He has been kind to me," she practically whispered, her voice hoarse from unshed tears. "And I had something that he could want."

Brayden let his eyes travel down her figure, resting on her breasts and waist. It was an insulting look, and she knew it, but she refused to give way. "I have no doubt there," he finally said.

"Arabella said that there were some men who would overlook many things to gain a title," she said through clenched teeth. "A title is one thing that I do have that is my own."

"The title belonging to a thief isn't worth all that much, you know."

"What are you saying? I have stolen nothing."

"You may not have, but your brother certainly has. He must have."

Jane wasn't sure that she believed him since he ran his hand through his hair as he said it, something she had seen him do before when he was unsure of himself.

She looked at him, her heart breaking as she did so. She had wanted Brayden to be something more and knew now that was not to be. He did not seem particularly upset at what he said Robinson had planned.

"If you'll excuse me, my lord, it's been a long day." She gave him a quick curtsy and headed for her room. No matter what he said, she wasn't convinced Robinson did only want her as a mistress. She supposed that was not out of the question since that could be seen as quite a feather in his cap—perhaps even more so than a wife.

She made it through the ballroom, then excused herself to Arabella. She didn't want the Arabella to worry when she didn't see her.

She dropped onto the bed, sitting there, unsure of what to do next. If that was the way Brayden felt, would Mr. Robinson be any different? She did not think so. Nor did she think it was something that she should mention to Arabella. She was still an innocent. Not that Jane wasn't, but Brayden had realized that she had seen more of the side of life not quite genteel. She gave a tired grin at her own thoughts. That was one way of putting it.

If she slept on it, she suspected that she wouldn't come up with a different answer. Seating herself at the small desk, she took out a piece of paper and sharpened the point of a pen. Carefully, she listed all of the duties that she knew how to perform, which made for a lengthy list. She would present it to Brayden with the request that he write to his relatives and friends looking for a companion. If he truly felt that she was not marriageable, perhaps he would be more helpful in finding a position. She had agreed not to discuss it until after the house party. That was officially over tomorrow.

* * *

Brayden left the ballroom, headed for his study and sank down in the chair, feeling more wretched than he had in some time. That went remarkably unwell he thought. Now Jane was angry with him, which was not what he wanted or intended. Of course, he was also angry with her. How could he not be? He gave a snort. She seriously thought of marrying Robinson. How could she? Now all he had to do was keep her from hearing that the nonsense he had told her was just that. As far as he knew, Robinson would ask Jane to marry him, and then where would he be?

Once the fire died down, he stood near the hearth, and picking up the poker, pushed at a few of the logs. They would burn faster and be done.

Now all that remained for him was to convince Jane that she needed to stay with him.

Leaving the lamps lit, for Harold would be in to take care of everything, Brayden made his way from the room. It was then that he saw something sticking out from one of the cushions. Reaching over, he plucked a sketchbook from between the cushion and the back of the chair. Perching on the arm of the chair, he flipped the book open, figuring that it belonged to one of the young girls.

It didn't.

He flipped past the first few pages, only mildly interested, not really registering what he was seeing. After looking at the fourth sketch or so, he stopped. He brought the book to the table in the room and turned up the lamp to better study the sketches. Jane was an amazing artist, he thought, and was glad for it. He looked again. The pictures were sketches of the dockworkers, unloading and loading barrels and crates. If the light drawn in the picture was accurate, it would mean that she would have been on the docks in the predawn light and early morning. He was certain there would have been no one with her. He restrained himself for bellowing for her, for demanding an explanation immediately. He was glad he did.

The next picture took his breath away. He was glad he was seated, even if it was on the edge of the table. Morris was in one. Another showed Nigel, Collin and several of the other riders, though he didn't know if she knew them as such. There was no mistaking them. He picked the book up and held it closer to the light, trying to determine the objects in their hands. It was definitely something. He reached for his magnifying glass to be sure of what he was seeing—he was. It was the Indian statue. If not the one he returned to the Regent, then another that looked terribly similar. That meant that they did know what it was.

Had Nigel truly been guilty? The next page showed Nigel and another group of men on the dock. Brayden had never known that his brother had spent any time there, let alone enough to be sketched on two different occasions, and they were different. The men's clothing was different, as was the sun, and on closer inspection, even the boats in the dock. What had he been up to? He would ask Jane, but perhaps he should wait until the morrow when he was calmer.

He moved to the next few pages, trying to see if there were any others of Nigel or Collin. There weren't. What he did find was a score of pictures of himself. Some when he was in a pensive mood and others where he was laughing. He smiled to himself. She could pretend that she wasn't interested but now he knew better. The question was if he should try to approach her now or wait until the morning.

He needed to share the information with Kit, but would not share the rest of the sketches. In light of what he did discover, he was even more angry that she had been on the docks.

Deciding that she surely would not yet be asleep since the orchestra music still permeated the house, he tucked the book under his arm, made his way up the stairs to her room and softly knocked on the door. Not getting an immediate response didn't stop him. He pushed the door, which opened easily under his hand, and slipped into the room, softly closing the door behind him.

He passed the desk with the paper lying on top. With the aid of the moonlight he could see that it was a list of some sort and could even make out some of the words. The chit was going to ask him for help, he just knew it. He was glad now that he decided to visit her this night.

Walking to the bed, he looked down at her, unsure of what he should do now. On the one hand, he wanted to shake some sense into her. On the other hand, he applauded her efforts. Leaning over the bed, he shook her with one hand on her arm. "Jane," he whispered, but she did not stir. He called her name a bit louder this time. She turned.

He wanted to step back, and yet step closer. When she turned, she managed to lose half of the bed covers. He knew she was covered, yet when the blankets slipped, and with the moonlight streaming through the windows, he could make out the outline of her breasts. He swallowed convulsively. Then he remembered her list.

"Jane..." He hissed her name this time a bit louder and she stirred more. He squeezed her arm and shook her awake.

Sleepily she opened her eyes, trying to focus on the face in front of her and understand why he was there.

"The girls!"

Instantly she pushed the covers aside and started to rise, but Brayden did not retreat from where he sat.

"The girls are fine," he told her. It was *she* who was in trouble.

She scooted up in the bed, pulling the covers with her, holding them practically to her chin.

"You can relax, you know," he told her. "I'm too angry to do anything but yell, but I am trying to keep that to a minimum."

"What is wrong?" Unlike him, she did keep her voice even lower.

He tossed the sketchbook on the bed. "You left this in

the study."

She glanced at it, but did not reach for it. The glance back to him still held a trace of fear. He ran a hand through his hair before saying anything, not exactly sure where to start.

"I looked at your pictures. I did not know they were yours when I opened the book. You left it downstairs."

Seeing the protest starting to form on her lips, he stopped her by placing his index finger on her lips. He hurriedly snatched it away, they were much too soft.

"I cannot believe that you went to the docks. Were you alone?"

She nodded as he continued. "Tell me about it. Did you see everything that you drew? Was my brother there?"

She drew her brows together. "I don't know who your brother is. One of the men in the pictures?"

"Yes." He cleared his throat and reached for the sketchbook again. Flipping past several of the pages, he held one out to her. "This one. You have a date on the bottom. Is that the date you drew the picture?"

Again she nodded. She still didn't look sure of his intent. Not that he blamed her, but at least she relaxed somewhat. He held the book out to her. "Tell me about the pictures," he said, releasing the book to her hands.

She looked at him for a moment as if gauging what he would do, but he merely held the book out to her, trying to be non-threatening. What was she afraid of anyway? Surely not him. He didn't continue to think along those lines, merely waited for her to speak.

She let the bed cover drop and he almost wished she hadn't. She was nicely rumpled from her sleep. Maybe he should have waited until morning.

"This one—I was going to market, so I stopped to see what new things were coming in from the dock."

"You did this yourself?"

"Of course! Who else would go?" She gave him a look as

if he were daft, and at that moment he began to wonder if he was. What could she possibly prove with the pictures?

"I would go there at least once a week, just to look." She smiled up at him. "I'm afraid I'm a rather curious person. This week was particularly exciting. "She pointed out the different ships as she spoke. "There was one from china that week. That is always exciting. They unload the most exotic things. I cannot imagine where they go."

He could. He had seen women ordering wallpapers from the silks of china. His sister did herself.

"Then there was the ship from India. They come more often, but are still interesting with their spices and artwork..."

He tried not to show that was what interested him the most. She flipped the page to the next sketch. "This one —well, you can see my brother Collin there."

"Did he see you?"

She giggled and unconsciously moved closer to him so they could better share the book.

"No. he would have been very upset. He never liked me to know what he did. I don't know the other men with him."

Brayden pointed to the taller man on the left of the picture that she had captured so well. "That is my half-brother Nigel."

"I did not know. Would you like the picture?"

How to answer? He would because it might provide the proof he needed. On the other hand, he felt that he needed the entire book. "Not right now, but I would like it at some point," he finally said.

She nodded and turned the page. It was something he had not noticed before as he flipped through the book himself—pictures of individual items.

"See, they had put some of the articles on the barrels as they unwrapped them so I hurried and sketched them."

He took the book from her and studied it. "Isn't that unusual?"

"A bit. But I have seen them do it before, especially when

they are selling items right on the dock, or someone was waiting for a particular item."

"How long have you gone to the docks yourself?"

She shrugged. "Perhaps seven or eight years."

Seven or eight years! Good Lord. She had been quite young and no one ever stopped her? He tried not to shudder, thinking of the things she could have and probably had seen there.

"Who was buying or selling these items? They look valuable."

"I have no idea of their worth. I was only interested because they were there." She pointed to a short man on the right of the sketch. "This is the man who had it with him. At least, he was the one who unwrapped it."

"How can you remember?"

She smiled at him. She was so close now, that he caught his breath, and in doing so inhaled the scent of her. This was not a good move, but then she was talking again, drawing his attention to the sketch before the current one.

"See...if you look closely, you can see that he's holding it while coming across the gangplank."

Brayden took the book from her and held it to the little bit of light, trying to make out what she was showing him.

"I think we need some light in here," she told him softly and started groping for the matches near the lamp.

He put out a hand and stopped her. "No. Let's meet in the morning." He had already spent entirely too much time in her room. He didn't need to have the light under the door draw attention to that fact. "May I hold the book until then?"

She hesitated, but finally nodded in agreement.

He pushed himself up from where he had been sitting on the edge of her bed, and tucked the sketchbook under his arm. Leaning over, he kissed her swiftly, and exited the room.

Chapter Thirteen

Jane didn't even want to look at herself in the mirror in the morning. How could she possibly face him? He undoubtedly would have studied that sketchbook. She didn't care about the pictures in the beginning of the book, pictures of the docks and markets—they were of no concern to her. The fact that his face was in the back of the book, numerous times, was of definite concern. How could she possibly remain here for any length of time? She sat on the chair by the desk, staring numbly at the list she had started to make the night before. Even as she made it out, she had half-thought there might still be a chance to marry. After Brayden's visit last night, she doubted that would be possible. Would she ever be able to think of anyone the way she did Brayden? Probably not. But until she learned otherwise, Mr. Robinson seemed a likely candidate. But what if Brayden had told her the truth about the man? He had no reason to lie to her. She wished she could know. Arabella might, Kit certainly, but how could she ask them? The best thing to do would be to meet with Mr. Robinson again, if he would invite her to do so. As for the sketchbook and its telling drawings, she would have to pretend they did not matter.

With new resolve, she made her way down to breakfast, delighted to find only Arabella sitting at the table, munching on her toast.

Jane poured herself a cup of tea and brought it to the table.

"That's not all you're having, is it?"

Jane looked at the tea as she stirred in a lump of sugar. "I'm not particularly hungry this morning."

Arabella rolled her eyes. "You need to eat. We are going

to go shopping and you will need to build your strength."

Chuckling, Jane assured her friend that she was not going to fall in with her plans. "I have no idea how you do it, Arabella, but I cannot spend another day shopping." She would never admit that perhaps if she had the proper coin she might feel better about the venture.

"Then what will you do for the day?" Arabella sipped her tea.

"I thought I would spend it with the girls. After all, I cannot stay here indefinitely and I would like to see them more."

"Do you think Mr. Robinson will come to scratch?"

Jane nearly choked on her hastily swallowed tea. "What are you saying, Arabella. That is absurd!" Although that was what she told Brayden she hoped for.

"Is it? The man follows you around whenever you are in the same room."

"I do not know enough about him."

"You would have time to learn. If he comes up to scratch, will you accept?"

Jane did not answer immediately, but that did not deter Arabella in the least. "Just think," she continued in an excited voice, "you will have achieved everything—more—than you planned. Wouldn't that be marvelous?"

"What would?" Brayden's deep voice joined the conversation as he walked into the room.

Jane had assumed that he had breakfasted and was gone. She immediately tensed at his voice. Would he say anything about yesterday evening? Or would he wait to discuss the sketches in private. She hoped for the latter.

"Brayden! We were just discussing the possibility of Mr. Robinson coming up to scratch. Wouldn't that be wonderful for Jane to have her future nicely settled?"

"Wonderful," he said wryly.

Jane was relieved when he did not repeat what he had said to her last night. "So, you approve?" he asked Arabella.

"Of course I do. I think it would be great. He is absolutely besotted with Jane. Anyone with eyes can see that."

"I hadn't noticed," he said quietly, seating himself at the table across from Jane.

Of course he hadn't noticed! He had been too busy watching her himself to notice anyone else's reaction until they came in hailing distance of her. If Jane truly loved the man, he hoped that his pack of lies would not deter her. He wanted his Jane happy, even if that meant another man.

He clapped his hands together and rubbed them. "It looks to be a delightful day. Would you like to join me in a carriage ride this afternoon?" He asked them both, but his eyes strayed to Jane.

Arabella pretended to pout. "We've already made plans, Brayden. Most of the guests have already gone. There is only Kit."

"I know," he said. That's why I'm only here now."

"Remember, Squire Reynolds is hosting an assembly tonight."

Why had he thought being at the Hall was quiet? Normally it was, he reminded himself. It was only because he had brought the house party that there was so much entertainment that the local gentry decided they must increase it. "Shall I see you both then?"

Nodding their agreement, they waited until Brayden was done with his breakfast before leaving.

"Jane?" Brayden stopped her as she was about to leave the room. "Would it be convenient to meet now?"

At her nod, he led her into his study. He didn't care what Arabella thought. At night was one thing, but this was the bright light of morning and his own house. Arabella could think what she liked, but he was not inviting her to join him.

He headed toward the settee and invited Jane to join him. At her hesitation, he pointed out that it was the only logical place for them to share the book. He made sure not to sit too close to her, though he would like to. He certainly didn't want to frighten her in any way.

Opening the book, he laid it open across his lap, asking more questions. Now that it was brighter, he could indeed see where the passenger she had pointed to the night before held the statue he had found.

"This is very important, so please try to recall the day," he told her. "Did the man leave with the same artifact?" He flipped the page and pointed to the small statue clearly outlined on the other page.

She thought about it for a moment. "Not that I can recollect, she told him. "But I had to leave early—to get to market, you know."

He didn't know. He had never been to the market in his life.

He did know he had an overwhelming sense of deflation. He hadn't really expected it to be that easy, but he had hoped!

Sensing his disappointment, Jane took the book from him, ignoring the brush of his arm as she reached for it. "I do remember that it was there several days later," she said. "I had to go to market again and saw the same gentlemen. I was rather surprised because the ship was no longer there. See..." she flipped through several sketches until she found the one she sought. Indeed the date was several days later than the first.

"Most of the same men are here, but Collin is not, and neither is Nigel."

Brayden took the book from her hand and studied it. "This is wonderful, Jane. May I keep the book a while longer."

"Am I to know why?"

Brayden shook his head. "It would be best if you did not at this time. But I will keep it safe."

She raised her eyes to meet his squarely. "Did you look at the other pictures?" If she did not ask, she would never know what she thought.

"Yes, I did. They were wonderful. I can see why everyone

wanted you to sketch them."

She breathed a sigh of relief. Perhaps he did not understand why she had drawn them, why they were so numerous. She did not feel compelled to enlighten him.

Brayden closed the book and let it rest on his lap. "This may help me tremendously," he told her. "I assure you I will return it as soon as I can."

Jane nodded. What else was there to say? At least she knew that she would have the pictures back, the ones that mattered the most to her, the ones of Brayden and the girls. She rose to leave, and he let her, assuring her that he would see her at the assembly that evening, and she should save him a dance.

More fool he, he thought later. He neglected to tell her to save him the supper dance. Instead, Mr. Robinson was down for that. Grabbing Kit, he also grabbed a few glasses of champagne and joined some of the other bachelors against the wall, watching the dancing.

"Why aren't you dancing with my sister," he asked.

"Because I'm standing with you," Kit answered reasonably. "What's the problem? You dragged me over here like it was life or death."

"It is. His," he said, pointing to Robinson.

Kit stifled a laugh, which he quickly turned into a cough when Brayden glared at him. "What has he done now? Not that I recall him doing anything that could annoy you."

Brayden scowled at his drink and didn't bother answering. How could he? To say the man breathing annoyed him just wouldn't do—not without an explanation.

"I discovered something today."

Kit suddenly lost all sense of humor and looked at his friend. "Should you discuss it here? I take it has something to do with our visit the other night?"

"It does."

That was as far as he got before he was joined by a few of the Demons with the cryptic message that they planned to ride that night, and they moved off. They had no fear that someone as unassuming as Kit would understand them. If he were not already exasperated with them, Brayden certainly would have been so now.

Brayden looked at Kit. "Perfect timing."

"I'm not so sure. Why would they pick tonight? There will be a half moon, and there do not appear to be many clouds. They may as well go in broad daylight."

"Actually, they have," he told Kit.

At the man's startled look, he instructed Kit that he would tell him after he met with the Demons. Kit would offer protection while he was with him—he knew that without asking. He didn't see how he could impart the information before then without giving away the fact that Kit was very aware of the Demons and their activities.

When Kit left to claim his dance with Arabella, Brayden made his way to Jane's side. She didn't precisely scowl at him.

He moved as close to her as propriety would allow, perhaps a step closer than that. She took a step to the side and he followed.

"Stop running away from me," he whispered to her. "I'm merely here to claim a dance. Now let me see your card."

She held it away from him. "There's no need."

"Are you afraid to dance with me?" He was incredulous. That couldn't be it.

She shook her head. "Of course not. If you must know, I don't desire to dance."

He grasped her elbow and started to walk toward one of the alcoves around the inner perimeter of the ballroom. "That's fine with me. I would prefer to talk."

She tried to move her arm, but he held it firm. "That's not what I meant."

He wasn't going to tell her that he would like to do a lot of other things too.

Once they were sufficiently far from the crowd, though that was nearly impossible in the same room, he released her, making sure that her back was to the wall where she could see out on the floor. He didn't want her to make an easy escape. If she left now, she would have to go through him; something that wasn't going to happen.

He leaned closer to her, wanting to inhale the scent of her. She turned her head away from him.

"Jane, listen to me—"

She tried to push past him. "I don't want to listen," she told him firmly. "I do want to go back to the dance."

"But not with me?" He didn't care if he sounded wistful.

"No, my lord."

"Brayden," he hissed. "Say it."

She stared at him.

"What seems to be the problem, Raby?" a voice he knew too well spoke behind him. It was Robinson. He nearly ground his teeth in frustration. The night simply was not going the way it was supposed to.

"Lady Jane was looking for a reprieve from the dancing and we were strolling about the room. Is there something I can help out with?" He half turned toward the other man. He didn't want to seem that he was hiding Jane, but he didn't want to flaunt where they had been either. That would do her no good.

He stepped around Brayden to better see Jane. "I've come to claim our dance, but if you would rather walk about, I would be agreeable. The Squire has set the lights out around the garden." He held his arm out, and Brayden watched Jane take it. To her credit, she did not look back at him.

The gardens were lovely, but not where she wanted to be, and not with this person. She glanced at him guiltily. That was not a kind thought, especially since she was thinking that she might agree to a proposal from him, if it were a legitimate one and not as Brayden hinted. More than hinted, blatantly stated.

"I'm sorry, Mr. Robinson, I'm afraid I was wool gathering."

"Charles, please. I think of you as Jane. It would please me if I could call on you tomorrow."

She nodded numbly. This would be her chance. She was sure he meant to offer for her. "That would be wonderful," she told him, trying to sound as enthusiastic as she should.

He grasped her hands. "You know what I want to say, don't you?"

How could she answer?

He raised her hand to his lips, kissed it and then turned her so they were heading back to the house. "Until tomorrow," he said. "In the meantime, I have the last dance to look forward to."

He left her with Arabella and Kit.

"I have the headache," she told Arabella. And it was the truth. She never suffered from such illness, never had the time or the luxury for it, but tonight it was very real.

"I think it would be best if I were to return to Raby Hall," she said. It hurt to even say the name.

Arabella glanced at Kit, then back to Jane. "If you want," she told her friend, "I will go with you."

"No," she insisted. There was no reason to ruin her friend's night too. She knew that leaving early would not please Mr. Robinson—Charles. She hadn't realized how much until the next day when he came to call as he promised.

"I cannot believe you did not tell me you were leaving!" Charles said as he paced around the parlor in front of her chair.

"I'm terribly sorry," she told him, looking up from her seat. She wished she were not at such a disadvantage, but he did not seem to move far enough away to give her room to stand.

"You knew I looked forward to it." Now he sounded like a petulant child.

"I knew. I did too," she said, not caring about the little white lie. She had been in mixed emotions about the entire thing.

Stopping in front of her chair, he picked up both of her hands in his. "Jane, I thought you understood why I was here today." He didn't wait for an answer, but continued. "Nothing would please me more than if you would consent to be my wife."

She looked up at him, unsure of what to think, what to say. She had expected the proposal, but she wasn't ready. She did not want to give the answer she knew she must.

He tugged on her hands gently. "Say something, darling." This time he tugged her to a standing position so that she was forced to stand very close to him. He didn't smell like Brayden. But this is what she wanted, wasn't it?

"May I think about it?" she asked, her voice not quite steady.

"Certainly." He leaned over and gave her a quick kiss that landed on her cheek when she moved her head.

"Should I speak to someone? Your brother? Lord Raby?"

"I'm sure it would be fine if you did, but why would you want to?"

He smiled down at her, and she did not like the patronizing look of it. "Why to talk about your dowry and settlements and the like."

This time she grasped his hands. "Charles, there is no dowry."

His smile slowly faded. "Of course there is. That has been the word for the past several weeks. You were a sly one not mentioning it when you first started doing the rounds. Granted, it's not large, but combined with your title it will be a wonderful beginning for us."

"You are mistaken. I have no dowry, nor will my sisters when they are of age."

"Your sisters are of no concern to me."

"But they would be your concern if we were to marry."

"I have it on the best authority that Lord Raby will continue to care for them. We only need to concern ourselves with us."

She pulled her hands from his grasp and looked at him, not knowing where to begin.

"Perhaps it would be best for you to speak with Lord Raby," she finally said. "It seems that he will have more answers than I."

He reached a hand out to touch her on the nose. "Don't be silly, darling. He can only tell me about the arrangements, he can't tell me yes or no. That must come from you."

"In that case," she said coldly, "the answer is no."

He dropped his hand and gave a startled chuckle. "Surely you are joking. You have not had sufficient time to think on it. But I have to warn you, Jane, I do not cater to odd humors."

She shook her head at him. "That is my answer. No. I would appreciate if you would leave."

"I believe I should talk to Lord Raby first. Perhaps he can talk some sense into you."

"You may do as you please, but Lord Raby is not my guardian. I am of age to do as I please."

"In that case, I will leave you, madam," he said, practically stomping toward the door.

After he left, with a resounding thud of the heavy front door, Jane remained standing in the same spot. She put her hands to her face, staring at nothing. Had she done the right thing? Most likely Arabella would tell her that it was the most foolish move she could have made. And she would be right. There was nothing to tell if anyone else would offer for her, title or not. And where had he got the idea that she had a dowry. She would have Brayden correct that immediately. There was no way she could have accepted him if it meant leaving her sisters. Brayden only consented to care for the girls because no one else would. If she married, he would fully expect her husband to do so. He was certainly under no obligation in any quarter to do so.

That was how Brayden found her nearly a half hour later. Still in the middle of the room.

He came up beside her, stood near her, looking in the same direction. She didn't turn and look at him, yet seemed to know it was he.

He put his hands behind his back. "So, did Charles come up to scratch?" Why did he torment himself? He knew that was why the man had come by. Aside from his intent being very clear, and the flowers he brought, which he noticed were not sitting in water, but lying on the table, it was in the betting books. Charles had been after a title for several years. If Arabella weren't his sister, he would have thought of strangling her.

"Yes, he did," she said quietly.

He frowned. He didn't really want to hear that. "Then why do you look so glum? Surely that is cause for celebration? I have heard Arabella talk of nothing else."

She wrapped her arms around herself and turned further away from him.

He had to step around her to keep in her sight. He wanted to see what she was feeling, thinking. It was better that way because then he wouldn't consider his own feelings.

She gave a tight laugh. "Do you know that he thought I had a dowry?"

"Yes."

She turned to face him now, puzzlement on her face. "Why would he think such a thing? I thought that he was interested in me because of my title."

"Oh, he was, Jane. That much I do know. There are many other reasons too, you know."

"But a dowry?"

"I told him that," he said quietly.

"You!" The word exploded from her. "Why ever would you do such a thing? You were the one who encouraged me to make plans and then you spread rumors so that I would have to tell a suitor differently?" She ran her hand along the back of her neck. "I do not understand you."

"Well," he practically drawled, "if you truly did not have

a dowry wouldn't it say something about his character that he wanted to marry you regardless?"

She nodded slowly. "Perhaps. But it smacks of dishonesty."

"I have told him because it was true, Jane." His voice was low and quiet.

"How can it be? Collin left nothing."

"I offered one."

She closed her eyes in shame. She opened her eyes when he began speaking again.

"If it would make you feel better, I would let your brother settle with me later, when we find him."

She sank into the chair that was nearby. "We don't know if Collin will ever return," she whispered. "Why would you do such a thing? Post a dowry as such?"

He stood closer to her, looking down on her sweet, confused face. How could she not understand? He wanted to tell her it was because he loved her and wanted the best for her.

"It would make it easier for some of your suitors, I thought."

So, he had wanted her away from him so completely he was willing to pay for the privilege. That was difficult to take.

With new resolve, she looked up at him. "As it is, my lord, you will be pleased to know that you can save your money. I have refused Charles."

"Why ever would you do that?" There was no mistaking the shock in his voice.

She gave him a tight smile. "It turned out to be rather easy, actually. Do you know that he had no intention of taking my sisters?"

Brayden shrugged. "They would be cared for here; you know that."

"But they are my sisters. You cannot care for them indefinitely. If I were to leave this house, then they would come with me."

"Then don't leave."

She stared at him blankly for a moment, as if his words had not registered.

"Do you have a position here for me? Is the governess leaving?" She didn't give him time to answer. "But she is your sister's governess." Her face cleared a bit, though she had a difficult time hiding the pain she was sure was still in her eyes. "Oh, you mean me to go with them? Would my sisters go too?"

Brayden shook his head. "You have misunderstood. I want you to stay with me, Jane. Your sisters would be welcome to stay too. Just think; they would have no concerns and when they were of age they could be presented and make a marvelous debut."

Shock made her feel cold. It struck to the very core of her. She didn't know when she would feel warm again. She didn't answer, just stared at him. Rising, she walked from the room. She could hear him calling her name, but didn't stop. Didn't want to stop. He was no better than Charles, or what he suspected were Charles's original intentions. That must have been how he arrived at that conclusion, since he was of like mind himself. She would leave immediately.

Brayden watched her leave. There was nothing more he could do. He had tried everything he could think of. At least as long as she was under his roof, he would be able to try and woo her. He had thought she was fond of him at the least. That she would see how well her sisters got along with his nieces. How well they all fit into this family. And it simply was not enough.

The clock striking the hour stopped him from any further thoughts. He had agreed to meet with Kit at his home and decide what was to be done with the Demons. They were the last thing he needed at this point. With a heavy sigh he left the room. It seemed that what he needed he was not going to get.

* * *

Sitting over their coffee in Kit's library, Brayden gave him some idea of the information he had from Jane. Going to his case, he pulled out her sketchbook and brought it to him. He would not show him anything but the pictures of the Demons, as he thought of them, his brother included.

He turned the first few pages and showed Kit what Jane had showed him.

When Kit finished looking at them, studying what Brayden pointed out, he covered the book in the wrap he had and placed it back in his case, then sat to finish his coffee.

"That is absolutely unbelievable," Kit said. "Does she know what she has there?"

Brayden shook his head. "Of course not, nor did I tell her. I found the book by accident and when I returned it she showed me the pictures." That was not quite correct, but close enough. He would not think of how he had followed her to her room and woke her. Now that she had refused him. It still hurt.

"Are you going to show the Regent, or should you show Liverpool?"

"Both. I think I have to, don't you? Especially in light of our last conversation. Now he can see for his own eyes."

"He'll keep the book, Brayden."

Brayden shifted in his seat. He had thought about that, but dismissed it. He would have to ask Jane once more if she could take what pictures she wanted from the book, or if she would allow him to remove those that would do him the most good. It would be an excuse to talk to her on a companionable—he hoped—level.

"I'll talk to Jane about it, but for now, we need to discuss tonight's ride. How can we best disband this group? I believe you are right and that is Prinny's concern. Somehow that must have been his only concern."

"It does seem the statue was merely a plant to get you to

do what he wanted."

"Aha, but don't forget that property, Kit. He very much would not mind having it. Since he tied that to the statue, I don't think he can renege on it."

"Can you just tell the riders that the Crown is not pleased?"

Brayden nearly choked on his laugh. "You are not serious?"

"I can see that would not work. But there must be something."

"Let's hope it comes to me while we're out riding. I wish you were with me instead of having to hide in the bushes."

* * *

The night was as dark as pitch. They certainly watched the sky well, Brayden thought. The clouds were moving in, making it even darker. Just thinking about the possibility of rain seemed to bring it on. In short order, it was a complete downpour. If only they would pay half as much attention to their estates as they did to this nonsense. And nonsense it was as far as he could tell, although, the newer members did make him uncomfortable.

"Are you taking the lead, Dere," one of the newer men asked.

He gave them a brisk nod. He would like to lead them into not doing anything. Why not?

"I would prefer to be somewhere dry," he told them. "With something warm in my hands."

His comment was met with laughter. "You're getting old, Dere," one of the men said to him.

"Now, now Parke, sounds as if you're still wet behind the ears. Probably everywhere else tonight, too. I'm all for finding a good assembly."

There was silence, save for a few of the men shifting in their saddles, the creak of saddle leather, and the sound of the rain.

"You ain't serious?"

"Actually, I rather think that I am. This was fun while it lasted, but there is no need for it. And as I said, I would prefer to be dry." With that, he clicked his tongue and turned his horse in the opposite direction. He held his breath, waiting to see who would follow. He could hear some discussion behind him, but he continued to walk his horse.

"I say, I have to agree," Mitchell said.

"And I say not."

"What? Are you afraid of riding?" There was a definite sneer in Parke's voice.

"I say that it's not as much fun as it used to be."

"That's because you would rather spend time with the fair Caroline."

He took the rest of the ribbing good naturedly. "That's enough reason for me. I think I'll join Dere."

Brayden heard him turn his horse and follow. That was one, then he heard a few more. There could only be two men left. He could hear them talking.

"I'll stick with you, Parke. This is just beginning to be more interesting than when Dere was in charge—either one."

Dere walked to the edge of the tree line and waited for the others to catch up. They stopped, but he urged them on. "This is for the best," he told them. "It was fun, but things change."

Agreeing, the men passed him. He raised his hand in salute as they trotted past. There was no need to tell them how irritated the Regent was getting. They were done. As for the other two, they were on their own. If the Regent or Liverpool pressed, he would give their names. The same if they gave any more trouble, but he had a feeling that once the ton knew the Dere Demons had disbursed, the men were not going to have such an easy time of it.

After the last man left, Kit emerged from the trees. "That was peaceful enough."

"Amazingly so. That must have been the first thing to go right in the past week." They walked their horses, side by side in the dark and rain. The hooves made plopping sounds as they moved along. After the day he had, Brayden found them unexpectedly soothing.

Refusing Kit's hospitality, he headed for home. He never let the grooms remain up when he went for these rides. The less they knew the better. He dismounted, and walked his horse back to the mews. As he removed the saddle, he heard a sound, and was instantly on his guard. No one who belonged should be moving about at this time of the morning. Arabella would have returned to the front of the house, and a quick glance showed him that the carriage horses were in their place trying to sleep, but shifting restlessly at the noise. It wasn't loud, but enough.

His horse nickered, and Brayden put a steadying hand on his neck. Even as he did so, he heard someone shush the animal.

"No need to wake everyone," the voice whispered. Brayden froze where he was.

"No need at all," he said, his deep voice carrying.

He heard the quick intake of breath and the sound of her getting ready to flee, the turning on her heel. He stepped around his horse and lunged for her, missing her by inches, forcing him to run after her.

"Stop, Jane," he said right before he grabbed her by the arms.

She tried jerking away, but he held fast, breathing hard. He could hardly tell if it was from the slight exertion or from the anger he felt welling up inside of him.

"You weren't thinking of running away."

"N...no," she said, her teeth chattering.

God, he wanted to shake her.

"Then what were you doing?" He refused to let go of her arm even though she pulled against his hold. He used both of his hands to grasp her upper arms, keeping her from wiggling away from him.

For the first time, he looked down at what she was wearing. "Where did you get those?"

"They were Collin's."

"I figured that much. Why are you wearing them, and why now? Where were you planning to go?"

She refused to answer, so he gave her a slight shake. "Answer me, damn it."

"You're hurting me."

He knew she was probably right, but he couldn't seem to stop himself. Perhaps if she hadn't hurt him so deeply earlier he would not feel that way now. Realizing that he didn't want to truly harm her, he took a deep breath, and eased his hold, to quickly tighten it when she tried to break away.

"Listen to me, Jane. Come into the house and talk to me."

"There is nothing to say. You made that very clear earlier today."

"This is something different." When he saw that he had her attention, felt it really in the stillness of her body, he said, "It affects Collin."

"I'll come," she said quietly.

He trusted her, but he felt better holding her arm as they walked to the house.

Chapter Fourteen

He didn't say a word, merely walked her into the study and closed the door after them with a decisive click.

He took a good look at her in her brother's old clothes. There was no possible mistaking her for a boy, so what was her plan.

He asked.

"It helps disguise me. No one really looks at another boy walking down the street, especially if I stay in the shadows."

She was standing in the middle of the room and he came to stand near after closing the door. He got the feeling that she wanted to turn away, but she held her ground.

"Jane, no one in their right mind would mistake you for a lad. Not with those hips." He grinned at her. He couldn't help himself. He wasn't in a better mood, but she was so appealing.

She looked down self-consciously, but he slipped a finger under her chin and brought her face up so that he could see her lovely green eyes.

"As much as I would like to talk about your body, that's not why I brought you here." He watched her blush at his words, and was somewhat amused by it. His Jane was such a mixture.

"I had to show your sketchbook to a friend of mine tonight—" He didn't want her to be self-conscious by telling her it was Kit.

She gasped at his words, so he hastily assured her that he did not show the entire book, just the first few pictures with Nigel and Collin. He felt the pent up breath leave her body.

"Does it really matter if anyone saw the other sketches?"

She shook her head. "It's just that they are private,

Bray...my lord."

He would definitely get back to that.

"I brought the book back with me. My friend and I agreed that the few pictures we looked at would be very valuable in clearing Collin's name—and Nigel's."

"I don't understand."

"I don't suppose you do," he told her. "Let me get you something to drink and I can tell you about it, and you can tell me why you were leaving."

She made no comment, but did agree to let him lead her to the settee where he joined her after handing her a small glass of brandy. She looked up in surprise.

Surely she didn't think he would sit across the room from her?

Quickly, he outlined why he had been searching for Collin to begin with, and how Nigel had been accused by the Crown of stealing the statue. He did not want to mention anything more about the Demons than he had to. If she did not know, that was best.

"But how do the pictures clear your brother? He was there."

"Remember I asked about the Indian man and you pointed out that he had been holding the artifact when he got off the ship?" When she agreed, he continued. "Neither Nigel nor Collin were in that picture, and the date was there."

"But does that mean they were not there? I cannot recall."

"That part is not important. We don't believe he was there. And the fact that the man was holding the artifact is sufficient. Supposedly he is the one who lost it prior to that date."

Her eyes widened in surprise. "Could he have had another?"

"There is only one. Actually, there are several, but the others have been accounted for. It was only this one that was missing. There are a few other pictures that are equally important. The one with Lord Hawke, for example."

"He was there? I don't recall, but then, I did not know him at that point."

"He was standing next to Nigel. He is the one who held the statue in his hands." Which explained why he was frantic about getting it back. "Since we found the statue in your house, he must have indeed been the one to give it to Collin for safekeeping." No wonder he wanted the house. Once that all became clear to the Regent, Brayden had a strong suspicion that he would be happy to give the house back to the Worsley's, but he didn't tell that to Jane. He didn't want to raise her hopes.

He did not want to get into what the prince had to say about the whole affair, and that was before he had the proof. He would spare her that. He and Kit could take the pictures if she would permit them.

"Please, take what you want, but may I have the book back? There are pictures of the girls there that I would like to have."

He reached out and played with her hair. She didn't draw back as he expected.

"You may have them, naturally. I had hoped that the other pictures would be as precious to you."

She continued to rotate the glass in her hand, so that he had to reach out and take it from her.

Finally, she looked up at him, her eyes tortured. "They do mean something to me. I will treasure them."

There! She said it. Let him make of it what he wanted. She would be leaving so it would not matter. She knew that she could draw his face from memory any time she wanted, but she wanted what she already had, for those pictures had been done in happiness, more so than any she would do now.

"May I have them tonight?"

"No. There is not much left to this night. You can have them after breakfast and after I remove what I need. Now that I'm here there is no need for you to run off in the night."

He let his finger run down her cheek. "Why were you?"

How to answer that? "Because there is nothing here for me."

He looked at her closely, studying her face. "You could have waited until morning."

"And have you ask me to stay again?" She covered her mouth with her hand. She hadn't meant to say that. It just slipped out. She didn't want to meet his eyes. Instead, she looked down at the floor, and tried to move away from him. Both efforts were futile.

He stopped her, by holding her arm. And then using his finger, he raised her chin so that she had to look him in the eye. She didn't want to. Didn't want him to see what she felt. Instead, she shifted her gaze away from him.

"No." The word was a caress against her cheek. He used his thumb to rub a circle on her jaw, and she could have melted on the spot. Felt herself growing much warmer at his touch.

"Look at me, Jane."

She didn't want to comply but the softness of his voice, the whisper of his breath across her cheek compelled her to do so.

"That's so much better, darling."

Her eyes flew open at the endearment. It wasn't said in a sneering way, but as if he meant it, in earnest. It took a moment for her to check her pulse, to remember that men often said what women wanted to hear to get their own way.

She pulled her chin away from his touch, and he let her go, only to drop his hand behind her neck, holding her there so that she had to look at him. It surprised her, but shouldn't have, that he was smiling at her. A warm smile that reached the depth of his clear gray eyes.

"Jane, what did you think I wanted from you this afternoon?"

"You said it well. For me to stay." She tried to keep the bitterness out of her voice, but it was difficult. She had felt betrayed. There was no other word for it. Yet, she could not blame him since the feeling was all on her side. He never promised anything by word or deed that would mean anything different.

He let his head come forward so that his forehead touched hers. It was an easy matter for him to draw her close to him since he held her by the neck.

"Jane, I want you to stay here. To marry me."

She tried to pull back again, this time in definite surprise. "What are you saying?"

"I want you to be my wife. Why is that so difficult?"

"I cannot," she finally told him on a shuddering breath.

"Cannot or will not?" His voice had a hard edge to it.

"Cannot." She put both of her hands on his arms that were holding her steady. "It would be best if I married, certainly easier. I know that. But after yesterday, after Charles proposed, I realized that I could not hold myself so cheaply." She looked at him this time, in the eyes, and told him, "I feel that I could only marry for love, Brayden."

He took a breath. She didn't wait for him to refute her reasons. Instead, she placed her finger over his lips to hold him silent. She was taken aback when he kissed it. She hastily dropped her hand to her side, but continued to speak. "It's not enough for me to love someone. I have seen first hand that it doesn't work when only one party loves the other and the other feels nothing." There was no use in pretending that she was not in love with him. He had seen the sketches and it would not take a brilliant person to figure out why there were so many of him. While Brayden was many things, stupid was not one of them.

"Jane, I love you—"

"No, Brayden. You have made it clear that you do not."

He shook his head in denial. "I do, Jane. I think I'm old enough to know my own mind. Why would you even think I did not?"

"You are never here when I am," she practically

whispered. It still hurt.

He tucked a loose strand of her hair behind her ear. "No, love. I was not here when I did not have to be because I did not trust myself. Why do you think I told you those stories about Charles?"

"They weren't true?" What had she done? She had believed him. "But they must have been. He went on about the dowry and how he didn't want to be with my sisters."

"To my shame, what I told you was not the entire truth. I cannot say what Charles's thoughts were to begin with. That was between him and you. Obviously, he failed some test, and I am glad of it. For now you will stay with me."

"What of Collin? Will that not present a problem? Will you want to be the brother-in-law of a thief, for that is what you think of him?"

"No, in this case, he was not, Jane. He was innocent of the affair except for the fact that he was soft-headed. Not unusual for men of his age."

"What will become of him if I marry you?"

"I do not know, dearest. That is only one of the reasons we must find him, but a man shouldn't lose his inheritance in a moment of stupidity—especially a drunken one at that."

"Truly?"

"Truly, Jane. Now, if everything is to your satisfaction, will you marry me?"

"Yes, Brayden.," she said and smiled up at him.

Epilogue

"Hold still, Emily!" Jane finished tying the sash of her sister's dress, then sent her off to gather with the rest of the children without waiting for her twin. There were quite a number of children present today.

"Arabella is so pretty," Evangeline said while Jane adjusted the bow in her hair. "She looks really happy today."

Jane could only agree before completing the task and sending her off too. Radiant would have been a closer word. How different this wedding between Kit and Arabella was compared to her own several months ago. Given that it had not been that long since Nigel's death, neither she nor Brayden had felt comfortable with a large wedding at St. Mary's Cathedral and opted to be married in the village, which greatly appealed to the local people.

For his sister, Brayden had insisted that the wedding be held at the cathedral and the wedding breakfast be held at Raby House, where they were currently gathered. The staff had outdone themselves in preparing the house.

"You did a marvelous job," Brayden said as he came up behind her. She felt his breath whisper across her cheek sending shivers down her spine.

"I did very little," she told him. She still wasn't used to running such stately homes and governing the numerous staff. "Anne helped, but the staff did most of it themselves."

"They love 'Bella," he said. Then he leaned closer, his lips touching her ears. "And I love *you.*"

She knew she blushed.

He stepped away and took her hand in his. "I wanted to talk to you," he said as he led her across the hall to his study.

She wasn't sure she liked seeing him this serious today. It couldn't be anything good. "Can't it wait?"

Brayden shook his head as he held the door open for her. "I think it's something you would want to know."

She stopped just over the threshold of the doorway and looked at him. "Collin? Have you heard something of my brother?"

Brayden put his hand on her waist and gently pushed her all the way into the room, then leaned against the door. When she whirled about to face him he handed her a folded note.

With trembling fingers, she took it from his hand, opening it at his encouraging nod. "Did you read this?" She didn't wait for him to answer, but quickly scanned the contents, then read it again more slowly. "He did buy colours," she said, wonderingly. "Did you know that?" She glanced at him and back down to the paper in her hands, not waiting for his response. "He'll have leave shortly and will see us then…in London." She looked at her husband. "Why ever would he choose London?"

"Perhaps because of this," he said reaching into his coat pocket, and pulling out another letter.

There was no mistaking the royal seal. She reached for it with trembling fingers. If it had been good news, surely Brayden would have just told her. She opened it, read it twice, then threw herself into her husband's arms. "Thank you, thank you, thank you," she said, kissing him each time. "I don't know what you did, but it must have been something, because I can't imagine any other reason for the Regent to be involved."

"Your brother was caught up in a bad situation, sad to say, partly because of *my* brother. Once the Regent had his statue back, thanks to you, he was inclined to be generous. According to this he can sell his commission and move back to his home because he will have his property back, but the Regent is insisting on an audience." He set her apart from him, and tucked a stray tendril of her hair behind her ear. "I think it would be helpful if we were there." Then he opened the door and extended his arm to her. "Shall we join the rest of the party?"

~ The End ~

About the Author

Always a daydreamer, author Tara Manderino loves to create stories and situations for the people running around in her head. She first began writing in third grade when she realized she couldn't afford her reading habit.

She currently works at the Library District Center where she assists in promoting the wide variety of programs offered through public libraries. When not in front of the computer, you can find Tara reading, watching old movies or doing needlework.

Tara resides in her native town in southwestern Pennsylvania with her husband and two sons. Besides enjoying a good romance novel, Tara seeks ways to avoid housecleaning and cooking; she thinks her crock-pot is her best buddy.

To date she has written several contemporary and regency historical novels, all available in electronic format and paper.

Other Regencies by Tara Manderino:

The Heir
Whisper My Name

~ Experience Historical and ~Regency Romance~

Awe-Struck E-Books, Inc.
and Earthling Press

In nearly all the electronic formats you could ever need, including Palmpilot, pdf, html, and of course, PRINT!

The Heir by Tara Manderino
Thwarting Magic by Ann Tracy Marr
Clementine by Isabel L. Martens
His Majesty, Prince of Toads by Delle Jacobs
The Forgotten Bride by Maureen Mackey
The Unexpected Bride by Jennifer Lynn Hoffman

And *many* more!

E-books are increasing in popularity and can be ordered easily and received instantly!

Visit our site for easy ordering information of electronic and print titles! Find your favorite historical and Regency e-book or **print** book at:

www.awe-struck.net
and Amazon.com

2235007

Made in the USA